Deaf identities

Deaf identities

Edited by

GEORGE TAYLOR AND ANNE DARBY

DOUGLAS MCLEAN • COLEFORD

8 St John Street
Coleford
Gloucestershire GL16 8AR
England
www.ForestBooks.com

British Library Cataloguing in Publication Data
A catalogue record for this book is available from the British Library
ISBN 0–946252–53–X

Typeset in 10.5/14pt Monotype Albertina
Printed by Cromwell Press
Typography and cover by Ernst Thoutenhoofd

Contents

Preface

This book is a follow up to *Being Deaf: The Experience of Deafness* published in 1991 as part of the Open University course Issues in Deafness. This marked the launch of what has become known as 'Deaf Studies', and to the exploration of what it means to be Deaf. Issues in Deafness was very successful and has since become established in other universities. This, coupled with an increasing interest in the study of British Sign Language means that the demand for *Being Deaf* continues, and *Deaf Identities* is a companion volume to it, rather than a replacement. Instead of a simple up-date, it is a completely new edition, with a more specific focus upon issues of identity.

The formulation of identity is an ongoing process of negotiation between individual perceptions and social structures, and deaf people have available to them, as with hearing people, the possibility of inhabiting multiple identities. This potential for diversity is problematised by attempts by those who employ simple definitions of deafness, and seek to stereotype members of the Deaf community. The rising level of awareness of the needs of Deaf people, and the discrimination and oppression they face, heightened by the previous and long standing Government policy to refuse to recognise their language, is mirrored by changes and developments within the Deaf community and within the context within which it operates. Significant to this development is an increase in the mainstreaming of deaf children in education, surgical interventions in the form of cochlear implants, and the formation of politically active groups, such as the Federation of Deaf People (FDP) in 1997, to respond to these developments. These factors represent a considerable challenge to static notions of deafness, and reinforce the need to re-assess issues of cultural identity for deaf people and within the Deaf community. The achievement in March 2003 of the FDP's first campaign as the British Government formally recognised British Sign Language may lead in the short term to a reinforcement of a stereotypical notion of Deaf people,

but in the long term allow the Deaf community to explore the potential
of its diverse nature and to expand its membership.

Throughout this book we use the D/deaf convention. Upper case 'D' is only used in relation to those deaf people who identify themselves as members of the Deaf community, and lower case 'd' is used when referring to the general deaf population.

Like *Being Deaf* the book is organised around a series of accounts by deaf people, about their experiences and the meaning this has given to their lives. Whilst most of the contributors are British, there are also contributions from deaf people from the USA, Spain, Germany and Russia whose testimonies help to broaden our understanding of the experiences of deaf people. This international dimension provides a varied cultural context within which to explore issues of identity and the lives of deaf people. But the real power of this book is in the richness of the accounts, and the determination of deaf people to live their lives in the way they choose.

Acknowledgements

Many people have assisted in the preparation of this book, not least the contributors, who have responded generously to requests for material and our persistent demands to meet deadlines.

In particular, we would like to thank Celeste Asensi Borrás, Rachel Coombs, Sue Gregory, Martin Atherton, Jens Hessmann and Antonio M. Ferrer Manchón for their help in locating contributors and gathering material. And Raquel Rodrigo Canet, Patricia Latorre and Rafæl Romero Zunicha for valuable assistance with interpreting and translation.

We are grateful to the following for permission to reproduce extracts in this book: deafbitch, 'Barriers', *Boadicea*, Issue 43 Oct/Nov 1999; Loris Malaguzzi, *The Hundred Languages of Children* © Edizioni Junior srl. Bergamo, Italy; Riki, Clive and Piers Kittel, 'Cochlear Implant—A Family's Experience' © Riki, Clive and Piers Kittel; Joanne Robinson, 'The Turning Point: Deaf Pride', *Deafness*, Issue 1, Vol. 11, 1995 © Forest Books; Dorothy Miles, 'The Hanglider' and 'To a Deaf Child' in *Bright Memory* 1998 © British Deaf History Publications; I. King Jordan, 'Dean or Deaf' and 'The View from the President's Office', *Gallaudet Today*, Winter 1997/98; Eudoria Antiaudio, 'Don't Look' in *Deaf Arts UK*, Autumn 2001 © SHAPE UK.

Team members of the MÁS Project *Broadening Access to Learning, Training and Employment for Deaf and Disabled People* (funded by Leonardo da Vinci II) have made a significant contribution to the production of this book. We are grateful for their support, encouragement and friendship.

I WHAT DOES IT MEAN TO BE DEAF?

Introduction

The question of identity is a thread that runs throughout the various chapters of this book, but it is seldom straightforward, and the issues raised are complex. There are those identities with a cultural or national root, such as Muslim or Spanish, and those identities related to employment, such as teacher, psychologist and social worker. Berger and Luckman (1967) refer to the former as 'collective' identities; those which have an historical basis, whereas the latter are a result of an ongoing negotiation between the individual and society and are therefore susceptible to change.

> Identity is, of course, a key element of subjective reality and, like all subjective reality, stands in a dialectical relationship with society. Identity is formed by social processes. Once crystallized, it is maintained, modified, or even reshaped by social relations. The social processes involved in both the formation and maintenance of identity are determined by the social structure. Conversely, the identities produced by the interplay of organism, individual consciousness and social structure, react upon the given social structure, maintaining it, modifying it, or even reshaping it. (Berger and Luckman 1967).

This negotiation is not, of course, conducted within a neutral environment. Society is politically loaded, and individuals are subject to a variety of forces and constraints when attempting to locatwe themselves within a social order where power is unevenly distributed. Individual behaviour patterns are subject to scrutiny within a framework of the dominant constructs of knowledge supported by the most powerful groups in society. This process produces a set of 'facts', which, when applied to individuals or groups, becomes their reality. Raquel Rodrigo Canet describes how, for her, becoming deaf had two distinct phases; becoming audiologically deaf occurred in childhood and the social phase took place at university where she mixed with Deaf people who, despite their lower academic status, acted as positive role models enabling her to start to take control of the situations in which she found herself with regard to communication, and to receive positive reinforcement for being Deaf. Chris Baxter and Candelaria Villæscusa Pedroche also emphasise their first contacts with other Deaf people and their movement into the Deaf community.

These identity types often contain contradictions which are overlooked in favour of consistent characteristics which are used to define the subject(s) according to the needs of the dominant groups. We see this regularly demonstrated by society's attitudes towards its poorest members, and the application of constructs such as 'the underclass' as a social category. It is 'a very elastic term' (Novak, 1997), which is employed to mark the distinction between the deserving and the undeserving poor, based upon their behaviour and not simply their circumstances. It is a powerful concept because it is offered as an explanation for social problems, such as rising crime levels, and supports simplistic solutions. In the USA the term 'underclass' usually refers to poor black people, it remains to be seen whether this will also be the case in the UK, where clearly contradictory constructs of black communities are deeply embedded in British society. For example; the respect for the perceived stability of Asian families is counteracted by a deep mistrust of other aspects of Asian cultural practises, such as arranged marriages and the position of women. Similarly, British people of African-Caribbean descent are often viewed as either exuberant or fun loving, or violent and unreliable. It is possible to exercise such a contradictory view in this way because stereotypes are held at an ideological level. They are based on strongly held beliefs, 'gut feelings'; a notion of what constitutes knowledge that is robust enough to resist being affected by logic or scientifically produced information.

According to the psychoanalyst Jacques Lacan (in Zizek 1989) we construct our ideologies as reality in order to deal with the Symbolic Order (e.g. patriarchy, capitalism) in order to divert us away from the lack of consistency and coherence in our existence. We are prepared to believe in an illusion because we have always done so, and because it affords us an order to our lives which we would not otherwise achieve. Karl Marx referred to ideology as a camera obscura (in McLellan 1977). He makes the distinction between the actual material conditions of

16 existence—work, production—and the superstructure that defines it—politics, and the legal framework. He argues that we come to know about the foundations of society through the 'lens' of capitalism, with its politico-legal structures, through the construction of ideologies that enable us to understand ourselves and the world in which we live. Identity, using this type of analysis, is politically formulated and subject to forces exercised by the powerful in society. The level of individual agency in identity formation is therefore limited to the choices made available to us by the dominant groups in society. For example, black people living in Britain cannot lay claim to an identity that is available to the white British population, because the ideologies that surround black British people constructs them as immigrants and foreigners, even though both (white as well as black) may be second or third generation British subjects.

Models of deafness

This is directly relevant when discussion notions of D/deaf identities. What are the choices available to deaf people in terms of how they are located within society? The Medical Model of deafness, with an emphasis upon impairment and deficit (Knight 1998) constructs an identity for deaf people that suffers in comparison to the hearing population. Whereas, the notion of Deaf people as a linguistic minority (Baker and Cokely 1980) promotes a positive image of Deaf people and Deaf culture, but only if you are a sign language user. This marking of difference is significant in the construction of identities, and the debates are often reduced to simple differences identifying polarised positions. Woodward (1997) argues that the notion of difference becomes a central plank in the construction of identities through symbolic systems of representation and forms of social exclusion. Identities are formed in comparison to other forms of identity, as different from, and in opposition to, other identity groups.

> Identity marks the ways in which we are the same as others who share that position, and in the ways in which we are different from those who do not. Often, identity is most clearly defined by difference, that is by what it is not. Identities may be marked by polarization, for example in the most extreme forms of national or ethnic

conflict, and by the marking of inclusion or exclusion—insiders and outsiders, 'us' and 'them'. (Woodward 1997, p2)

Jennifer Dodds in her account identifies as Deaf, not through the status of being born deaf, but by living, working and socialising with Deaf people. From her earliest years, she did not want to recognise herself as different from her hearing peers, but also recognised the empathy with her deaf peers. She defines the difference as Deaf people's own language and culture and argues that the polarisation of deaf and hearing people can increasingly be minimised as Deaf people develop English skills through bilingualism, with access to the mainstream technology of faxes and mobile phones. In addition to this, as Deaf people become professionals themselves, services provided to Deaf people can be moved forward, from the paternal 'us and them' division between Deaf service users and hearing professionals, to the more collaborative relationships described by Volker Maaßen.

The notion of there being a single D/deaf identity is, of course, not helpful, any more than it would be to think of, for example, all British Asians as having just one cultural identity. The British Asian community is diverse and represents a number of different ways of being Asian and British. Likewise for D/deaf people. Deafness describes a physical condition, but is not a helpful term with which to identify a section of society who may have little else in common. Research into the linguistic structures of sign languages, and the increased recognition of sign languages as legitimate linguistic forms, has supported the development of Deaf cultural identities.

Amparo Minguet Soto, in common with other writers throughout this book, reflects the facets of these arguments in her account of a developing Deaf identity through recognition of language and what Volker Maaßen refers to as 'solidarity' with the community. Sign language projects of the type Volker describes have developed in many countries following the recognition by linguists of sign languages and have brought the active involvement of Deaf people into teaching of sign languages and into other professional roles within the Deaf community, as Jennifer Dodds also recounts.

What Deaf patients at Rampton Hospital have in common is an identity imposed by their individual histories and reinforced by the

18 outside world: an identity that implies danger and a need for exclusion. Whereas most other accounts in the book are written by Deaf individuals, the account from Rampton Hospital is written by two of the professionals working there and gives their ongoing story of bringing a notion of a Deaf identity and development of a sense of Deaf community to patients within the hospital through the teaching of BSL.

The growing awareness for some Deaf people of a cultural and linguistic heritage has promoted a sense of community with sign language at its centre, and marks a significant distinction between those Deaf people who claim sign language as their primary means of communication and those who identify more with hearing communities. This has fuelled the debate about the relationship between Deaf people, who claim a cultural identity, and the wider disability movement. According to Corker (1998) this hinders the potential of any real social change for deaf or disabled people because it holds out the possibility of there being a 'cultural' identity to which Deaf people can aspire, and excludes the majority of disabled people.

> This has two main outcomes. Firstly, very substantial areas of commonality between deaf and disabled people are disguised and ignored. Secondly, the complex experiences of people are reduced to simple categories, often binary oppositions, which are both a result of and determine how these experiences are controlled or regulated by the dominant culture. Two main forms of regulation are identified: the sovereign power of medicine and science which focuses on overt control, and the more subtle disciplinary power which directs community concerns inward towards self-regulation and self-discipline. (Corker, 1998, p32)

It is the tension between essentialist and non-essentialist definitions of identity that underpins this debate. An essentialist definition of a deaf identity would be one that lists a set of characteristics that all deaf people share, unaffected by the passage of time. Such a definition could draw upon either the medical model or the cultural model of deafness, because both lay claim to some essential truths about deaf people. The main difference being that an essentialist medical model definition of deaf identity would simply locate deaf people as hearing people, functionally impaired by the impact of deafness. An essentialist

cultural model of deaf identity is much more difficult to sustain, unless
you confine it to those families who have deafness across a number of
generations. Otherwise, how is the culture transmitted if not by external forces?

> In these circumstances, identity ceases to be an on-going process of
> self-making and social interaction. It becomes instead a thing—an
> entity or an object—to be possessed and displayed. It is a tacit sign
> that closes down the possibility of communication across the gulf
> between one heavily defended island of particularity and its equally
> fortified neighbours. "Otherness" can only be a threat when identity
> refers to an indelible mark or code which is conceived as somehow
> written into the bodies of its carriers. Here, identity is latent destiny.
> Seen or unseen, on the surface of the body or buried deep in its
> cells, identity forever sets one group apart from others, who lack
> the particular chosen traits which become the basis of a classifying
> typology and comparative evaluation. (Gilroy, 1997, p308)

Within a medical model, where the essentialising trait is deafness,
it constructs deaf people as the 'other' in relation to hearing people.
Within a framework of Deaf people as a linguistic minority where the
essentialising trait is sign language, those deaf people who do not use
sign language as their primary means of communication are cast as the
'other' in relation to cultural forms of Deaf identity. A non-essentialist
definition would note how deaf identities are historically specific, are
affected by political and social factors, and would emphasise common-
alities as well as differences between deaf and hearing people. Asif Iqbal
argues that the Deaf community is passive, and that individuals need to
be more pro-active, to be socially involved and to promote diversity,
challenging negative behaviour and attitudes within the Deaf community as Asif does within the Asian community. Asif is a person who uses
all the opportunities that occur. He is interested in, and uses, everything
possible to enhance his present and future development, whether this be
contacts with the British royal family, the Duke of Edinburgh scheme for
personal development, organisations like Friends for the Young Deaf,
the Conservative political party and his local Member of Parliament,
or the opportunity to be the representative of his residential house at
Derby College for Deaf People. He describes his work with an organisa-

tion working with people with AIDS and HIV as the opportunity which developed his commitment to diversity. He joins with Hope Ahmed in stressing the importance of Deaf role models for hearing people.

The first account in this book, by Jennifer Dodds, resonates with many of the other accounts. She raises issues and themes returned to by other writers: being deafened at a young age by illness, the struggle to accept the fact of medical deafness, seizing rare opportunities to iden- tify with other deaf people, and the struggle to overcome the paternal- istic oppression by hearing professionals and other adults in the lives of deaf children to reach a solid sense of identity and pride in being Deaf. She charts her educational experiences, raises the issues of integration both in primary and higher education and the importance of literacy. She notes the increasing number of Deaf people in professional roles within the Deaf community, and argues that mainstream advances in technology that is directly relevant to Deaf people has moved the focus of integration of Deaf people away from issues of difference towards a campaign for equality.

References

Baker, C. and Cokely, D. (1980) *American Sign Language*. Silver Springs: T.J. Publishers.

Berger, P. and Luckman, T. (1967) *The Social Construction of Reality*. London: Allen Lane.

Corker, M. (1998) *Deaf and Disabled or Deafness Disabled?* Buckingham: Open University Press.

Gilroy, P. (1997) Diaspora and the Detours of Identity in Woodward, K. (Ed) *Identity and Difference*. London: Sage Publications.

Knight, P. (1998) Deafness and Disability in Gregory et al (Eds) *Issues in Deaf Education*. London: David Fulton.

McLellan, D. (Ed) (1977) *Karl Marx; Selected Writings*. Oxford: Oxford University Press.

Novak, T. (1997) Poverty and the 'Underclass' in Lavalette, M. and Pratt, A. (Eds) *Social Policy: A Conceptual and Theoretical Introduction*. London: Sage Publications.

Woodward, K. (Ed) (1997) *Identity and Difference*. London: Sage Publications.

Zizek, S. (1989) *The Sublime Object of Ideology*. London: Verso.

barriers

by deafbitch

I've had enough…
negotiating, compromising
suggesting gently in ladylike tones
reaching consensus
hinting it might be a good idea if…
doing research
writing reports
proving the business case
explaining the law
taking the barriers down inch by painful inch
brick by careful brick
I want to
SMASH
DESTROY
ANNIHILATE
BOMB
SUNDER
DEVASTATE
RAZE
CONSUME
DEMOLISH
all in one go on one perfect day of ecstasy

Being Deaf and Proud

Jennifer K. Dodds

I am Deaf and proud of it. I was born hearing in 1975, to a hearing family, in Edinburgh. At the age of five, I became deaf through meningitis, but consider myself Deaf rather than deafened. This point sometimes leads to teasing from my friends, as I have a strong Deaf identity, so they say 'You're not really Deaf because you weren't born Deaf like us'. But I am. Being Deaf is probably the most important part of me! I live with other Deaf people, work in the Deaf community and socialise with Deaf friends. I value my life, thus feel fortunate to be Deaf; if I was hearing, I wouldn't know the people I know now, nor would I belong to such a vibrant, varied culture which I am lucky to know.

Here, I will try to recount my life in brief. I believe I am a typical Deaf person of my age (26 at the time of writing) and nationality, and so my own experiences are very similar to those of my peers, though everyone is individual of course.

Coming to terms with me, myself and I

My childhood wasn't very exciting really! I grew up in the town of Berwick-upon-Tweed, just south of the English/Scottish border. When I became deaf, I continued to attend the local primary school for one year. During this year, I found my communications with my friends deteriorated, and I became more subdued than I used to be—I was always a very lively hyperactive child (and still am as an adult!). A pro-oralist peripatetic teacher of the deaf visited me, I think once a week. I hated it. She was a pleasant enough woman, but it made me different. I didn't want to be different—I wanted to continue with the way I'd been living before I became deaf.

After this, I was transferred to another primary school, the only one in the area that had a PHU (Partially Hearing Unit). Funnily enough, it was in a village fifteen miles away, which meant a bit of a drive each morning. Every day, a teacher would drive me and two or three other

deaf children who lived 'far away' to school. I spent most of my time
with hearing pupils, because again, I didn't want to be different. However, I struck up a strong friendship with a boy called Craig who was also deaf and was the same age as I was. Craig and I created one or two iconic signs to describe school related things, though they were strictly private between us, because we knew it was 'wrong'. No-one else did it, and we were instinctively aware that it was 'our thing' even though we did not have Deaf identities at that time. You see, remote areas such as the one I grew up in in the North East are extremely vulnerable if you happen to be deaf. Unless you live in a city or a large town, it's very unlikely you'll be exposed to sign language because there aren't enough people to sign to! There is no Deaf community, hence no signs. Auralism rules! And the parents accept it because they know no different. I would like to emphasise at this point that I hold no grudges whatsoever to my lovely family or any of the teachers I had in the North East, for the decisions they made on my behalf.

Moreover, I am especially relieved that my parents did not decide to have me cochlear implanted at an early age. I have extreme objections to medical intervention, too long to explain here, but I am glad my parents told me I 'didn't have to have a box in my head if I didn't want one'. I recall telling them I'd heard about the 'boxes that make you hear again,' but I wasn't keen on having one, and if a doctor wanted me to have one, they were to say no, thank you very much! I find it interesting how my childlike (I must have been about eleven years old) anti-implant stance has continued and strengthened into my work today. Even as a child, the very idea frightened me, and as an adult it still does. Who has the right to interfere with a child in such an extreme way, when deafness is not life threatening, and implantation can lead to severe physical and psychological problems? Very small children have no choice in the matter because they are too young to understand. Adults however, can understand and have the right to choose.

Anyway, after this primary school, I went to the local secondary PHU in the same village. However, I was only allowed to attend the PHU once a week for auditory and speech sessions. Although I wanted to be taught with the other deaf kids my age, the teacher of the deaf thought I was managing just fine in mainstream classes. But in fact, I had created my own survival method: from becoming deaf until the age of eleven

24   when I was transferred to Mary Hare Grammar School in Newbury, I read story books all the time. And I mean *all* the time; in lessons, at home, during travelling, wherever. That's probably the reason I have a fair grasp of English now, but at the time it was simply survival, because it meant I didn't have to talk to anyone or try listen to them talking to me. I was in my own little world and I was happy enough—I didn't like being deaf so I just retired into a shell.

I will not go into great detail about my experiences at Mary Hare (simply because there isn't room!), but I will say, despite the oppressively oralist environment, that school brought me a sense of being. After only meeting about twenty other deaf kids, I was suddenly surrounded by, and being taught with, over a hundred more! Communication was also easy—we fashioned our own 'school signs' and would help each other in classes. As a totally deaf pupil, my lipreading and auditory skills were poor, so I would constantly ask my classmates with more hearing than myself what was happening. Either that, or I'd just pretend to understand and then simply ask if we had any homework at the end of each class!

A drawback that really affected my confidence and identity came under the general school atmosphere. Mary Hare places huge emphasis on good hearing and speech skills, neither of which I had. I received speech therapy for years, and remember crying when being taught to say my name! They completely battered my natural North East accent out of me. For example, I used to pronounce 'Jenny' as 'Janey' which was, well, just how I said it. However, this was seen as a speech impediment and promptly removed, replaced by a kind of strange Queen's English. This 'problem' also prevented me from even auditioning for school plays—even though all the kids were deaf, I'd not be able to follow the dialogue of the 'good speakers' and I certainly wouldn't get any lines. So, I worked backstage. This was a real shame as I have always had a real fascination with the theatre and media, and enjoy writing songs. I now have over three hundred songs, off the top of my head, but I was rarely given the chance to excel in this area at school.

So, I turned my attentions on to English and media, working on writing rather than performing. It didn't help that the school careers service insisted it was impossible for me to be a journalist, but I am one now, because:

The realisations of a real identity

Ironically, Mary Hare introduced me to the Deaf community at large, though this was through my peers rather than the staff. When I was about sixteen, a fellow pupil joined us in the Mary Hare sixth form from another Deaf school. She kept in touch with Deaf friends from her previous school and as one of them attended the regular 'Deaf Pub Nights' in London, we went along. There, we made new friends—most of whom teased us about being oral and from Mary Hare—and our confidence soared.

My best friend in particular, Emma, struck up a relationship with a Deaf boy from a strong Deaf family. One weekend I chaperoned the young couple to his house. I was amazed. His mother basically sat me down in the kitchen and told me all about being Deaf. I was entitled to a minicom, flashing lights, to sign, to do whatever I wanted in the future, including being a journalist. I will never forget what that family did for me and they will always remain very special in my heart. I left their house a new person. I was Deaf! I'd met my first strong Deaf adults and I wanted to be just like them. I didn't want to be the pseudo hearing person Mary Hare tried to mould me into. My parents, bemused at first, thought it was fine and supported me. They have only ever wanted me to be happy.

My rapport with the Deaf community deepened when I attended the University of Luton straight after leaving school. On one hand, my speech-related confidence soared when I realised my hearing peers could understand me. I spent about a year sorting that out and establishing effective communication. Far from the rigorous speech therapy at school, my new friends simply roared with laughter when I mispronounced a word. I'd thump them playfully and they'd teach me how to say the word correctly. In return, I taught them basic signs. Sorted! On the other hand, I also went to the Deaf Pub Nights on a regular basis, and from there I went to parties and made many new Deaf friends. I gradually picked up more and more BSL (British Sign Language), discarding the Mary Hare slang signs I'd come to rely on. From University (I graduated with a BA Hons. in Media Production, in case you were wondering, and I had a Communication Support Worker, not the notetaker Mary Hare recommended!), I moved to London where the fun started:

When pride meets politics

Like many other Deaf people my age who graduated around 1996, I was plucked into a new Deaf related job before I'd even finished University. Through my degree work and my experience as a youth columnist in the British Deaf News (BDN), the British Deaf Association employed me as Community News Editor of the BDN. Looking back, that was a great deal of responsibility for a naïve twenty one year-old like myself, but I did enjoy it. My learning curve was, and still is, very steep, as I quickly became acquainted with people, organisations and all that was happening in the Deaf community in order to do my job. Since then, I've had several journalism/editorial jobs in the Deaf community and have developed a deep interest in Deaf politics, which was naturally followed by a commitment to fighting for Deaf Equality.

I am proud to be Deaf, thus it is natural—logical even—for me to want to work towards improving Deaf people's lives. Being a Deaf journalist has meant that I am exposed to many situations and pieces of information that I may otherwise not have access to. This has prompted my emotional 'This is not right!' reactions, which in turn have become political—and 'the personal is political' as they say.

The political uprising of Deaf people within society during the new millennium is to be expected, if you think about it. My generation is the first in which a large number of Deaf graduates have found work within the Deaf community. We are moving towards matching other minority groups' campaigns, for example, those of Black people, women and gay people. We grew up during the Scargill Miners Strike and thought, 'Well, if they can do it, we can, and we shall'. Our education has brought us a new-found confidence, and we want to use this to benefit the Deaf advance.

Our rising equality within society is also a direct result of past campaigns by older Deaf people, who I shall refer to as our 'ancestors' from now on. I am personally extremely grateful for this campaigning and very much admire their efforts as they were truly against the odds. It's now our turn to carry on the work and give something back, to thank our ancestors for campaigning for us when we were children. After all, they brought us the right to use BSL, minicoms, the possibility of entering higher education, and many other things we sometimes take for granted.

This rise is also indirect through the progress of technology and our understanding of English through better education. This enhances our status and accessibility to information and, hence, communication. We can use this in campaigning as a 'base', an advantage. This 'advantage' is perhaps so historically if you compare us to Deaf people who are more than fifteen years older than us. Pushed into menial jobs without realising their true potential, our ancestors truly had to campaign to get their voices heard. For example, our ancestors didn't even have minicoms. They had to campaign face-to-face, or through the post and so on. And it worked. Now we have positive role models, much better access and Deaf awareness.

However, if you consider our position in society now, we don't really have an advantage. We're just the same as hearing people, except we can't hear. But many hearing people can't do things too! Some of them have really hard lives. And does it stop them from doing what they want? No! If you take it as it is, we are naturally capable of campaigning at the level on which we do. It's no big deal, it's all part of progress, or evolution, if you like. Now, we have young Deaf teenagers who want to become Members of Parliament. Fine, no problem! I have a feeling they will, but this would probably have been unheard of years ago. To illustrate this point: an older—and very political—Deaf friend of mine once exclaimed 'Oh, wow, a Deaf person working with animals!' when I told him of a younger Deaf person's aspirations. My reasoning to this was, 'She can do what she wants; she's had positive role models'. It makes sense. Compare this with *See Hear* programmes made for the BBC fifteen or twenty years ago, when an entire programme focused on the existence of one Deaf farmer.

In fact, one of the things I love most about the Deaf community is that it's so varied. It's almost as if the Deaf community is a shrunken version of the entire world! I know Deaf people internationally and from almost all walks of life—accountants, teachers, plumbers, painters, postmen, lawyers, chief executives, models, mechanics, TV presenters, actors, many more, but no Deaf politicians yet. We have Deaf people like David Buxton but they are usually quite low key. We need to raise our profiles to the level of the 'deaf' Jack Ashley and people like him.

Our interactions with general society have also developed as more

28   Deaf people understand English (which means easier communication with those who cannot sign), and an increase of confidence due to our ancestors. Deaf young people who have Deaf parents have particularly high self-confidence, compared to those who don't. Throughout my years of discovery, I found that I am indeed:

Happily different

We are Deaf, we have the same abilities as hearing people, but while we continue to be different because we have our own language and culture, we are happily different, rather than begrudging our deafness and striving to become second class hearing people as we were taught in school. We see hearing people today as our equals. We want to 'be just like them', but not to be hearing! We just want to be equal with the same quality of life as they enjoy. We have confidence in being different, hence our continued campaigning for equality rather than for medical treatment.

One heartening thing that has continued to be passed down from our ancestors is the fact that we still have strong Deaf values and are loyal to our Deaf roots (even though Deaf clubs are dying out). We do have text messaging on mobile phones, emails and faxes, but face-to-face is still the best method of communication as it delivers clarity and equality to a community whose language is BSL. Even more so, when you consider that not all Deaf people 'have' English, and others like me are bilingual. Moreover, facial expression is just as important to us as tone of voice is to hearing people, if not more so.

We also have access to popular culture through subtitles and digital technology. We can watch *Eastenders* and *Top of the Pops* just like everyone else. Young Deaf people today, like myself, are much more interested in music than they used to be. We have access to it, but many of our ancestors didn't, so they shunned it. Deaf people who like music are often considered to be 'less Deaf' identity-wise, when that's simply not true. Music is an enjoyable pastime. We have our own ways of enjoying it and are still Deaf!

With all our technological advances deafness is becoming less and less of a difference. In the past, hearing people had to learn how to master the minicom or Typetalk in telecommunications. Deafness was a 'nuisance' because you had to have lots of equipment and learn how to use it. Now, we have the same access as they do via email or text messaging, and we can watch DVDs knowing they automatically have subtitles. And the technology moves with us, within our culture. A Deaf friend once said to me 'I feel like a proper Deafie now, I've got a mobile phone!'

However, technology sometimes backfires. Computers crash, emails are misread and private information is accessed by hackers. This can be particularly dangerous when staging a demonstration, for example, if information is given to the wrong person! However, mobile phones have been an extreme boon to us when networking, planning and operating in demos. I won't give away our secrets here, though!

So with these things in our favour, we continue our campaign for equality. It's natural in this modern day and age that people will not be walked over. We've seen Black people overcoming racial harassment, gay people against homophobic abuse and women arising through feminism. We see no reason why Deaf people should be different in this sense—why shouldn't we have equality demonstrations and marches too?

In addition to this, Deaf women, Deaf people from ethnic minority groups, and especially gay Deaf people, are often more prominent when campaigning. I am not sure why, it could be because they face double discrimination and want to do something about it, or perhaps through learning from their Black, Asian or gay peers. Whatever the reason, it's worth noting that most people within the large and varied Deaf community largely embrace difference. There is very little oppressive behaviour like racism and homophobia—we can't afford to discriminate against each other, there aren't enough of us! It would also be hypocritical because so many of us have been discriminated against by hearing people all our lives, so we know what it feels like. Obviously this is not universal within the Deaf community, but it is worth noting.

Confidently relating

Thanks to the technology I mentioned above, I enjoy closer relations with my family now than I have done in the past few years. They all still live in the North East, while I am in London, which made communication quite difficult. Hey presto! They now have mobile phones and email. This is a wonderful way of communicating with them as print media is something we all have access to. My two grandmothers

30   have also written to me weekly since I went to Mary Hare at the age of eleven, which I really value. They have also subscribed to the magazines I write for and take a keen interest in what I'm doing.

I rejected hearing-aids when I left Mary Hare, and have not worn them since. My new found relationships with hearing people are, I believe, linked to my confidence within my Deaf identity, rather than being a passive oralist. For example, as a teenager I spent school holidays in Berwick with my family, where I had a smattering of hearing friends. Mary Hare imposed on me that I should behave like they did, so I tried, but invariably failed as I had no idea what to do so I would simply shrink back and nod vaguely at anything I didn't understand. At University this tactic didn't work because I was thrust in the midst of hundreds of hearing people who I needed to communicate with for various reasons. Vague nods are unacceptable if someone is asking you if you've got notes on a lecture that they missed! At the same time, my Deaf identity was soaring, so I had the new confidence to say 'I don't understand, I'm Deaf'.

This stance has escalated within who I am today and has developed into an assertive attitude when communicating. I gesture a lot, and often adopt a stern voice/expression and say 'Write that down!' if I don't understand what hearing people are saying, as if it's their fault that they cannot sign…! It was interesting to note that I did this with some local 'hard men of the community' during a recent visit to Berwick. I was delighted when they meekly accepted we had to argue on paper (we were discussing London landmarks)! I can speak, but I dislike doing so. Speech is not my natural language, and I only use my voice if absolutely necessary, or with hearing people that I really trust.

I am fully at ease when communicating with Deaf people, and am able to be flexible when doing so. My communication can slip between BSL and SSE (Sign Supported English) at times, depending on who I am talking to. Because I have many friends and colleagues from many parts of the country, I can also understand most local BSL dialects, some of which have found their way into my own vocabulary, and International Signs (I love signing to foreign Deaf people).

Filling gaps

My situation within the Deaf community is quite complicated because of the number of roles I have. At the time of writing, I have three part-time jobs, I do lots of 'one off' work and am on several committees. Why? Probably because my area of work is very specialised—I am keen to see plenty of 'new faces' springing into Deaf journalism! My current situation is typical of many Deaf people working in the Deaf community today; I've often felt there aren't enough Deaf people to go round. For every strong Deafie you find who wants to work for Deaf children's futures, you'll find another two or three deaf people who don't want to know. Many of them are still stuck in the oralist trap from childhood, working in ordinary jobs and disappearing from the Deaf community. Others are simply apolitical and prefer to socialise and have a good time rather than do lots of voluntary work. Each to their own, I suppose, but personally, I can't sleep easily at night unless I'm involved in Deaf politics. For one thing, I embrace the Deaf community, and for another, if I see a problem or a gap, I have to sort it out or fill the gap. The political FDP (Federation of Deaf People) has certainly given me an outlet for this, and I am proud to be involved with them. It does get a bit confusing sometimes, for example if I'm working on the door at the Brothers and Sisters Club, and someone comes up to me and asks me questions about FDP membership or an article I've written! But that's to be expected and makes for an interesting life.

One thing I cannot stand is paternalism and the huge amount of control some hearing people have over Deaf lives. It shocks me that people with no understanding of the Deaf identity are so shamelessly allowed to destruct so many Deaf children's identities via cochlear implantation, for example. I have been appalled by the amount of 'do-gooding' I've witnessed by those who pity Deaf people and want to 'help' us. Deaf people do not need help! We are perfectly capable of doing whatever we want by ourselves. This is why I will continue to campaign on the springboard provided by our ancestors.

And one day, we'll all bounce together, so far into the sky that the enemy won't be able to catch us.

II GROWING AND LEARNING

Growing and Learning

This section draws on some of the themes introduced in the previous account by Jennifer Dodds. It focuses on the early attempts to construct identity, attempts by both parents and children to deal with the notion of what it is to be deaf within the family and within the culture that surrounds each family. These themes are also returned to in the later sections of the book. The experience of each of the writers in this section is of being born deaf, or in the accounts by Hope Ahmed and of Riki and Clive Kittel, of having a deaf child, but as Jennifer has pointed out, a child does not necessarily have to be born deaf to develop a culturally Deaf identity. The differing ways of developing Deaf identity are reflected in the differing accounts in this section.

All of the accounts reflect a positive experience of being Deaf within a family whose other members are not deaf. We know that these experiences do not reflect the experiences within the Deaf community as a whole. In the examples we have here, the families are shown to focus on the needs of the deaf child and to be motivated to enable them to maximise their potential as happy, confident adults. Often the social and economic conditions in which the family finds itself does not facilitate the particular needs of deaf children and their parents. Mark Heaton's account in the account with other Royal Cross School pupils demonstrates the gap between the resources available at the school and his own family experiences, in terms of the standard of living, the grandeur of the school, the facilities for play. For Ira's parents, Veniamin Tsukerman and Zinaida Azarkh, the issue was the struggle for life itself.

The role of Deaf families in conveying the reality of Deaf life was described by Jennifer Dodds. Hope describes how the school her daughter attends is not only providing Deaf adult role models at a much earlier age, but also providing them to hearing children and staff. Hope also discusses her experience of obtaining a cochlear implant for her child, a choice that Jennifer is glad her parents did not pursue for her. Each of

the Kittels describe the route that led to Piers choosing to have a cochlear implant.

The collection of accounts in this section reflect the changes in the
school experience. Whilst the accounts in the book *Being Deaf* polarise
mainstreaming and residential Deaf schools, the experiences of recent
years reflect a greater diversity in provision. Although schooling outside
of the child's local community remains a major feature, Hope discusses
a school which adopts an inclusive approach in which deaf children are
encouraged to develop their Deaf identity amidst their hearing peers;
where standards of education and expectation is high. Teresa Waldron
describes differing experiences of unit provision, which emphasise the
importance of expectations but also demonstrates how much power
was exercised by the individual teacher. The importance of relationships with staff are discussed by the diverse group of ex-pupils of the
Royal Cross School, and Joanne Robinson refers to the importance of
Deaf awareness for both staff and fellow pupils. She recounts days that
were 'nerve-racking' in her mainstream school, when she was humili-
ated, frustrated, depressed. Like Jennifer who felt she was being trained
to become a second class citizen, Joanne was the recipient of the good
deed of the day, and struggled to be a full member of the school. Also
like Jennifer, Piers attended Mary Hare Grammar School for secondary
education. Both accounts describe difficulties experienced by profoundly deaf children in that setting and the importance of a peer group.
Hope raises the issue of positive Black role models within schools and
the need to facilitate the development of multiple identities.

Teresa and Hope discuss the processes of identifying deafness, the
choices presented to parents, their expectations and isolation, their
need for unbiased information and resources not only during the early
years, but throughout the school years and particularly for the decisions
to be made at transition to secondary school. The Kittels too echo these
themes. They discuss in differing ways the development of speech and
the importance of bilingualism, adding to Jennifer's views gained from
her experiences.

Teresa describes her transition from school to work. Her contact
with disabled people facilitates the development of her identity as a disabled person, in which she adopts the political construction of deaf people as using the term 'Ddeaf' as both audiologically deaf, and culturally

36   Deaf, simultaneously. The use of the term is designed to include all deaf
      people within the political compass, both those who do not identify as
      culturally Deaf and those who identify themselves primarily as Deaf
      people. She also provides an illustration of the paternalism, patronage
      and control exerted over Deaf people referred to by Jennifer, whose de-
      scription of life in the Deaf community is expanded by Joanne.

The Hundred Languages of Children

by Loris Malaguzzi, at *The exhibition of Reggio Emilia Preschools*, Italy

The child has
A hundred languages
A hundred hands
A hundred thoughts
A hundred ways of thinking
Of playing of speaking.

A hundred—always a hundred Ways of listening
Of marvelling, of loving;
A hundred joys
For singing and understanding
A hundred worlds to discover
A hundred worlds to invent
A hundred worlds to dream.

The child has
A hundred languages
(and a hundred hundred
hundred more).

But they steal ninety-nine.

The school and the culture separate the head from the
Body.

They tell the child:
To think without hands
To do without head
To listen and not to speak;
To understand without joy…

38   They tell the child:
That work and play
Reality and fantasy
Science and imagination
Sky and earth
Reason and dream
Are things
That do not belong together.
And thus they tell the child
That
The hundred is not there.

The child says:
No way.
The hundred is there.

Memories of The Royal Cross School, Preston

Former pupils Jim, Molly, Bertha, Terry, Neil and Mark,
with Martin Atherton and Len Hodgson

The Royal Cross School in Preston opened in 1894, and remained on its original site until 1990. Nowadays it survives as a junior school for deaf children. In a series of interviews conducted by Martin Atherton and Len Hodgson for a video history of the school, former pupils recall various aspects of their lives as pupils at the school. The following interviews offer insights into the changing life of the school during the 20th century.

Jim Brown moved to the Royal Cross School at the start of World War I. During his time there, he was a member of the first Deaf Boy Scout Troop in the world, which was started for the pupils by the headmaster. Jim died in 1998, aged ninety-one.

—I came to the Royal Cross School in 1914, it was wartime, and I stayed until 1921. The headmaster then was Mr Shaw, he was the first headmaster and he had been there since the school opened. Mr Shaw set up a Boy Scout Troop for the pupils, and we wore a uniform with a big hat. We used to go hiking, camp out in tents—I used to really enjoy that, setting up the tent, knocking in the pegs to hold it up. It was really good! I was the captain of the Troop and we had about twenty boys in the Scouts. We used to have a Scout Hut in the school grounds, but now it has been knocked down. We didn't join in with the hearing Scouts, but after I left, the deaf Scouts joined in the local Scout Rally that was held every year.

Molly and Bertha met at the Royal Cross School in Preston before the Second World War. They have remained friends ever since, with Molly acting as relay interpreter for Bertha, who is both deaf and blind. In this

40 interview with Len Hodgson, Bertha tells how far her eyesight deteriorated and the treatment she received.

B: We met at the Royal Cross School when we were five.

M: It was 1928, and we both started at the same time. The headmaster was Mr Barnes.

B: Yes, his sign name was [Bertha puts her finger to her lip, as though saying 'hush'!]

M: It was an oral school, and we used to have to lipread the teachers. They were all the same; nobody used sign language in the classrooms.

B: I could see until I was five, and then my eyes started to go worse. I used to have to stare at the blackboard, and the teacher noticed I couldn't see very well. He got fed up and he sent for Mr Barnes. The teacher told him I couldn't see very well, so Mr Barnes wrote a letter to my mother. She came to the school and she took me for an eyesight test. The man who did the test looked in my eyes and said my eyesight was very poor.

M: Your grandmother was blind, wasn't she?

B: No, my grandfather, he was partially blind.

M: We didn't travel to school every day, we used to stay here.

B: Every month we went home for the weekend. My parents thought it was better if I stayed at the school, so that the teachers could help me with my work.

M: You finally went blind when you were twenty-six, didn't you?

B: Yes, I started to get pain in my eyes, so I was sent to the doctor. He sent me to an eye specialist at the hospital, and he put some drops in my eyes. They were no better, they just made my eyes water. He said it would be better if I had an operation on my eyes, but gradually I went blind. Because I couldn't see, I had to feel everything. My sister used to make me feel lots of different things, so that I knew what they were. I also had a teacher of the blind, Miss Walmsley, who taught me to read Braille. I've used it for fifty years.

Terry arrived at the Royal Cross just as the Second World War was ending. Here, he recalls his only real experience of the war, which looking back he finds quite amusing!

—I came to Royal Cross full-time in 1945, although I had been here in 1944 for a couple of weeks to try it out. Because I was only five, I don't really remember much of the war, but I do remember one incident after I had started at the school. We were all playing out one day when some planes flew over the school. The teacher said they were English, so we all waved to them. We were quite excited. Then we realised they were German planes—you could see the crosses painted on the wings! The teacher panicked and made us all run inside, but they didn't drop any bombs on us. The teacher said they were heading for Liverpool to bomb the docks there. We had an air-raid shelter at the school but we only ever used it a couple of times for drill practices, and the war ended soon after I had moved to the school.

Neil has some unhappy memories of the oral education provided by the school in the 1950's.

—I came to Preston Deaf School in 1953, when I was about ten. It was better here than at Manchester Deaf School, where I had been before. Here the school was surrounded by fields and countryside, whereas in Manchester the school was in the city. It wasn't a very good place for me there. Here was better, but it was a boarding school. That meant I didn't go home for months and I didn't see my family very often. The education wasn't very good, and it was difficult for me in the classroom. The teachers were not allowed to sign. That meant we had to lipread, and wear headphones and microphones.

All the children were the same. It was an oral school then, but at playtime we all used to sign. In the classroom, it was a different language and so a different way of teaching. Outside, we all used our own language and we had our own culture. In the classroom, they used oralism and so we had to use their language instead. That's why it was so hard for deaf children—they had to have two languages and two cultures. They missed so much.

One of the hardest things was written English, and we tried to learn, but whenever we were alone, we used a different language. It didn't fit in with what they were trying to teach, so the education for me wasn't very good. I don't blame the headmaster or the teachers, it was the local Education Authority who made the rules. They banned sign language

42 and said deaf education should be oral. They didn't understand how deaf people think or see things, so deaf people left school unable to read or write. So their education was wasted, which was a shame, because many deaf people are clever.

Mark Heaton offers an alternative view to Neil, showing that deaf children could derive some benefits from being sent to an oral school. His first experience of the Royal Cross School came when he became a boarder at the school's nursery in Blackburn. He remembers his first day there, and looks back on what was a happy time for him.

—I was only three but I can remember my first day at school really clearly. The school was in Blackburn and was called Wilmar Lodge. It was part of the Royal Cross School in Preston. The main school was for children from nine up to sixteen. There was another school called Ribby Hall, that was for children from six up to about nine. Wilmar Lodge, where I started, was for children from three up to six.

On my first day at school, my mother drove me in the car from my home near Chorley. When we arrived there, it was a really posh house! It had its own grounds, a big gateway and a long drive with trees on either side. I remember being able to smell the moss! The house was all painted black and white on the outside, it was really impressive. My mother got me out of the car and took me inside. There was a really big hall, with a large staircase leading off it. Everything was made of lovely brown wood—the doors, the walls, the windows. There was a big fireplace made out of marble. I saw someone coming towards us— it was the matron. She smiled and made me very welcome. She was really nice, and I took to her straight away. She took my hand and we went off together. We were walking along and I suddenly realised my mother wasn't with us. I started to panic—I realised I was staying there and that I wasn't going home. What was happening to me? No-one had explained to me what was going to happen, I didn't know I was going to be left there. But the matron was really nice and gave me a cuddle and explained that I was staying there. She said I was very clever and I hadn't to cry. So off we went and she took me into a room. It was full of children and they were all signing. I realised they were all deaf, the same as me!

I stayed there from Monday to Friday, and went home for the week-
end. I certainly didn't realise when I first arrived that I would be sleeping there, or that I wouldn't see my family during the week, but I soon picked up the routine. On Fridays, my mother would come and collect me and on Mondays she would take me back to school. This happened every weekend from me being three until I was eleven, when I moved to Burwood Park School in Surrey.

There were only two classes in the Nursery School, and only two teachers, and so it was more like a glorified all day playground than anything else. I found out later that the teachers there had trained at Manchester University under the Ewings; so of course, they didn't use sign language at all. In the classroom, all the children used to sit around facing the teacher. She would write on the blackboard and draw pictures. She would draw a picture and write a word next to it. There was no signing, it was all oral. Everybody was the same, we were all learning the same simple words. The teacher would draw a house and write 'home' next to it, so we would link the two together. She would draw a woman and write 'mummy' and it was the same every week, always the same. We also used to play with bricks, making houses and all sorts of things, and I liked that. I used to love it when we painted as well.

We used to play outside and that was brilliant, because we had a slide, swings, a sandpit—all sorts of things to play on! The sandpit was my favourite. I had two good friends there, Doreen and Susan. We were always together, from being three until we were eleven. It was brilliant at Wilmar Lodge, and I felt like I really belonged. I was part of a close and loving family, and although I was the only deaf one, my mother never treated me any differently. There wasn't really any communication though, especially as the teachers at school didn't use signing. Also, I grew up on a farm, so I was used to being able to go off on my own and do much as I pleased. It was only when I went to Wilmar Lodge that I had any real friends, and of course we managed to find ways of communicating, even though we were only very young. Doreen and Susan came from different backgrounds to me, and because Susan was very clever and well educated at home, I learnt so much from her. I think it is true to say that I was very lucky to have them as friends when I was young and that I wouldn't be the person I am today without their influence in my early life.

Finding the Link

Hope Ahmed

I noticed on the maternity ward that my child did not wake up like the other babies did. One would wake and the crying would wake the others, there would be a chain reaction. I mentioned it but the reaction was 'happy mum, happy baby', I was relaxed and contented, so was the baby. At one month I recognised that there was a problem. If Julia woke crying, she would be reassured by the light coming on, but not by the sound of my voice. I went to the Health Visitor but she reassured me. It wasn't until the routine health visitor test at eight months that Julia was diagnosed as severely deaf.

She rejected the post-aural hearing-aids, taking them off and hiding them. When she was one year old, they did another test and discovered that she was profoundly deaf, so they gave her body-worn hearing-aids. Although she responded to them by humming, we all hated them; they were so obvious and everyone would stare at us like Julia was an alien from outer space. I really felt so negative, like I'd done something wrong. I tried so hard to be positive because Julia was so in tune with my feelings she could pick up whenever I was feeling down. By being positive, no matter what I was feeling, I could create a positive aura around us so that Julia would be more content and happy. Behaving and looking positive helped Julia to accept her difference. This really was the foundation which contributed to Julia adjusting to her deafness within a hearing family.

When she was given hearing-aids, I expected to see a difference. I expected her to listen, develop spoken language and feel less frustrated, but this wasn't happening. She still didn't know where her dad was going when he left for work because we couldn't get the message through to her. She didn't know where we were going until we arrived at the shops or her nanny's house or wherever. I found it very frustrating. Her concentration span was short. Talking to her felt unnatural. Something was missing, something very important, I could sense a link, I could feel it but I didn't know what it was.

The tradition in my husband's family is that at the end of the year, no matter where we all live, the family comes together at my mother-in-law's house. There one evening my sister-in-law suggested sign language. She had been learning it herself and had reached stage one. She showed me how to sign 'milk' and gave me some of the vocabulary we needed, 'daddy', 'gone', 'work'. Basic signs like 'bed', 'toilet', 'want', signs for colours and foods, just basic communication. I had finally found my link. The skies opened up and Julia became less frustrated. Even her facial expressions were different: she'd be sitting in her rocking chair and she'd respond to the content of what I was signing, she'd wave her dad off to work.

We both come from large families. I am one of five mixed-heritage children; Joe is one of eight from an Asian family. Both families are close-knit and I would take Julia to my family home frequently. However, what really hurt was that not a single member of the family asked to learn or showed any interest or sharing of responsibility in trying to communicate directly with Julia. They tried to communicate completely orally. I understand this, from a hearing perspective, but it meant that I always had to appear over their shoulder, signing for them. Wherever we were, Julia would look for me, I became the link, the interpreter. It was a huge responsibility, it meant that at bedtime I would have to be the one who always settled her to sleep, stroking her for an hour. Joe would try, but he couldn't understand what she wanted because he couldn't sign. My sister-in-law lived too far away to be able to help.

After that New Year holiday, when the term started and the teacher of the deaf came for her weekly visit, I told her what had happened and asked her for teaching through sign language. Of course she was taken aback and said she'd have to discuss it with her Head of Service and then I received a phone call trying to persuade me to stick to the oral approach but I was not going to have my link taken away. I'd had the cotton wool taken from my eyes by sign language. I knew what I wanted, I knew the benefits for Julia. I would have gone on my knees if I had to, but he was persuaded and we were allocated an extra teacher, a profoundly deaf teacher who had been to the Mary Hare School but who could sign. She came for an hour a week and I could see why Julia looked forward to her visits more than those of our other teacher.

46   Jason was born when Julia was just over two years old. I maintained Total Communication naturally because I wanted both children to have equal access to me so of course he signed before he could speak.

When she was three, Julia had age appropriate language and about five spoken words 'mama' 'papa' 'nana' 'baba', and 'bu' for bus. She called her brother 'baba' but she could sign his name, Jason. At a routine appointment with the Ear Nose and Throat consultant and the Head of the Hearing Impaired Service, as Julia's speech wasn't developing, we were offered the choice of a vibrating tactile aid on the wrist, or a cochlear implant.

After going through the whole assessment programme, meeting families who'd had the operation and reading the literature they gave us, we decided to let Julia have the operation. Naturally as parents we were terrified of facial palsy, the risks of anæsthetic, the pain and trauma but thank God everything worked out well and the operation was a success.

When it came to the first tuning session, we were very anxious because this was the moment when Julia would experience her first sound sensations. They asked Joe to play with Julia because I was so tense. They were playing with blocks when the processor was switched on. She instinctively looked up. The expression on her face said it all: she was so frightened by the noises she buried her head in my lap. It was a heart-wrenching experience. Had we made the right choice? It was traumatic, as she had no context for all the noises she could suddenly hear, and no understanding of what was happening. They said that this was normal and that all the children react the same way.

But if I had to, I would go through the cochlear implant process again because it has been so worthwhile. We noticed a big jump in her speech, loads of vocabulary and then two-word constructions. It was hard to get her to use the cochlear implant at first. For the first three weeks she refused to wear it and she would run from me. She was naturally afraid of it, but I had to be patient. They gave us the speech processor and we gave her rewards for increasing use. Bribery works! I would phone the implant team everyday, and they would reassure me, don't push her, go with her flow. That's what we did, then it clicked and she wore it increasingly. Now she asks for it in the morning and wears it all the time.

We continued to sign. The hospital staff, particularly the cochlear implant teams were helpful. The audiology scientist uses sign with Julia.

Signing has supported her speech development. For her, hearing a new word is like us hearing Chinese, but a new sign she understands. Once she has the sign, she works on the sound of the word and because she has sign language her understanding and development of spoken language is much more natural and not forced.

I have reservations about the bias of the advice I received from the education service. When they say to you, 'if you sign you'll delay speech', that is nonsense. We were not advised to use sign language and no literature was given to us about deafness (other than literature produced by the National Deaf Children's Society). No tuition in British Sign Language was offered to us as a family, I've done it all on my own. I've wanted to do it so that I have BSL as a language and to support SSE (Sign Supported English). I need BSL for my child's present and future Deaf friends. It gives me, Julia and us all as a family access to a wide range of events in the Deaf community, but more than that because I've always signed to Jason too so as not to exclude Julia. It means that sign language is at the heart of our family, we have adapted our way of being to accommodate her needs and by doing that, we have given her access to our family lifestyle. It means that, in the way we are bringing her up, she is being treated no differently from any other child.

Parents of deaf children don't have the same choices for schooling as parents of hearing children. First, it is virtually impossible to meet all of the Deaf child's needs within one existing provision, particularly if travel is involved. We are meeting Julia's educational needs and her needs as a Deaf child, but sadly her social needs and her cultural needs as a Black child cannot be met in full. Secondly, decisions are made by the professionals according to what they think deaf children can cope with not what is the best education for that child. Then what happens when they can't cope? They get dumped in a school for the deaf so the special schools are coping with all the children with behaviour problems and massively delayed language. How can they then offer suitable education and a peer group for deaf children like Julia, who is scoring at the national average in all subjects except, surprisingly, English in which her score is actually above average for her age?

Our experience of primary education has been very happy and positive. Julia attends a mainstream school with a Deaf unit and I'm extremely pleased with the Junior School provision that has been de-

48 veloped so recently. The school's attitude is so positive and their approach is really, really good. Their integration policies are very desirable. There's a lot of support from teachers of the deaf and classroom support staff who sign, but most importantly, there are Deaf staff who teach BSL, assess the children's language development and provide cultural awareness. Julia has two sessions a week in a Deaf group which aims to develop and continuously assess their skills in BSL. The school reinforces the opportunity for the children to interact with high achieving Deaf people who act as role models and who pass on their skills and experiences to the younger generation. There is a need for Black role models too so that the whole community has a view of Black people as teachers, lawyers and dentists rather than as drug dealers, criminals and murderers. The whole school signs: everyone from the Head to the dinner ladies has some signing ability.

Due to the distance between home and school and the travel involved, Deaf children have a home/school book to replace the daily contact. The teacher of the deaf records the events of the day, both academic and social. Any problem that crops up is mentioned, any materials or equipment that is needed for the next day. They also use it to ask for the support of parents, whatever is needed at that time, for example some testing of the multiplication tables or work on spelling. The school writes down what they've done and the progress that Julia has made. It is a form of communication for me too, if I have been worrying about her I can write it in the book. The book recognises the partnership between the teachers and the parents. If I write anything in the book, the message always gets passed on.

I go in for assemblies, sports days, or if I need to speak about any of my worries I can ask for and get an appointment.

The school also provides reports on the child's progress in key areas and we are invited to comment on the school's methods as well as on the individual's progress. My child is the only Black child at the school. It is an extended family environment but it is very white. The school has been very accommodating. I insisted that her ethnic status and her religion were put on her educational statement, which was a first. I talked to the dinner ladies about her dietary requirements. They were very good about it and my child knows herself not to eat pork.

The parents and teachers in primary school have high expectations of the deaf children. They demand a high standard and they don't stand for any nonsense. Deaf children are disciplined and rewarded in the same way as the other children, there are no exceptions to the rules and they have an incentives scheme which works to the benefit of each child. When Julia started there the school gave us a lot of useful information on everything from the school's summer fetes to the holiday schemes available for children and several useful contacts within the Deaf community.

However good the school is, the education system can't be totally responsible for the progress of the individual deaf child. In order to be the advocate for the child, parents have to make sacrifices. A lot of hard work and commitment is essential. Nothing is ever simple or easy and certainly nothing is ever handed to you on a plate.

All I want is for people to listen to me and not to feel that they know better than I do. There's always one child in ten that's successful. If my child does well academically and the professionals feel that she can go on to mainstream school with support, what happens if I'm not happy with that? I want a unit so that she has permanent support always available, and excellent Deaf awareness in the school. I don't want her to be dependent on one interpreter whose signing may not be suitable for her or compatible, or a teacher of the deaf who might go sick. Julia has a good peer group of Deaf and hearing children who have come through the school system together and whose attitudes and levels of understanding towards deafness are very positive and not bigoted. Being Black, I know what racism feels like. As Julia is Deaf and Black I don't know what she will face. I hope she doesn't go through all the pain that I had at school.

At the moment very good foundations are being laid at home and at school which include Deaf culture. There are no conflicting models, no family division. I feel in my heart that whatever she decides to do she will be a success. I want Julia to be in a position to leave secondary education with a good level of attainment so that her choices of career and employment are wide and she can get a job which interests and fulfils her. I don't want her to grow up with mixed views, with hang-ups that lead her to feel that she doesn't belong in the hearing world, that she doesn't belong in the Deaf world. I know that life can never be perfect, that she will hit obstacles, barriers and oppressive attitudes, but I want

50 her to have the confidence and resilience to overcome them. I also want the resources to be available to her. For example, we only get one showing of a newly released film with subtitles. Other people can go to see that film anytime during the period it is shown, it may run for three to four months. We have to drop everything to attend the one subtitled or signed showing, or we've forever missed the opportunity.

I do feel I should have been given more contact with Deaf adults and children in the pre-school period. There's a real need for an Early Years Centre for parents and children when deafness is discovered. It would make for easier contact with all the necessary people, Deaf adults and children too, all there in one place. That would be wonderful. I'd like people to give both sides of the story, not in a biased way. The for and against of each method, Total Communication, the oral/ aural approach, BSL, SSE. Information should be accessible, e.g. times and dates of signing classes, so that families get the whole cake rather than the crumbs according to the bias of the policy, whatever it is, even if it is a signing policy. Parents should be encouraged to go to the Deaf club. People should not view deafness as a medical thing, something that is not normal, something to be ashamed of. It's OK for my child to be Deaf. I want the message to be broadcast, there should be more publicity. Some famous people should be encouraged to sign like Princess Diana did. My hope for Julia is that she lives as happy a life as possible. I used to worry that she'd marry a Deaf person and deafness would always be around but now I'd welcome that. If deafness were perpetuated through the generations I would be happy. It is painful to live a life with ignorance. They say that 'ignorance is bliss', but it's not.

Cochlear Implant—A Family's Experience

Clive, Piers and Riki Kittel

The following account has been taken from presentations given to the LASER workshop in March 1995. It has been included because of the continuing debate within the Deaf community about cochlear implants in relation to Deaf identity. Many of the attitudes and concerns expressed in the account have been heightened within the Deaf community as the age at which children are implanted decreases and criteria are changed to facilitate the implanting of a wider group of deaf children.

The decision—Riki Kittel

When Piers was eight-and-a-half months old, we were told by a teacher of the deaf that he was profoundly deaf. She told us not to worry; that if we worked hard, used his hearing-aids at all times, then he would develop quite normally but at a slower rate than his hearing peers. She also told us categorically that using sign language with him would mean he would never learn to talk. Both statements are false.

What she said 'felt' wrong to us. We decided before he was born, that we would try not to impose our own needs over those of our child; that if important decisions had to be made, we would consider their impact on the future adult he would be. Having got over the initial shock of the diagnosis we settled down to life with our deaf son, never for a moment wishing to change him into a hearing child.

We read as much as we could about deafness. We read about deaf education and the poor results achieved with using the oral/aural approach shocked us and we sought advice from many people, including deaf adults, believing them to be the best people to understand the full implications of the situation and advise us properly. We were given a lot of varying advice but we decided we must add signing to our programme and started at once.

Friends with a hearing child were bringing him up bilingually, each using a different language with him in the home and we aimed to do the same with Piers, but our main problem was that we had no knowledge of the second language! Because I am very poor at languages, and because we intended to continue to use Piers' hearing-aids to help him utilise his residual hearing and try and develop his lip-reading skills, we chose Sign Supported English as the signing code we would both use at first. However we did not want our ineptitude to keep Piers from having access to both his mother tongue and good deaf adult role models as soon as possible, so we asked some of the deaf people we had met to help us.

Soon deaf acquaintances became friends, helping us to ensure that Piers regularly had BSL bedtime stories, contact with signing deaf children, visits, outings and as much exposure to good BSL as we could manage. As he grew older, Clive's ability to communicate in the new language increased and both he and our deaf friends helped me to incorporate many BSL features in my SSE, so that my signs gradually became less inappropriate. Piers rapidly learnt the art of code switching, using SSE when he and I played, worked at our daily oral/aural lessons or read together and BSL with deaf people and for his increasingly intense conversations with Clive. When he was two and a half we rented out a room to a young deaf man, who lived with us very happily for over two years.

Piers began to read very early and adored books; whenever we went out shopping I would buy him a book as a treat and very soon I had to take him to the library two or three times a week to keep up with him. He had one or two hearing friends and with one of them attended an ordinary playgroup for a couple hours a day from two and a half to four and a half.

Piers went to Heathlands School in St. Albans when he was four and a half. There he was taught using Total Communication methods. We continue to spend a small fortune and many hours travelling time to locate good, soft earmoulds in a continuing attempt to get some sound in his even poorly functioning ears. Signing never, ever stopped him using his voice. After he went to school he began to try very hard to speak, working hard at formal speech therapy and taking informal corrections from us. His speech and lip-reading ability were fairly average for a very deaf little boy but his understanding and his school work above average. Some of his speech was understood by his teachers, family and close friends, some, particularly as his sentence construction was advanced, would have been impossible to understand without the clues that signing gave us. None of us suffered frustration because we were unable to understand each other, although we did find it tiring constantly having to explain what was happening on TV at the theatre or in mixed deaf/ hearing gatherings.

We attended the Nuffield Centre annually for Piers to have an audiological check. When he was nine, his audiologist, Dr Lim, said it was a pity that he was over their age limit for referral for a cochlear implant as she considered him a perfect candidate. I was shocked. Both Clive and I were strongly opposed to parents taking decisions on invasive surgery for children unless it was a matter of serious illness. We believed it breached the Rights of the child. She pointed out that although she could not refer him to Nottingham, if I wished she could let me know of other options for cochlear implant tests for him. I said 'No thank you' and gave it no further thought.

When he was ten we arrived at the time for another crucial decision to be taken. Which secondary school would he go to? Leeds was impossible as it has no residential school. We all went up to Scotland to look at Donaldsons School, which Clive and I thought would probably be the best place for him to continue his education but Heathlands began to press for him to take the entrance exams for Mary Hare. He and his school friends seemed very keen to go there and we all went to have a look without really considering it as a viable option. We noticed that all the children signed to each other outside their classes and all seemed relaxed and happy.

Piers passed the exams and was offered an interview. I was very opposed to going any further but Piers was equally opposed to going to Donaldsons. We explained about the oral ethos of Mary Hare, about how it really breached our principles. Piers began to reason with us, explaining that he had been to a signing school, and that he now really wanted to develop his speech and lip-reading. He assured us that he would be able to cope.

We allowed him to go for the interview, they too thought he would cope and he was offered a place. We decided to allow him to go for one year, reckoning that we could afford to lose a year at this stage if it proved a disaster. We reconciled ourselves with the thought that sign-

54 ing had not only helped him to achieve this standard of education but that it had also given him the ability to understand and make his own reasoned decisions.

He did well at school although he came home every weekend, usually bringing one friend or another. The next summer he came home from school looking forward excitedly to returning in the autumn. That was that; the die was cast, he stayed on at Mary Hare.

School work may have been going well, but all was not one hundred percent happy at school. Amazingly Piers was getting bullied at school for being deaf! It couldn't have been his speech, most of his friends at school had speech no better than his, combined with very poor signing abilities. I found I had enormous difficulty in communicating with them. It may have been a result of this bullying that when he was halfway through his second year, he came home one weekend asking about the possibility of having a cochlear implant. It transpired that a boy in his class had one and it helped his hearing. The thought of having more hearing was very exciting for him.

I was not at all keen and I was pretty certain that at twelve he was far too old to be an acceptable candidate but I agreed to think about it. We then discussed the whole idea within the family throughout the weekend and it was agreed that I should approach the school for their advice. I was referred to the deputy head. Initially he was as surprised as I had been and pointed out that the boy in Piers' class had not only had meningitis at nine years old but also had experienced enormous problems adjusting to the implant. He said he thought Piers' deafness would be borderline for acceptance on any programme. We decided it would be best to discuss the matter fully with both Piers and Clive present the following week when he would also have a copy of Piers' most recent audiogram.

At this meeting Piers listened very carefully to all the pros and cons. I thought there was a lot against it as it was a major operation which would remove all the hearing from one of his ears and it was totally irreversible. It would leave a very large scar on the side of his head. Other operations might come along in the future that were better and if he had this one, he would not then be able to have another. He might die on the operating table. He was almost certainly too old to be accepted on any of the existing programmes. There would be a long process of selection to go through, lots of travelling to and from hospitals, and after all that he still might not be accepted for the operation. If he had the operation it might be unsuccessful or there might be post-operative complications or infections which could mean having to re-operate to remove the implant and leave him with even less hearing than he had now.

If the operation itself was successful it might still be of little benefit to him. He might be too old now to ever learn to understand spoken language. There would be at least two years of speech and language work following the operation; more travelling to and from hospitals in the school holidays.

What there was on the plus side seemed to me to be pretty chancy. It was most likely to be successful. There was only a very small risk of death, post-operative infections or other complications. He would almost certainly be able to hear environmental sounds, car horns and fire alarms, warning of danger; door bells, telephones and the like. With luck he might be able to hear a great deal more and his brain might, in time, begin to understand the things he was hearing, possibly even speech.

Then came the solemn warning that there was no way that this operation was going to miraculously change him into a hearing person. If he did eventually have it, he would hear more than he could now but he would still be deaf.

Well, that came as a great relief to all of us! However, Piers said it sounded good to him and he wanted us to go ahead and find a programme that might accept him. The deputy head said he would make some phone calls to various centres.

Mrs Court, the head of the CI team at Addenbrookes Hospital in Cambridge rang us a week later to tell us that if we could get funding agreed for the initial testing procedures, then they were prepared to put Piers on their programme. She warned us that it was not very likely they would accept him, as he was much older than the children they had operated on in the past. She explained that we could not have an appointment without an agreement for funding. This would have to come from our GP, who is a member of a fund-holding practice, and all the money for Piers' tests would have to come from their practice budget.

This seemed an insurmountable hurdle but I went to see our GP, talked it over, they had a practice meeting and agreed to pay for all his tests! I was also told that if Addenbrooks accepted him for the operation,

56 then North Hertshire would be prepared to fund all the costs for both the operation and all the post-operative visits. It was amazingly simple!

One month later we all went to Addenbrookes Hospital and met the CI team. It was the start of the arduous procedure of assessment and it necessitated many trips to and from Cambridge over the summer and autumn of 1993.

Six months later Piers had the operation, and in the 1994 Easter holiday the cochlear implant was 'switched on'.

I am glad that the decision was one hundred percent Piers'. I have done my best throughout the intervening time to support him in that decision. From the first time he has been absolutely determined, sensible, brave and always quietly optimistic. He listened to all the advice he received from deaf and hearing people, from friends and acquaintances, for and against. Then in a matter of fact way, he decided to go ahead. There was only one moment, when the needle was in his hand and the anæsthetic began, that I spotted the fear in his eyes and realised for the first time just how difficult and frightening the decision must have been for him too; his determination had hidden those apprehensions.

Piers is different now but he's not different because he's changed into a hearing person. He's still the same son; my deaf son. Piers is different because he's happier. Of course he's still deaf but now, at long last he's got a decent hearing-aid. For the very first time he has a hearing-aid that actually works. For us, this means that he now hears me shouting his name; before he couldn't. He tells me this is what he wants. Certainly he now actually goes looking for new batteries; before he didn't even know when the battery was flat.

Piers tells me that with his cochlear implant he no longer feels isolated, cut off from the world; he feels that at last he is part of what is going on around him, a part of life. He tells me that he has no regrets, that he made the right decision, that he would do the same again if he had to make a choice.

Sometimes I worry that he wishes I had made the decision earlier, on his behalf. But I did what I believed was right at the time and I too would do the same again.

The experience—Piers Kittel

When my mum brought me to Addenbrookes Hospital, I felt very shy when I met people there. They were a team and the team 'boss' was Ivy Court, the surgeon was Dr Gray. The others were Lesley Shipgood, the speech and language therapist, and there was Zeb, the audiologist who operates the computer. There were other people in the team but I saw them rarely. When the formalities finished, we had a talk, then we went to a clinic, to see if I was good enough for my cochlear implant. I had to take five big tests. I felt very nervous about taking them; I thought they were like school tests, the ones you had to answer questions, but they explained what they were. The clinic was where I took my first test to see if I was good enough for a cochlear implant. I felt frightened, as I didn't know what tests were, but the tests were to test my hearing.

The first test was which most of you deaf people have been through before, the nasty headphone test. I had to put on a headphone and Zeb made my headphones do different sounds, whatever. The next test was the bone conduction test, to see which side of my skull could absorb the heat from the drill and which was the best area for the cochlear implant. The next test was for Lesley to say some words, and I had to answer what they were. For the first part of the test I had to look at Lesley with my aids on; the results were okay. The second part of the test was to look at Lesley without my aids on, and the results were quite okay. The last part of the test was not to look at Lesley, but I could wear my aids.

The test was *terrible*, which means that I couldn't hear a peep out of my aids. The aid was a Phonak Superfront PPC-L-4, which is a very powerful aid. Because of this test, I thought I would fail the other tests, so I was worried, but I passed the rest.

I passed my first test, so I had to take my second test, which was a few weeks later. I went to Addenbrookes again, and went to the scanning department. There, I took a CT scan, which was a bit like having an X-ray. I had to lie on a bed and it went through a hole in the scanner. My head went in the hole, and a scanner went round my head. I felt frightened. As my mum said, they found out that I was born deaf, and my hearing defected by a matching gene. (Your mum's and dad's gene must not match, so you can develop properly, but my mum's and dad's cochlear genes matched, so I was deaf). I was deaf by a blob of bone at

58   the top of my cochleas. A tiny bone can make me deaf. My cochleas were suitable for the cochlear implant, so I passed my second test. I felt very pleased to find out how I was deaf, not pondering which way I was deaf. Born deaf by gene, or jaundice.

My next test was a bit strange, so strange I almost didn't understand it. The test was very simple, you didn't need expensive equipment. I lay down on a bed, and a tube was entered in my ear. A jet of cold water went in my ear and out. It was a bit like having your ear wax taken out. I was made to look at a little light on a ceiling. Nothing happened, so the same process was done to my other ear. The whole process was repeated, but with hot water. Nothing happened so I passed the test. Afterwards Zeb explained why, and I was surprised! If your ear is cold, the balance organs in your ear become cold, and the blood vessels in the ear become cold, and they travel to the eye. If you have good balance, the eye nearest your ear will start to move towards your ear. With hot water, it is the opposite. My dad and I were amazed about it, we almost didn't believe it. As I had no balance, the test was correct, so I passed the test. I felt that I was making good progress after I passed the last test.

At Mary Hare, I was doing my English lesson; the senior audiologist took me away from my lesson to the school's audiologist area. I thought it was an ordinary process which all pupils have to take (twice each year?). The audiologist was Mr Powell. He did the normal things, checking if my cochlea is normal, doing the normal headphone sequence, etc., then he sent me back to my lesson. The next time I went to Addenbrookes, I asked when I would take my fourth test; but Lesley and Ivy said that I had already finished it, and that I had passed! I was amazed and felt happy that I had passed my fourth test.

Soon after, I had my last test, which was a bit painful. I lay on a bed (again!) then a round object was placed on my ear, and a thin needle was entered in my ear, past the eardrum to the oval window of the cochlea. I only felt the pull of the ear drum when the needle passed it—it felt a bit like having an injection. Electric currents of different 'volumes' were passed down the needle to the cochlea, to stimulate the cochlear implant. It was a test to see which cochlea accepted the electrical signal best. My right ear was the best for hearing, but the left ear was the best for accepting the electrical signals. So the agreement was made, I would have the cochlear implant in my left ear. I didn't just do five tests; I did some other small ones.

Just before my operation, I had to sign a contract, and two parts of the contract, which I remember well were No. 14, 'There is a one-in-a-million chance you may die under the anæsthetic', and No. 16, 'At the switch-on, you must stop signing'. For No. 14 I didn't die because it was a very small chance, a smaller chance than that you may win a million pounds at the National Lottery, which is one in twenty thousand. When I remembered No 16 of the contract I made my mind up: I would sign to my parents and friends, and deaf people, but not to strangers like bus drivers, and teachers at Mary Hare. I felt excited about my operation. I hoped it would come out good, and that it was not a fake—like the ones on *Crimewatch* or other things—but I trusted them because they were nice, and they showed my speech processor and a broken receiver, the thing that would be put into my head (they wouldn't actually put the broken receiver in my ear, it was only a display!).

I was given the choice of being put in an adult or a children's ward, as I was over twelve and so I could choose, but I chose to be in a children's ward. I was put in C2 which means 'Children's ward'. I was lucky, as that ward had a PC, a TV, a VCR, a Super Nintendo, and a small shopping mall below us, which had about ten or twelve shops! I liked the ward there and the people there, but the only thing is that the saying 'hospital food is terrible' is true! Just before my operation, which was at about two o'clock, I put on a gown, and a painkilling cream was put on a cross on my hand where the needle would be pushed in. I was wheeled to a recovery room, then I said goodbye to the world. The needle was put in the cross on my hand, and the anæsthetic was injected into my hand.

I felt my hand becoming a rock, then my lower arm slowly became a rock, then when the rockiness reached my elbow, I was blown away to dreamland, but I didn't dream. The operation took five hours. My mum and dad went to lunch, then at four o'clock they came back. The operation finished at seven o'clock, but I had to sleep the anæsthetic off. At half past seven, I stirred, so the nurse on duty tried to wake me up, by tickling my feet, but she failed, so she transferred me to the children's ward. At ten thirty I woke up, feeling groggy, but I talked to my mum and dad and went back to sleep.

60   At the next day, I woke up, and Dr Gray came round to see if I was okay, and see my scar. Before the operation, he said that the bandage had to stay on for 2 days. He saw my scar and said that the stitches were good and it was sewn very nicely on! He decided that my scar healed enough not to bleed again. He removed my bandage. (Later, I found out that my other cochlear implant friend, Richard, had the bandage on for three weeks! He was jealous of me).

The result after the operation was having a lump on the side of my head, and at the same side, having a cold side! My hair was shaved off, but it was a terrible haircut, not done by a haircutter! I had to wear a hat to hide my scar and keep my head warm and to stop people seeing my scar when I went out. I felt very embarrassed when I went to the shops with my hat on, on a sunny day!

Anyway, the next day I went home. I felt fine, with no pains, or problems. I couldn't wait until my switch-on. One of my friends, Gregory, came to my house to see me and cheer me up. We had a good weekend that time.

After a nice birthday, and a card from Addenbrookes (thanks!) I went back to the hospital, and I heard for the first time. Some of you may have seen Nicholas Carter on *Tomorrow's World* last year, and the second part was on the same day as my operation! What a coincidence! Anyway, I looked like him when he heard the first time! I jumped when I heard it, I heard quite loudly which I haven't heard before, I only heard quiet sounds, not loud ones through my hearing-aids! My mum almost bawled when my switch-on had finished.

I felt very happy when I got my cochlear implant. At the start, I had some problems like batteries, clips breaking, but they soon went away. When I went to school with my cochlear implant, people began to act strangely, and keeping away from me, at that time. I felt quite lonely, but soon, they accepted me, so I am now part of a group of normal hearing-aid friends. They found out that I didn't change a bit from my operation or having my cochlear implant, and I was the same as before; they learnt that nobody changes after an operation. I felt quite pleased with them accepting me, and learning how to cope with me (!).

I think that deaf people get worried about nothing, about cochlear implant people leaving the deaf world and joining the hearing world. This is simply not true, as I remind you of contract part No. 16, 'At your switch-on, you must stop signing'. I ignore this rule, and continue to sign. I still receive *Talk* (magazine of the National Deaf Children's Society), which I enjoy, and I still have deaf friends, I have got lots of deaf friends, only two hearing friends, one I became friends when I was born, another about five years ago. I still like deaf people same as before. I agree with some of you, children shouldn't be allowed cochlear implants when they can't decide if they want one or not, and I think it should be against the law for children under eight to have cochlear implants and if they are over eight, they should choose if they want one or not, not their parents.

Now I can hear many more things than when I had my aids. With my aids, I only heard pneumatic drills, and they sounded like a quiet hum; but now I switch off my MSP when I hear it, it is too loud! Before, I had to rely on the 'black box' on the top right of the TV screen when it had nearly finished; now, when films finish, I hear a hum getting louder, then the credits start. Before, when my mum wanted me, she had to bang on the stairs to get me down, but now she just shouts 'Piers!', and I will come down. Also, I now can hear the computer bleeping, and the phone ringing, which helps me to help my friends hear the phone at school.

Before, when I wanted to phone my mum, I had to ask the care staff to help me pick up the phone, dial my mum, then ask her to ring back. When I got my cochlear implant I couldn't hear my mum's phone ringing when I picked it up and dialled her at first, but after my MSP was turned up I could hear it. Now I only have to pick up the phone, insert 10p, then dial the number, then try to hear the ring; then when it stops, I say, 'This is Piers, at Mary Hare Grammar School, please phone back at...'. Then my mum will ring back. There are many other things I can hear—it would take a very long list to write them down—but I wouldn't understand them if I heard them for the first time: I search for what the sound is at first. The only thing I understand straight away is the phone ringing.

Reflections—Clive Kittel

When Piers said he wanted a cochlear implant (CI) my first reaction was surprise—why should he want one? Surely he was coping well at Mary Hare Grammar School (MHGS) and could sign with us and his friends?

62   We were OK as we were. We had all invested so much nervous energy
      in TC over the years that I did not want to change. An almost certain
      improvement in environmental awareness—car horns and fire alarms
      etc., is obviously important—but not an overwhelming benefit com-
      pared with the risks of the operation.

         His desire for the implant forced us all to reconsider his future.
      Clearly he was doing well at MHGS but he was finding life increasingly
      difficult. After MHGS what? Hopefully he will be looking for higher ed-
      ucation, of which very little is likely to be available in a signing environ-
      ment. 'Mainstream' with an interpreter is a possibility but this has severe
      limitations. The problem is that everyone—children and adults—learn
      as much from their peers as they learn directly from teachers. Interpret-
      ers can usually interpret a lecture satisfactorily but in informal groups
      and discussions they cannot cope so well. In a group of hearing people,
      discussion revolves very fast—one contributor chipping in before the
      previous speaker has completely finished. An interpreter has to wait
      until a sentence is almost completed before commencing the interpre-
      tation and must also indicate who is speaking. Almost invariably the
      discussion has moved on before the deaf person has even received the
      information, making it almost impossible for them to make a contri-
      bution—so the deaf person cannot fully participate in a spontaneous,
      unstructured discussion amongst hearing peers. I feel that it is vital for
      Piers to improve on the extent to which he can cope on his own—with-
      out special provision. A CI seemed to offer a chance of improvement.

         This, for me, was the crucial factor. Gradually I became more com-
      fortable with the fact that a CI is only an additional aid for Piers. He is
      still deaf—he will still have a deaf identity and will, I am sure, want to
      sign whenever possible. Taking this with the arguments Riki and Piers
      have outlined, I added my support to the decision for Piers to have the
      operation.

         Riki and Piers have described the tests and the operation itself. My
      most vivid memory is of waiting for news of an operation that normally
      takes no more than three hours, but for Piers lasted for over five hours!
      Riki and I spent those two extra hours in quite a worried state. Had
      something gone wrong? Had the implant been abandoned? Then there
      was a slow realisation that all was well when he came back to us—albeit
      with a shaven head and mammoth scar.

What is the situation one year after the operation? It is, in fact, only nine months since the implant was energised to a level which really gives him a significant benefit. As predicted, he is becoming much more aware of environmental sounds—not overnight but gradually. Most of these sounds he had no reason to suspect even existed—the hiss, for example, given out when I pour on water to extinguish the Barbecue fire, or the roar of the wind when Riki winds down a window in the speeding car. He feels more in touch with the world and will be very much safer as a result.

His receptive skills using sound alone have improved somewhat from a base close to zero. His lip-reading without sound is improving also, much as expected with age, regardless of the implant. However when the two inputs are combined there has been a dramatic improvement. We see this both in test conditions at the clinic and in real life.

I am perhaps even more encouraged by the improvement in his speech—particularly the production of 's' and 'sh' sounds. He has been taught to produce these sounds since a baby, but they never became second nature, were never included during spontaneous speech. I can see him developing a feeling for those sounds and beginning to include them spontaneously. He still has a long way to go.

In dealing with most hearing people, his receptive skills have always been greater than his expressive skills. I can now see the imbalance being redressed. People who see him occasionally comment that he is becoming easier to understand.

His school work has deteriorated somewhat during the year, due principally, I believe, to the nervous energy which has gone into the implant. He is now into the first year of his GCSE course and the signs are that his work is picking up again, much to our relief.

The future looks good for him, but the implant also brings long term problems for him. All being well, Piers should live for another seventy years. The external processor and ancillaries will certainly need to be repaired, replaced and updated during this time. It is highly likely that the implant itself will also fail. If, by that time, Piers has become heavily dependent upon it, he will need a further operation. Although the technology will have advanced, it will probably carry the same risks and cost the same in real terms as the initial operation.

It seems unlikely that the NHS, if it exists at all when he needs the

64   next operation, will provide the funds—£30,000 at current values. Piers may need to take out insurance to cover this, as well as paying out for the running costs of the external elements. This is likely to be a significant, but not a crippling burden for him.

Another significant long term concern is the effect on the Deaf community of large numbers of CIs—particularly in very young deaf children. The reactions expressed by Deaf people, '…we don't need this operation'; '…we are OK as we are, particularly with the spread in the use and acceptance of sign language'; '…we don't want to be involved with a new type of deaf person, one who may not want to join the Deaf community' and so on, do need some response. I am however certain that Piers, with his strong background of signing and contacts within the Deaf community, will not turn away from it because of his implant. Matters are very different for a child implanted at, say, four years of age. There is a very real danger that professionals with auralist views will find it easy to discourage early signing with the promise that everything will be OK after the operation. Children with this sort of experience may well be lost to the Deaf community.

There seem to be three options open to the Deaf community. The first is to ignore the operation and shun those who have it. I suggest that this is both short-sighted and negative. The second is to oppose such early implants. I do not want to go into all the issues here, but however persuasive the arguments for opposing early implantation are, I imagine that only a small proportion of parents can be persuaded to postpone the implant. The Deaf community certainly has a duty to ensure that parents are made aware of the issues. However, if opposition is made the main focus of the community's campaign, I feel that a lot of vital effort will be wasted with very little success and that, far from arousing sympathy, many parents and professionals will feel confused and alienated.

The third option is for the Deaf community to challenge the assertion that early signing is unnecessary. Even with the earliest implantation currently envisaged, the device cannot be implanted until about four years of age. Only children who are profoundly deaf are currently considered for implantation. Without signing, such children will have virtually no useful communication for at least their first four years. The operation is no miracle, so even in favourable circumstances communication can only gradually be established. Thus there can be little real communication during the first five years. There is considerable evidence that such a deficit can never be made up. Early signing, as we found with Piers, can establish excellent communication and permit near-normal development during the early years. I am certain that a child who has used sign as their main means of communication for their first four to five years will always find a place for signing in their life, and will therefore gravitate to the Deaf community—regardless of the impact of a CI.

I therefore believe that the Deaf community would be advised to accept implants as part of the Deaf scene, concentrate their efforts on campaigning for good signing to be introduced from diagnosis, and on maintaining contacts with such children and their families throughout childhood.

I have found the attitude of professionals at institutions like Addenbrookes Hospital and MHGS extremely puzzling, in that while they are often impressed by Piers' grasp of English and his general education, and acknowledge the important part that signing has played in achieving it, they still want us to stop signing. We have had to reiterate our belief that the CI is an extra help to complement, not supplant, signing. Sign has been crucial to Piers' development so far and we see no reason for this to change. Professionals have tolerated this view and have agreed to a compromise—we accept that signing is not used in certain formal situations including, for example, his speech therapy sessions that we carry out at home; they accept that we sign at other times. I fear that parents who are less firm in their views on signing than we are may be put under more pressure to drop signing and may need support in resisting such pressure.

Some professionals still seem to have an inherent fear that signing discourages the learning of English—a good knowledge of which is vital for the implant to be effective. These fears will be fanned by programmes which teach English as a second language, i.e. English may follow in time but that there will not be enough English in place by the time of the implantation.

Clearly all educational programmes for deaf children place enormous stress on the acquisition of English, but it seem entirely possible that, particularly in the initial stages, some programmes may not form the best preparation for an early implant. So implant professionals

66   will continue to mistrust them. On the other hand such programmes should not be forced to change merely to suit those children who will go on to have implants. On top of this, we ourselves have seen the impact that having an implant has had on Piers' education for over a year now. Teachers clearly have great problems managing a class containing a number of children at various stages in their implant programmes. Thus, as well as the irrational mistrust that has existed for years within deaf education, I now see real and valid conflicts of interest.

Dare I hope that there can be enough dialogue to dispel the mistrust that will certainly damage the deaf children we are all trying to help?

Riki and I are very grateful for the years of help and support we have received from the Deaf community, the teaching profession and now the implant team. All have been important in moulding our son, and will continue to be important in the future. We hope that in sharing our thoughts on the operation itself and some of the diverse issues surrounding it, we can contribute to better relationships between all those involved, as this is so crucial for our son and others like him.

The PHU Experience

Teresa Waldron

I was born in 1969 and was a hearing baby. In fact, I passed the hearing test that is given to all babies, with flying colours. I began to talk and apparently had quite a good vocabulary by the time I was one year old. Then I developed a bad cold and my mother noticed that I didn't seem to be hearing as well as usual. I was taken to the doctor, who said I had bad catarrh and prescribed nose drops. These seemed to work well and my hearing returned once again.

Two months later, I caught another cold which was accompanied by tonsillitis. When I eventually recovered, my mother noticed that I was deaf again. More nose drops were prescribed but this time my hearing didn't return. The doctor said it was severe catarrh and that it would go in time, so my parents weren't unduly worried.

The months went by, until my parents were expecting their second child. During one of my mother's anti-natal check-ups, she mentioned to the doctor that my hearing still hadn't returned and that she was concerned about it. He prescribed yet more nose drops and told her to continue with these. During the following check-up my mother said there was still no change and that she thought that maybe I was deaf. The doctor said she was worrying unnecessarily. He then clicked his fingers and I turned my head. 'There you are,' the doctor said, 'I told you—nothing to worry about. She can hear'. My mother protested, saying that I had caught sight of his hand movement out of the corner of my eye. The doctor said this was rubbish and that she was just being a neurotic mother.

My mother went home with mixed emotions. On the one hand, she wanted to believe the doctor but on the other hand, she had a gut feeling that I was indeed deaf.

It wasn't until after my sister was born that something was eventually done about my situation. My mother came home two days after the birth. The midwife came in each day and at the end of the week there

68 was a call from the health visitor. She asked if there were any problems. 'Not with the baby,' my mum said, 'She's thriving. But my little girl,' (by this time I was two years and eleven months old) 'she doesn't seem to be able to hear properly'. The health visitor watched me as I tapped my mum and mimed for some scissors. (I had a red plastic pair with which, I am told, I loved to cut pictures out of magazines). The health visitor was amazed to discover that this was how I communicated all the time, through mime. The speech which I had previously developed during my first twelve months had nearly all vanished. Any words which I did say, were now said back to front—'Daddy' and 'lolly' were now pronounced as 'De-da' and 'Le-lol'.

The health visitor asked if I had seen a doctor and my mother told her of her experiences at the anti-natal clinic. She seemed quite shocked and said that it may be that my bouts of tonsillitis were making my tonsils swell, partially blocking my ear canals. She suggested making an appointment with a different doctor at the surgery.

So, the very next day, off we went to see another doctor. My mum told him the health visitor's theory about my swollen tonsils. He said this was rubbish. He asked how I communicated and my mother informed him that I mimed for everything. He then asked if she gave me the things I mimed for. My mum told him if they were things which I should have, then yes, she did. He asked what would happen if I mimed for something and she didn't understand what it was I wanted. 'She screams with frustration' my mother replied.

'I wouldn't allow a child to scream at me,' said the doctor, 'I would apply the master hand'. Mum told him that she didn't think that was the answer. 'That's my advice', said the doctor 'It's up to you whether you follow it or not'. She told him she would definitely not be following his advice. She told me that she left the surgery that day feeling very frustrated and very alone.

The next day, when we were getting ready to go the shops, Mum decided to test my hearing for herself. She asked me to go and fetch the shopping bag which hung behind the door. She says she did not use any exaggerated lip pattern and nor did she use her voice. I apparently did as she asked and fetched the shopping bag. My mum said she was stunned when she realised that I was a competent lip-reader.

We didn't make it to the shops that day. Instead, we walked just two hundred yards up the road to the Health Clinic. My mother asked to speak to the health visitor who had come to the house after my sister's birth. Mum also explained how she knew I could lip-read and about her unpleasant experience with the second doctor. She then demanded a hearing test and the health visitor agreed to book an appointment. The health visitor said that it should really be booked by our family doctor but because of his attitude she would have to go over his head.

Two weeks later we had still heard nothing back from the audiologist, so my mother returned again to the Health Clinic. The health visitor explained that appointments could sometimes take months to come through. Mum wasn't happy about it, she felt too much time had been wasted already, so the health visitor agreed to try and hurry things up and two weeks later I had my hearing test. There was an audiologist present and also a peripatetic teacher of the Deaf. It was a very in-depth test and the audiologist told my mother that I had a shock response to sound. I could only hear things like very loud bells ringing or a door bang and I couldn't hear a human voice. The audiologist said I would be fitted with a body-worn hearing-aid and the teacher of the deaf would come and visit the following week to start working on my speech at home.

Mum said she felt upset when she got outside the clinic because she didn't know anything about deafness. She didn't know what sort of future I would have or what to expect. On the way home she cried but that was the first and last time she cried about me—well about my hearing anyway!

The next morning my mum decided that she was going to be positive. She carried on as though I wasn't deaf at all. She made sure I had the right education to meet my needs but apart from that I wasn't treated any differently to my younger sister. She wanted me to have a good education and to believe that you can be anything that you want to be. I find that I now tell my son the same thing.

The audiologist said that I had a good chance of being an oral child and advised that I would probably do better in a Partial Hearing Unit (PHU), a unit placed within a mainstream school than in a School for the Deaf. The PHUs back then did not allow signing. The emphasis was on speech. In a School for the Deaf, the emphasis was on signing. Nowadays, children in a PHU are encouraged to speak and to sign.

I was fitted with a body-worn hearing-aid and my mum made little bags with animals sewn on the front to encourage me to wear it. On the way home from the clinic, Mum bought me a little book which was shaped like a rabbit. When the rabbit's tummy was squeezed, it squeaked. She said she would never forget the look on my face as I squeezed the rabbit over and over again. Also, when my father stopped for some petrol, a fire engine went past with the siren blaring. She said I was amazed and couldn't work out where the noise was coming from. When we first went shopping, she switched off my hearing-aid where there was a lot of traffic but turned it on when we were walking down the quieter streets. She said I stopped and pointed to my feet and then to my ears and she knew from that moment that life was going to be all right for me. I had such a curiosity about sound and speech that I learned really quickly.

I started Aldercar Infants School when I was just four years old, travelling there and back by taxi. My taxi driver was a wonderful man. His name was Mr Dawes and he came from Heanor. As I was the youngest and the only girl in the taxi, he spoilt me rotten. He defended me from the rough boys who shared the taxi, when my small voice would pipe up, 'Mr Dawes, he's hitting me!' When it snowed, I didn't like walking. I was scared of slipping. So, he would pick me up and carry me across the road! He is now in his seventies and to this day is still a very dear friend. He retired from taxi driving some years ago. He doesn't drive at all now due to cataracts and says the roads are too congested anyway. I visit him every Christmas and he always makes coffee with a dash of Tia Maria in it. We then talk and laugh about the old days, when he was my hero and defender from tormenting schoolboys!

I was a timid child when I first started school. I hadn't mixed a lot with children, apart from when I was at playgroup. I soon got used to it though and made lots of friends some of whom are my friends to this day. I did lessons within the unit, sums, reading and writing and also received speech therapy from my unit teacher, whose name was Mrs Brown.

She was lovely, kind gentle and being shy herself, in her, I found a kindred spirit. There was also a nursery nurse called Mrs Bacon, who was also lovely and a grandmother figure to all the children. She retired and was replaced by Mrs Tagg, who was a lively and fun person with

tremendous energy. She lived in my hometown and I used to go to her
daughter's birthday parties.

My speech began to develop well in the unit. I was integrated into
the main school for less intense subjects, such as painting, sewing and
physical education. My mother, although happy with my progress,
wondered how I would have fared at the Royal School for the Deaf.
One day when I came home, she had cause to tell me off about some
misdemeanour. She said I immediately put up my fists and declared, 'I
fight you!' As she knew I hadn't learnt this from the teachers, it must
then have come from the school playground. This was proof to my
mum that I was actually picking up speech from hearing children, perhaps not really the type of speech that she wanted me to learn, but it
was speech nevertheless. I stayed at Aldercar Infants School until I was
seven, and I think these were probably the happiest days of my school
life, cosseted and carefree.

I moved on to Langley Mill Junior School, which although sounds a
long way away, was actually only a few yards down the road. The teacher there was Mrs Hardy who, although much stricter than Mrs Brown,
only wanted the best for us in life. She demanded—and received—our
best efforts. I worked hard while I was there and she filled my head with
facts and figures, knowledge and information. She even made us learn
multiplication tables, which had been taken off the curriculum at that
time, because she believed they were vital to a child's mathematical
education. Mrs Hardy was a teacher of the old school, believing that she
was there to teach and we were there to learn! And learn we did! Being
deaf didn't mean that we got away with anything. She didn't pity or feel
sorry for us, she just wanted the best that we could give. She wanted me
to take the entrance exam for Mary Hare Grammar School, a boarding
school near Reading for very bright deaf children.

I was excited at first about going, but as the time drew nearer I began to think about how much I would miss my parents and my sister.
I confided my fears to the classroom assistant, Mrs Diggle, who was a
bit of a softie and she told my mum and dad during a parents evening.
My dad, I know, was disappointed. My mum was secretly relieved. She
didn't really want me to leave home at such a young age, but hadn't
liked to stop me from going in case I missed an opportunity for a better education. Mum had the task of telling Mrs Hardy, who took it quite

well, even though she was probably a bit disappointed. I am grateful that she believed in me enough to give me a chance in life, an opportunity a lot of pupils don't have. She did instil in me an ethos for hard work, dedication and determination. I hope I have never let her down.

When I left Langley Mill Juniors at the age of 11, I moved on to Heanor Gate Senior School. This was one of the most traumatic experiences of my life. I had to say goodbye to all my old friends at the junior school as they were moving on to Aldercar Senior School where there was no PHU. Three deaf children moved that year and I was the only girl. I didn't know any of the children in my class and I felt totally isolated. The other children didn't want to know me and some were unkind and called me names. As a result, I became isolated and withdrawn. I didn't want to go to school and it took me a long time to settle down. I did make friends with a girl who started the school having moved from up north. We were both lonely and struck up a friendship. I still wasn't totally happy though. The hearing children who had started school at Aldercar Infants accepted the deaf children in the PHU. They did not see us as being 'different'. They grew up with us and were totally happy with us—as we were with them. The very young know no prejudices, whereas older children learn prejudice in later life. It would have been much better if the PHU had been attached to Aldercar Senior School and I could have stayed with all my deaf and hearing friends there.

The teacher in the PHU at Heanor Gate, whom I will call Miss 'P', was not a patch on the other teachers of the Deaf at my previous schools. She had no real understanding of children, deaf or hearing. Her main concerns did not seem to be with our education but more with our presentation—clean shoes, straight tie and so on. She was very old-fashioned and out of touch. We had to do extra lessons with her in English and maths. I was taken out of French for two periods to do maths in the PHU. The French teacher told my parents that I was, quite surprisingly, good at French. She told my parents to ask if I could be taken out of music instead of French. I did not benefit from music lessons at all but Miss 'P' would not allow this. Similarly, the English teacher told my parents that I was showing promise in his English class but I was being taken out of his classes to do lessons in the PHU—in English! Again my parents requested, on the English teacher's advice, that I be taken out of a less academic subject to go to the PHU, but this did not happen.

Miss 'P' had low expectations of deaf pupils. When the time came for my year to sit exams prior to the end of our full-time education, it transpired that the school had never entered a deaf child for an 'O' Level at GCE (Ordinary level at General Certificate of Education) and only one had taken a CSE (Certificate of Secondary Education). This was really appalling, as the school had been open for 11 years. If the decision had been left to Miss 'P', I would not have been allowed to take school leaving examinations. My parents had to fight all the way for me to have the chance. They asked the deputy head if I could follow the advice given by the subject teachers, and be entered for the GCE examinations in English and Pottery. This was allowed and I passed them both. I took other subjects at CSE and I passed those too.

The options offered to me on leaving school was a Youth Training Scheme (YTS) or factory work. My parents would not hear of either of these and, as I loved books, they helped me to apply to Derbyshire County Council Library Service for employment. I was interviewed and started work at Heanor library. I spent a very happy time there and my confidence began to grow. I then transferred to Allestree library.

I passed my driving test and my dad bought me a car as a reward. Sadly though, my parents split up. This was more traumatic for my sister than for me as I am quite philosophical about most things. I was very happy though at Allestree and remained there until I eventually got a job at DCIL (Derbyshire Centre of Integrated Living) at Ripley. DCIL has an ethos based on the seven needs which are: Access, Counselling, Employment, Housing, Personal Assistance, Technical Aids and Transport. These needs are required in order for disabled people to live independently in the community. My confidence grew even more here as I found my identity as a disabled person. The ethos made me realise that all Ddeaf people need to have some of their needs met in order to live independently. There is one need that was not covered and that was Education. I think it is very important for all Ddeaf people to have equal access to Education. I firmly believe that if this happens, this would reduce their need to be reliant on services provided by mission based services or Social Services.

I feel honoured having worked at a campaigning organisation which gave me an insight into the rights of disabled people. I worked as a Community Development Worker in the Derbyshire Dales District and

74 made lots of good friends. During this time I became involved in doing part time youth work with young Ddeaf people. Eventually though,
I wanted to further my education and applied to go to De Montfort
University in Leicester to study Youth And Community Work. I was
accepted and did a year's study and then, much to the dismay of my
parents, I became pregnant. My mother was particularly distraught
and was convinced that would be the end of my chance at university.
I took a year off and had a son. He is, along with my sister's son who
was born two years later, the absolute centre of my parents' universe. I
think the world of him. No matter how old he is I think of him as being my little baby.

I returned to university and gained a diploma. I was about to begin
my final year to complete the BA Honours in Community and Youth
Studies when I saw a job advertised as a Co-ordinator/Development
worker at Chesterfield Law Centre. I decided to apply and was amazed
when I was successful. I left university and started work. I was a single
parent and I wanted to support my baby. I could have remained at university but there was no guarantee that I would be employed at the end
of it all. Seven years on, I am still employed at Chesterfield but if a better
job came along I would probably apply.

Throughout my career I have had to campaign for better conditions
for deaf people and to try and raise awareness. Together with Sarah
Roelofs and Phillip Gerrard, I set up a political group—Ddeaf Equality
Forward. This group is managed and run by Ddeaf people themselves. It
is very similar to branches of the Federation of Deaf People.

In 2000, Derby Deaf Centre were hoping to make big changes. I
was elected onto the committee. I was nominated again this year, but
the hearing interpreter objected and I wasn't voted in. It's always the
same—certain hearing people are allowed in but any deaf person, apart
from Deaf people with BSL, are obstructed—which on the one hand I
can understand, but on the other I can't. The last I've heard is that the
committee was struggling to get a Chair. They have a hearing person as
secretary now and they seem to be doing little on the campaigning issue
of getting Derby Deaf Club moved to suitable premises, which surprises
me as Derby Deaf Club premises are to close down sometime next year.
I was hoping that they would model themselves on Nottingham Deaf
Club where some services for Ddeaf people can be found within these

new premises. I was hoping that Derby Deaf Club would take the lead 75
on this. All we can do is to wait and see and hope for the best. There is
still a long way to go but I feel things are improving, albeit slowly.

Life or Hearing

Veniamin Tsukerman and Zinaida Azarkh

This is the story of Irina Tsukerman—known to friends as Ira—written by her parents. When it was first published in the USSR in 1984 they used the name Krainin, because at the time their work at the top-secret nuclear research station known as 'Arzamas-16' (actually the town of Sarov) could not be mentioned in print. Izrail Galynker (1909-67) was given the pseudonym Leonid to cover up his Jewish origins, but his tombstone bears his real name. He is one of the unsung heroes of the Stalinist repression. As a result of his help to Irina he was arrested in 1948 for 'preparing an attempt on the life of Comrade Stalin' and sentenced to death. This was commuted to twenty-five years imprisonment, and he was released in 1955.

Ira had been ill for four days, yet no-one could diagnose her illness. The old doctor from next door said,
—It's probably malaria.
The doctor from the clinic examined the little girl and concluded, without any particular confidence,
—It may be typhoid fever.
With each day that passed new and ominous symptoms appeared. Slowly but steadily her temperature rose, her headaches grew worse. On Saturday June 1 she began vomiting.
The Saturday night was terrible. Ira's mother and grandmother took it in turns to sit by her bed. In those few days the girl who had always been cheerful, lively, friendly, everybody's favourite, had changed beyond all recognition. From time to time she moaned, unaware of everything that was going on around her. That night no-one in the family slept. Something fearful, ineluctable was looming over it.
That first year after the war, 1946, had started wonderfully fair: not a cloud in the sky. The banner of the victory over Nazi Germany was

raised high over everybody. We'd all done our bit to achieve this victory. In January 1946 it was announced that my friend Lev Altshuller
and I had been awarded a USSR State Prize for the work we had done
during the war. And suddenly there was this sinister, incomprehensible
illness...

We had many loyal friends who knew what life was about. My
work brought me into contact with many distinguished academics.
When they heard of our misfortune, they all tried to help as best they
could. Following one good piece of advice, one sunny Sunday morning my wife and I hurried round to see Dmitri Dmitrievich Lebedev,
an outstanding pædiatrician and first-class diagnostician. The doctor
promised to come that very day. On the way back Vera bought a spray
of lilac whose buds had not yet opened. But Ira who had always liked
flowers, didn't even look at it.

—I've got a very bad headache, Mummy!

Lebedev came exactly at the appointed hour. A greying man of about
sixty, with a little pointed beard and kind, intelligent eyes.

—What other illnesses has Ira had?

—When we were evacuated to Kazan, after she'd had measles she had
tubercular bronchial adenitis. She was treated in the sanatorium at
Yudino, near Kazan. The X-ray of her lungs showed only the image of a
small calcified glandule, about the size of a one-copeck piece.

He gave the little girl a long and thorough examination. Then, going
into the next room, he said:

—I have bad news for you; it looks very much like meningitis.

—But meningitis can be cured, can't it? I asked hopefully.

—Simple forms, so-called cerebrospinal forms can be. But it looks to
me as if your daughter has tubercular meningitis. We can't cure that.

—How many days does the illness last?

—Usually death ensues on the 21st day, more rarely on the 23rd or 24th
day. Each year hundreds of children die from this disease in Moscow.
If any do recover it means there's been a mistake in the diagnosis and
it wasn't tubercular meningitis. Send the child to us at the Morozovsky
hospital. We'll do tests. Maybe I'm wrong.

The door slammed. Out with the professor went our old life, which
now seemed so wonderful. We were left with our grief.

Vera ran to Ira's side.

78   —Where've you been so long, Mummy? And why are you crying?

—I bumped my leg in the corridor.

We had to do something. I rang my relatives and my friends. They were all upset, sympathised with us and tried to instil hope in us. But what hope is there? For a mistake in the diagnosis—perhaps it wasn't tubercular meningitis. We clung on to that hope.

Everything that followed reminded me of frames from some fantastic film. In the evening, out of sheer habit, I turned on the radio. The shining white needle slowly crawled over the dial with names of towns. We stopped it at 'London'. A broadcast of scientific news, in Russian:

—In the USA a new antibiotic has been discovered: streptomycin. Unlike penicillin this antibiotic kills bacillary micro-organisms, including the one that causes tuberculosis, Koch's bacillus. Doctors hope it will help people with such incurable diseases as tubercular meningitis to recover...

Twice in one day I'd heard this terrible combination of words: 'tuberculosis and meningitis'. I recall that the wife of our deputy director of science, Tatiana Sergeevna was a doctor specializing in tuberculosis. She worked in a large TB hospital. I gave her a ring. Yes, she knew about streptomycin; the hospital had a small amount of the drug, but for the time being experiments were restricted to animals.

On Monday we took Ira to the Morozovsky hospital in the Institute car. It was easy for Vera to persuade her; for Muscovite children of 1946 a car journey was an almost undreamed of luxury. Before the journey Ira agreed to have her hair cut. Her thick auburn curls fell to the floor. Unnoticed, Vera put a lock of hair on one side. Would the hair ever grow again on Ira's poor head?

Ira's grandmother and grandfather saw the car off. They tried to smile through their tears. We crossed the Krymsky Bridge. A fresh breeze blew in from the river through the open windows of the car.

—That's nice. Even my headache's a bit better, said Ira.

The Morozovsky Children's Hospital, which was built before the Revolution, occupied a large green plot in a relatively quiet side street linking Kaluzhsky and Serpukhovsky squares (now known as October Square and Dobrynin Square). It was about three hundred metres from the entrance to the building where Dmitri Lebedev worked.

We went through the usual procedures for new patients: an examination, registration, a bath. A white ward, and in the corner by the window, in a pink hospital nightdress, lay our Ira.

The first cerebrospinal puncture was made. This was an injection between the third and fourth vertebræ in the region of the small of the back. The liquid ran smoothly, without the high pressure which is characteristic of meningitis. The Head of the Department Rachel Zakharovna Sherman tried to calm us:

—Why must it be tubercular meningitis? The basic indicators, albumen and the number of cells per unit volume (cytose) are only a bit more than normal. With this sort of illness, after 24 hours the film on the surface of the liquid in the test tube falls away. That's a sure sign of the illness.

Tuesday 4th June

All morning my friend Lev rushed round Moscow with one aim in view: to find out where one could get hold of streptomycin. In the regional clinics they still had never heard of streptomycin. They advised us to try the TB Hospital on the Yauza. There we were told: 'Yes, we've got one patient who is being treated with his own streptomycin'.

We found out this patient was Professor Lavrovsky, who was suffering from TB of the throat and that his Head of Department, Academician N.D. Zelinsky had obtained the streptomycin for him in the USA. We hastily got in touch with Academician Zelinsky, who made an appointment for us for the following day.

At midday it became clear that the film had not fallen away. Dr Sherman was pleased...As we left the department we met Dmitri Lebedev. He was already in the picture.

—Yes, Dr Sherman doesn't agree with my diagnosis, but I'm not retracting it yet. We must repeat the puncture. The albumen and cytose are up. Ira was again given an injection between the vertebræ.

The next morning, not yet having had the results of this investigation, I rang the doorbell of Academician Zelinsky's house. He lived on Mokhovaya street, right next door to the old building of Moscow university. The door was opened by a handsome old man wearing an Academician's skullcap. He was eighty-five, but his eyes were lively and bright. He invited us into his study. When he had listened to our request, he thought for a minute, and then said:

80 —You know I'm not sure that streptomycin is suitable in your case.

He opened a catalogue written in English. The Merck Company gave careful information about the properties and characteristics of streptomycin in the treatment of different forms of tuberculosis. Prolonged usage in large quantities was recommended. There was nothing about tubercular meningitis. But as far as we were concerned, if the terrible diagnosis was repeated, it was our only hope.

From further discussion it emerged that Professor Lavrovsky, for whom Zelinsky had got the preparation via some American colleagues, had got a little streptomycin left. Zelinsky advised us to ask for some and gave us a note.

In the sample taken the previous day the film fell away. Other indicators also showed us that Dmitri Lebedev was right in his diagnosis. We hurried to the hospital on the Yauza and Professor Lavrovsky.

That evening we got a glass phial with a rubber stopper. The Merck Company of the USA. But how was it to be used?

Where must it be injected and in what quantity? Lavrovsky was getting intramuscular injections of one gram, one million Oxford units, every day. But we only had one gram. Such a small amount would hardly help at all.

It became clear that there were in Moscow two schools of thought, two opinions about how to treat diseases of the brain. At the Institute of Physiology, run by Academician L.S. Stem, it was considered that drugs should be administered by endocranial injection directly into the fourth ventricle of the brain. According to the theory current in this institute, the barrier could thus be surmounted which prevents drugs reaching the infected areas of the brain.

The second school was the N.N. Burdenko Institute. There they asserted that drugs could be injected into the cerebrospinal canal; a much less dangerous procedure which could be done by any surgeon. But neither institute had experience of using streptomycin on humans. A preliminary test on a dog was essential. This would put off the use of streptomycin for several days and would diminish the already limited supply of the precious drug.

The terrible symptoms grew. Even a non-expert could see the rigidity of the neck; the child was unable to bend her head. Her mouth was slightly twisted. Fire in the brain. The accursed acid-resistant Koch Bacilli! For them the cerebral fluid is an excellent breeding ground. They multiply rapidly and poison the brain.

Thursday 6th June

One of the most remarkable days of my life and the life of all the participants in this epic. Early in the morning a phone call from Izrail Galynker , one of my closest friends.

—We must try and contact America by phone and get their advice as to how best to administer the drug.

I didn't know where to start. I had no friends in America. During the war, it's true, senior members of our institute had asked for information about the treatment of pigmental retinitis, a serious eye complaint, from the Mayo Brothers' clinic.

Maybe that was the way out of our difficulty. We had neither the time nor the drugs to do experiments on dogs.

—All right. But how do we do it?

Academician N.G. Bruevich played an active part in all this. So too did the Præsidium of the Academy of Sciences which approached the Ministry of Communications for permission to make a phone call to the United States.

My English wasn't up to a conversation like this; I only read technical literature. I asked the head of the English department at the institute run by the Academy to help out, as well as the doctor who headed the Clinic attached to the Academy.

I dialled the number. The operator asked me where the Mayo clinic was. With some difficulty I recalled the name on the telegram: Rochester

—What state?

I didn't know. New York, I thought.

—Who do I ask for?

—Ask for any of the doctors treating tubercular meningitis with streptomycin.

I realised that I was giving an address like the one given by Chekhov's Vanka Zhukov: 'to grandad, in the country'.

—Be at home near your phone between 17.00 and 18.00 hours. We'll try and connect you.

Several hours passed. During that time another little girl was brought into the ward where Ira was: Lena. Another case of tubercular

82 meningitis. Her father was the director of one of the big metal works in the Ukraine. The illness had started at the end of May, but the condition of the child was much better: the headaches were less violent, the rigidity of the back of the head less marked. She was talking dreamily about summer, about a trip to a dacha, about how she would go mushroom picking.

An hour before the appointed time Izrail and I rushed home in the Academy car. And for the first time in these four days, so full to overflowing with unrelieved anxiety, there arose within me the distinct feeling that with such friends even the impossible was possible. Many years later, reading the letters of Marina Tsvetaeva, I found her broad definition: 'A friend is one who acts'. My friends fitted this formula to perfection.

In our communal flat there was a long narrow corridor on to which opened the doors of five rooms. In the middle of the corridor was the communal telephone, the main participant in that day's events. Once again I checked that the call was booked.

—Everything's OK. Just wait.

Izrail, who had excellent English and a translator sent by the Academy had already clearly formulated six questions which we wanted to put to someone in America, it didn't matter who. The old wall clock struck five. Then, impassively, it struck the quarter hour and half hour. The telephone remained silent. I rang up again.

—Yes, your call has been booked, the American operator is looking up the number you want. Keep waiting.

Five minutes later came the prolonged ring of the international exchange. The operator told us that in Rochester, New York State, there was no Mayo clinic.

What could we do? I explained the situation to the operator: a child was dying, we had the drugs but no one knew how to use them. I pleaded with the operator to persuade her colleague on the other end of the line to find the clinic. It was a well-known medical establishment and there must be lots of people in the USA who knew it.

At 17.55 there was another ring: the Mayo clinic was in Rochester, Minnesota. That's almost 2000 kilometres to the west of New York. There it was now eight o'clock in the morning. Was there anyone at the clinic?

18.05. Another ring. Another operator told us that time was up for private conversations. From 18.00 to 20.00 the lines to America are only used for newspaper correspondents. We explained, we pleaded, we asked them to persuade the correspondents to wait a little.

At 18.15 came the long-awaited, life-saving ring. Professor Hinshaw was on the line from the Mayo clinic. He was the first man to use streptomycin in the treatment of TB. But in Moscow the receiver was being held by a teacher of English.

—Mr Hinshaw, Mr Hinshaw, she shouted. She turned an anxious face to us,

—There's some sort of crackling, distortion. I can't make out a single word...

We knew that a direct cable link between Europe and America had still not been established. During the war German U-boats had destroyed the transatlantic cable between London and New York. Telephone conversations went by cable as far as London; beyond that there was a radio telephone link to New York and beyond that cable links with the rest of America. But in 1946 the radio telephone was not very reliable.

—Give me the phone, please.

Izrail almost wrenched it out of the English teacher's hands.

—We have only one million units of this medicine. He repeated this phrase in English, three, four, five times enunciating each word clearly and separately.

—Damn it, he can't hear me, he said in Russian.

Again I prayed: so many miracles had happened in the last four days; just let one more happen; let this remarkable conversation take place!

Suddenly Izrail's face brightened up:

—He can hear me, he can hear me! He rattled off translations of Hinshaw's replies and the doctor from the polyclinic jotted them down. Hinshaw recommended that 100 thousand units of streptomycin be injected daily into the cerebrospinal fluid. That's 0.1 grams per day. On top of that daily intra-muscular injections of 2–3 million units were essential. Once again Izrail explained that we only had one gram of the drug.

—Do the injection into the cerebrospinal canal, came the answer,

—But I'm afraid you won't be able to avoid intramuscular injections.

84   —Many thanks!, Izrail shouted into the mouthpiece;

—One last question: using your method of treatment, what's the inci-
dence of recovery from tubercular meningitis?

—At the moment I'm treating two children, a little girl who fell ill three
months ago and a boy who fell ill two months ago. They're still alive.

The conversation was over. One problem had been sorted out; there
was no need to experiment on the dog. Streptomycin could be injected
into the cerebrospinal fluid. But how? Into the fourth ventricle, into the
seat of infection as Ya.A. Rosin, a physiologist of the Stem school advised, or into the spinal column? Besides that we had a one-gram packet
of streptomycin. Where and how were we to divide the contents of one
phial into 10 equal parts? We needed a sterile medium in which to parcel the preparation up into ampoules.

We remembered Professor Zinaida Vissarionovna Yermoleva. In
1942 she had supervised the cultivation and production of the first
penicillin to be manufactured in the USSR. We had already been to
her laboratory. She had addresses and telephone numbers. I called her
at home and told her about my conversation with Hinshaw and about
how urgent it was to divide sterilely one gram of streptomycin into 10
equal parts.

—Come to my laboratory on Vorontsovo Field at eight o'clock.

My brother took the precious gram to Professor Yermoleva at the
Institute. Lev and I set off on a triangular route: The Burdenko Institute,
the Institute of Physiology, and Dmitri Lebedev's flat.

The last word, the decisive word, lay with Lebedev. It was already
past ten o'clock in the evening as we drove up to his house. He listened
to our excited account of the events of the day. He reflected for several
moments, then said:

—I would do the injection in the way Rosin suggests, directly into the
head. It may be risky but it's nearer the seat of the infection and we've
only got enough medicine for ten days.

The streptomycin was packed in ten glass ampoules. We signed an
indemnity, to the effect that we would make no claims in the event of
an unsuccessful outcome. Uncle Yosif volunteers to go to 25th October
Street to fetch Rosin. At half past eleven they were at the hospital. We
were not let in of course. We waited beneath the windows. In the street
it was quite dark. Suddenly we noticed a figure dressed in white coming

towards us. We recognised Aleksei.

—Aleksei. what are you doing?

—I can't sleep.

At half past twelve Rosin came out. Everything was OK. The drug had been administered.

—When did you begin? asked Yosif interestedly

—At ten past twelve, replied Rosin.

—Very good, said Yosif. On the way home he explained.

—I'm glad that the injection was done not on a Thursday but on a Friday. For our family Thursday is an unlucky day. You'll see, everything will be all right now.

Superstition, of course. But who could have know then that eight years later Uncle would die from a heart attack, on 30th September 1954, a Thursday...

After the injection Ira lay semi-conscious. Although weak, her pulse could be clearly felt. About three o'clock it began to get light. The tops of the trees turned pink and, as a result; the leaves on the lower branches appeared blue. The first birds began to sing, ushering in the new day. Vera turned away from the window and looked at her daughter. Something had changed! Her lips had turned grey, the outline of her nose had sharpened slightly, her finger nails had turned blue.

Vera quickly seized her wrist: there was no pulse, or almost no pulse. During the terrible summer of 1941 Vera had worked as a nurse in an evacuation hospital. She knew that this was either severe shock or death. She yelled to the duty nurse:

—Nadya, bring some camphor! Quickly! She's dying!

It was a good thing that the duty nurse's post was right next to the ward. Nadya quickly gave Ira an injection, then summoned the duty doctor from the neighbouring building. While Nadya and the out of breath doctor Natalya Vasilevna Konopleva worked their magic over Ira, Vera hurried to the telephone and woke me up:

—She's dying. Get here quickly.

I woke up Vera's sister, Aniuta, rang Aleksei. Then we rushed to the Morozovsky hospital. By the time we arrived there, Ira had already come out of severe shock. But what were we to do today? Hinshaw had recommended daily injections.

In the evening an executive quartet got together: Izrail, Aleksei, my brother and myself. We decided to try to ring Hinshaw again. Alas, we had no success.

The operators explained there was no radio link with New York that day. Once again we explained the situation to the duty operator. She listened carefully and asked for our number. A few minutes later the phone rang:

—Do you know Yurovsky?

—No, we don't.

—He's in charge of international telegrams. Compose a telegram and go to the Central Telegraph Office. It only takes a few hours to exchange telegrams with any point on earth.

The familiar building of the Central Telegraph Office stood on the corner of Gorky Street and the then Gazetny Lane, now Ogarev Street. We found the right room and the right window. Behind the window stood a pale woman in black. We related our misadventures once again. Her eyes filled with tears.

—Two months ago I buried my son. He died from tubercular meningitis, she said quietly.

—I'll do everything I can to get your telegram through as quickly as possible.

This time we knew the exact address: Professor Hinshaw, Rochester, Minnesota, USA. We explained briefly that we had done the first endocranial injection of 100,000 units of streptomycin; there had been severe shock, from which we had managed to bring the child round. We asked whether we should continue to administer the drug. We paid for a hundred words of answer. We composed the text together and Izrail translated it into English.

An hour and a half later we got the following telephone message; 'Your telegram has been handed over to the addressee. He will reply as soon as possible.' An hour later Hinshaw's detailed reply was delivered by post. He had not done any endocranial injections; he had only done them into the cerebrospinal canal. The first injection might cause a state of shock but, as a rule this phenomenon disappeared after further injections. He recommended us to continue injections into the cerebrospinal canal, a concentrated intramuscular dosage of 2–3 million units of streptomycin daily.

Professor Rosin was clearly the first man ever to inject streptomycin into the human brain. We decided to continue the injections. On the morning of Saturday 8th June the second endocranial injection passed off without complications. Immediately after the injection Ira's condition worsened and a temporary squint developed. The headaches continued. The samples of the cerebral fluid remained bad; both the albumen and the cell count were increasing. The membrane was falling away regularly and Koch's bacilli were found in the fluid.

In the evening I managed to get Vera home for a few hours. In a vase on the window ledge was the branch of blossoming lilac. For the first time a faint smile played on Vera's lips:

—You know, I've made a prediction: if this branch which I bought last Sunday, Black Sunday, lasts a week, Ira will live.

On Sunday 9th June and on the succeeding days Professor Rosin continued the injections. 100,000 units of streptomycin were injected into the fourth ventricle of the brain everyday.

Tuesday 11th June

Yesterday Lena's father invited me to have dinner with him at the National Hotel… He almost agreed to begin experimenting with endocranial injections on Lena. Uniting our efforts to get hold of streptomycin could be useful to us both. But today, after seeing Ira's torment after the latest injection, Lena's father changed his mind.

—I don't want to torment Lena with such injections. Let's let nature take its course.

He didn't believe in streptomycin, but we did. We believed and we hoped.

Sunday 16th June

The 18th or 19th day of the illness. One gram of muriatic streptomycin, made by Merck, had been used up. We got another gram of the substance from Tatiana Sergeevna. This time it was a sulphate made by Pfeiffer. The same executive quartet decided to continue the endocranial injections. The headaches and occipital rigidity were almost unchanged. Compared with Ira, Lena felt much better.

Wednesday 19th June

Ira's condition remained essentially the same. Vera stayed by her bed-side day and night. That evening it seemed to us that her hearing had deteriorated somewhat:

—Mummy, why can't I hear the sound of your heels when you walk down the corridor?

But Lena's condition had deteriorated sharply. Her head was thrown back. She vomited continuously. She was transferred to another ward.

Thursday 20th June

Today was Ira's birthday, her ninth. In the morning we set off for the hospital with a doll and other presents. Vera was alarmed: during the night Ira's hearing had deteriorated even further. You had to shout; she was going deaf. What a birthday present this was. By the evening Ira was completely deaf. At the entrance to the unit we met Lena's father and grandmother. Her grandmother was in tears: Lena was dying.

Saturday 22nd June

During the night Lena died. Ira showed some improvement; her temperature had dropped from 38 to 37.5°C. Her appetite had returned. As he did his rounds, Dr Lebedev lingered a little longer by her bed.

—How many days has she been ill?

—24, 25.

—Interesting.

—Her temperature is down a bit.

—I see.

Surprisingly he did not touch her but stood a metre from the bed. That evening, as he was leaving the hospital, I caught him by the exit.

—Dr Lebedev, what do you think? Will her hearing return ?

—I don't know. As it is, it is surprising that she's still alive.

—How did you know that her temperature had gone down? You didn't touch the child did you?

—I could see from the vein throbbing in her neck.

Experience is a great strength. He had made the terrible diagnosis without any apparatus or samples, simply from the prehistory of the tubercular process and from the appearance of the patient. Later we learned that in his heart of hearts he did not pin any hopes either on streptomycin or on any other drugs.

Tuesday 25th June

The streptomycin was running out. We had to get hold of a new batch urgently. The Ministry of Health was due to get 20 grams; we had been following their transportation for a whole week. We knew that the drug was in Europe and that it was being delivered by air. But the pilot had got held up somewhere, in Paris or Copenhagen.

When I was with Ira she had asked me,

—Daddy, read me a book.

I made signs towards my ears.

—You won't hear anything darling.

She understood and burst into tears. Neither she nor we could get used to her deafness.

Friday 28th June

Three cheers! The streptomycin arrived. 20 Grams, the complete batch. The price was 250 roubles per gram. We paid 5000 roubles for 20 small phials. Luckily I had money from a State prize. We decided to do 10 intramuscular injections, one gram per day, alongside the endocranial injections. This was less than Hinshaw recommended but we had no right to use more on intramuscular injections.

A young girl, Dina, was brought into the unit. She was fourteen, pretty and clever. She too had tubercular meningitis. But the diagnosis had been made later; the illness was now into its 12th or 13th day. I offered her father some of the unpacked streptomycin, in 0.1 gram doses, for endocranial injections. He agreed to repeat our experiment.

The old nurse tried to talk us out of it.

—You haven't got any yourself and you're going in for charity.

But after all 0.1 grams a day for a month was only 3 grams. That could save the child's life. How could we not try to help?

Wednesday 3rd July

Two important pieces of news in a week. Zhenya, the theoretical physicist from the Academy of Sciences rang. We'd lived in the same student hostel when we had been evacuated to Kazan. His supervisor, Dmitri

90 Vladimirovich Skobeltsyn was going to New York to work for the United Nations. We went to see him urgently and explained our situation in detail. We asked him to get hold of 50–100 grams of streptomycin by any possible means and to send it to Moscow as quickly as possible. He promised to help.

The second piece of news was no less important. At the invitation of the Academy of Sciences the man who had discovered streptomycin, Professor Z. Vaksman was coming to Moscow. It was said he was an emigré from Russia, knew Russian, and was due to bring with him specimen strains and hand them over to Yermoleva. We sent him a detailed telegram asking him to get hold of at least a little of the drug in order to save Ira's life.

Thursday 11th July

Vaksman replied that there was very little chance of getting hold of streptomycin. The US President, Harry Truman, had banned the export of the latest medicine to the USSR and other socialist countries. The beginning of the cold war.

In the hospital Professor Rosin had taught Dr R. Rolnik the technique of endocranial injections. Now two patients, Ira and Dina, were receiving streptomycin by this method. Both were in a satisfactory condition, although their cerebrospinal fluid remained diseased, with a high albumen content and high cytose.

Saturday 20th July

Vaksman arrived. Despite everything he had brought about 50 grams of streptomycin. He explained that this was practically contraband. A strange unrefined brown powder, in semi-manufactured form. He handed it to the President of the Academy of Sciences, Sergei Ivanovich Vavil. This time it had become clear that the former Vice-President of the Academy, the legendary Polar explorer Otto Yulevich Schmidt, was ill with consumption. After Lavrovsky and Ira many people had developed an interest in the new method of treating tuberculosis. They wanted to give the drugs that had been brought in to Schmidt. Vaksman gave a report on streptomycin in the House of Scientists.

—Streptomycin is the first success in the struggle with tuberculosis, which after fascism is the most fearsome enemy of mankind.

Academician Stem invited the American scientist to the Moro hospital where TB was being treated with endocranial injections of streptomycin.

Saturday 3rd August

Yesterday was a big day. Vaksman came. We'd been preparing ourselves for this event for three days: we cleaned and polished the whole section like they do in the navy before the Admiral's inspection. Ira produced an excellent impression of him and read a poem about a fat cat in English.

—The child has already survived more than two months, said Dr Lebedev.

—We've never seen anything like this with tubercular meningitis.

Vaksman inquired in detail how deafness had occurred. When he learned that it had occurred when the streptomycin produced by the Merck Company had been replaced by the sulphate made by the Pfeiffer Company, he suggested that the Pfeiffer preparation was less pure.

Sunday 11th August

This week there was a big event, the decision by the President of the Academy of Sciences Sergei Vavilov to divide the streptomycin thus: 15 grams to Ira and 35 grams to Schmidt, on condition that I take on myself all the hassle involved in purifying and checking the sterility of the drug. I, of course, agreed.

Sunday 18th August

Dina died yesterday. Clearly treatment had begun too late. The death of an adult is always terrible. But the death of a child, who knows almost nothing of life, is a fearful blow, an irreversible blow for parents and friends alike.

Thursday 12 September

Last night we almost lost Ira. Events developed rapidly. In the night the headaches got worse and suddenly she began vomiting again. To cap everything she started having convulsions. She lapsed into semi-conciousness. It was barely six o'clock in the morning when Vera ran into the main block of the sanatorium. She knew that Professor Arendt was

92 resting there. She ran to his room on the first floor. Fortunately he was already up. She gave a garbled account of what had happened. Arendt fully understood, quickly examined Ira and gave her anti-convulsant drugs. We needed to get her to hospital quickly.

When we got Ira to the Morozovsky hospital, she was unconscious again. The thin thread on which her life hung was stretched to the limit. Would she survive? An eye specialist who was called out to her confirmed loss of vision. We doubled the dose of streptomycin, which we injected into the fourth ventricle, to 0.2 grams. Analysis of the cerebrospinal liquid showed a doubling of the albumen to 1.32%. If we continued to inject in doses of 0.2 grams there would only be enough Vaksman streptomycin left for ten injections.

What then? Where and how could we get hold of streptomycin?

On Wednesday the 18th, there occurred an event of enormous importance for us. In the morning there was a phone call from the Ministry of Foreign Affairs:

—A parcel has arrived addressed to you.

Dmitri Skobeltsyn had kept his promise: he's sent 50 grams of streptomycin by diplomatic post. Riches beyond price.

Now it was possible to inject the streptomycin intramuscularly as well, even in doses of a million units a day, and still keep a supply for endocranial injections. Today, when the eye specialist examined Ira, he retracted his conclusion about loss of sight. Active therapy had again triumphed. Ira could see, although it was still difficult to determine whether her sight had been completely restored.

Thursday 13 February

Again a day which burned itself into my memory. At work I got a call on the internal telephone to go to the municipal telephone centre. Disconnected fragments of thought flashed through my mind: phone calls from the hospital were extremely rare... They've not rung at all during the last 4–5 months... What could have happened? Probably it was the cursed 13th.

But when I picked up the phone I heard the calm cheerful voice of Anna Guseva:

—I've decided to cheer you up. Today's tests on Ira showed that the albumen cytose content has halved. Congratulations.

This was the first objective improvement for eight and a half months.
And only a week and a bit has passed since the dosage of streptomycin had been increased. Long live science! Long live life!

In the following weeks and months the albumen and cytose levels began to fall, slowly but surely. By May we had begun to talk about Ira's discharge from hospital. The basic profile of the cerebrospinal fluid was normal.

Vera had lived with Ira in the Morozovsky hospital for more than eleven months. She had taught herself the technique of injecting strep-tomycin intramuscularly. We had about 80 grams of the drug left and Dr Lebedev was insistent in his recommendation that injections should continue for a further two to three months.

By September 1947 Ira had received by intramuscular injection all in all more than 200 grams of streptomycin. As for endocranial injections, we had probably set a new record (58).

For the first few months in the new place, Ira was so weak that she couldn't walk. But by the autumn she had got perceptibly stronger. We had to start thinking about her education. Up to the eighth grade, Ira went to an ordinary school. In 1952 the family returned to Moscow. Ira entered the 8th class of school No.337 (now school No.30) for deaf chil-dren. The school had an excellent teaching staff and the quality of its graduates was as good as in any school in Moscow.

August 1955

Examinations for The Bauman Technical Institute, Moscow. Together with Ira we had chosen this institute because it willingly accepted deaf students. The famous interpreter D.N. Stopanovskaia had worked there for more than four decades, since 1934. Thanks to her unstinting efforts some 150 deaf specialists—designers, technologists, engineers—had received their engineering degrees. The Institute was proud of its deaf graduates.

Ira passed the competitive entrance exams and became a student of this, the oldest higher educational institute in Moscow.

The Institute's programme is wide-ranging and complex. Not for nothing are its initials in Russian MVTU, interpreted as standing for the Russian words for 'courage', 'will power', 'hard work' and 'persistence'. Ira possessed these qualities in plenty. At times it was very difficult, but

94 she managed. She got top marks for her degree project. No concessions were made for her deafness. They simply applauded her louder and longer than the others at her *viva voce* exam.

In the autumn of 1958, Ira got married. Her husband was also a deaf engineer. In 1962 their daughter was born. Ira works in a Moscow Research Institute on questions of training deaf people. In 1966 the first international congress on training deaf children was held in London. Ira went to England to read a paper on 'Technical means for training deaf people in the USSR'. She read the last two paragraphs of her paper in English. In a break between sessions, the chairman came up to her and wrote in her notebook: 'It was completely unexpected for me to find that such a young and charming lady in distant Russia was concerned with the human problems of helping the deaf. We understand your English better than the language spoken by many of our own deaf people'.

February 1969

Successful completion of Ira's doctorate. The theme was 'Telephone links for the deaf'. Ira became a senior research fellow. She has written dozens of articles and two brochures on communicative problems of deaf people.

20th June 1977

Today was Ira's fortieth birthday. We decided to mark the day by collecting together those who had taken part in the struggle to save her life. Unfortunately there were not many of them left. Ten years had passed since Ira's great friend, the splendid Izrail Galynker, had died. Academician Stern and Dr Sherman had not survived to see the day. But one of the people most responsible for saving Ira, Dr Lebedev, was alive and in fine fettle. Despite his 94 years he climbed the stairs to the fifth floor, scorning to summon the lift. Dr Rosin, who was almost 80, also came. At the table were, of course, Aleksei, relatives and deaf friends. Dr Lebedev proposed the toast: 'To the miracle-workers'.

That evening my thoughts kept returning to the most difficult year of our life; with deep gratitude I remembered those who helped us to save Ira's life.

In the last three decades the approach to the diagnosis and cure of tubercular meningitis has changed drastically. Before 1948 the medi-

cal textbooks said: 'do not diagnose tubercular meningitis hastily; it is
untreatable'. But now the pædiatric textbooks say: 'an early diagnosis
of tubercular meningitis, plus treatment with streptomycin and other
anti-TB drugs, is a guarantee of success'. According to the testimony of
Dr Rosin, as early as 1948 more than 900 children in the Soviet Union
were saved by endocranial injections of streptomycin and by active
anti-TB therapy. Trutnev was right; an early start to treatment, as a
rule, preserves hearing.

The record player was turned on and two or three deaf people, including Ira and her husband, danced. Who would have thought that the
sense of rhythm was so developed in deaf people?

They conversed energetically with each other in sign language and
they had plenty to talk about. They were cheerful, active, happy in their
friendship with one another and understanding of its value; the days of
each one of them were rich in impressions and interesting encounters.
Their faces were illuminated with the joy of being.

Today was another anniversary: 31 years since Ira lost her hearing.
Deafness. Yes, it is a high price to pay for life. But did those who had
gathered here today feel this fact so keenly?

The Turning Point: Deaf Pride

Joanne Robinson

I am going to describe my journey from seeing myself as 'hearing-impaired' to Deaf as in culture and community but, in order to understand how I reached this point, I'll tell you a bit about my background. I went to hearing primary and secondary schools with the help for half an hour a week of a peripatetic teacher. I managed through lip-reading, sitting in front of the class and with help from my friends. The only deaf person I knew was my sister, whom I didn't consider as a deaf person, just as an older bossy sister!

I was the first deaf child taught at my local primary school. The teachers had no specialist knowledge of deafness, and from an early age I had to take responsibility for my hearing-aids. I made many friends there. One in particular helped me, passing on any information I missed in lessons.

Throughout most of my school years I considered myself to be just like my hearing friends. The teachers were absolutely smashing and tried not to make me feel any different even though you could tell I was different with a big hearing-aid on my chest! Over the years, I had a few mishaps as a result of my deafness. For example when I was in the infants I misunderstood my PE teacher telling the class to get undressed for PE (Physical Education). And I did, literally! I stripped off all my clothes.

There were times when my deafness held me back from being an integral member of the class. I remember vividly when I was ten years old, not being allowed to advance to a more complex instrument than the recorder. I felt extremely left out when my close friends progressed to instruments like the violin and the flute and as a result practised in the music rooms at dinnertime. This was the first time in my life that I felt different from other people, I was made to think I had a proper disability and I rebelled strongly against this, refusing to believe that I wasn't the same. At the same time I had a form teacher who had a beard and was impossible to lip-read. This made me depressed, and worried my parents. My friends' musical phase eventually passed but I remember feeling really unnerved by the experience.

Starting comprehensive school was extremely nerve-racking as there were a lot more teachers and pupils. Luckily my elder sister who is profoundly deaf paved the way for me and the teachers already knew they had to face me at all times so that I could lip-read—though some of them forgot. Basically I was happy at senior school. I was made to feel normal although problems did occur. In English classes, where oral discussions were part of the GCSE syllabus, I felt excluded. I could never follow and this would make me very uptight and frustrated. When asked questions I repeatedly had to ask 'Pardon, could you repeat that please?' until everyone was looking at me. I felt terribly frustrated and a lump appeared in my throat. Sometimes it was unbearable and I would burst into tears in front of everyone and that was humiliating. At that stage of my life I lost confidence and it was during my last year at secondary school that I began to feel different. It was as if I was on the outside looking in, a glass wall between me and my friends. My deafness had never really been a problem when I was young because breaktimes were spent playing games so it was easy to get involved. Deafness in that respect had no barriers, though I don't suppose I was very conscious of what I missed, being deaf! I tended to avoid group situations for conversations. These were usually with close friends on a one-to-one basis which made lip-reading possible. As I grew up I had more and more a feeling that I was different. I had the feeling that people talked to me as their 'good deed of the day'. It was as if everyone had tried to cover it up in the past, saying I was like them when it was only a pretence.

In my last year of school, the fifth year, I was chosen to be a prefect. Breaktimes were spent in cloakrooms sending the younger ones outside, thus all the prefects used to stand around in groups chatting. Naturally, I felt isolated, which had never happened before.

During this time I had been attending sign language classes with my Mum for a year but it was just basic signs and I hadn't taken the CACDP Stage I exam. When I left school I didn't achieve the grades I wanted for GCSEs so in order to re-take them, I opted to go to a different sixth form college than my school friends. The one they attended was a Catholic college, catering for the Catholic schools in the area and it had

98 big classes and no specialist support. The college I chose was a small, non-Catholic college which had a teacher in charge of the five deaf students. In hindsight, I made the right decision as my sister went there at the same time as me and I felt at ease with the other deaf students, a situation that had never occurred before. I made friends with another deaf girl and I finally began to learn to accept my deafness. I went to classes in British Sign Language with my mum and my sister. Through the teacher I began to understand Deaf culture. In the first year, I went through a metamorphosis in that I left my old self behind and became someone new. In the process I asked, 'Why am I deaf? What does being deaf mean to me?' I was having new insights into my situation from mixing with deaf friends, going to sign language classes, to the Deaf club for the first time. I discovered many different facets to my deafness. What were these facets?

Little did I know what was to come. I went from someone who had a hearing problem to someone who was Deaf with a capital 'D'. I swayed constantly from being proud of being Deaf, to that person I had been all those years, the one who couldn't hear very well. I desperately wanted to be accepted by the hearing people at college, wanted to be like them, but in order for that to happen I had to make it known that I needed to lip-read, therefore my deafness was at the fore again. I wanted to hide my deafness but at the same time there was an instinctive part of me which said I should be upfront about it. This resulted in me being classed as 'one of the deaf ones' so it was a double-edged sword at times. Being very mixed up, the scholarship trip to Gallaudet University when I was nearly seventeen was a blessing in disguise.

The scholarship to Gallaudet University in Washington, the only university for deaf people in the world, was perfectly timed. The trip for six deaf people was organised by the RNID (Royal National Institute for Deaf People) who made a £500 award to all candidates winning a scholarship to Gallaudet University, to meet half the cost of attending the course in America and to study Deaf culture, community and history for a month. Time was short for the application so I took two days off college to write an essay about myself and why I wanted to go. Little did

I know that this trip would change my life.

I had preconceived ideas about Deaf people who used BSL (British Sign Language) as their first language, which in retrospect I am extremely ashamed of. I used to think that because I could speak well and went to a hearing school l had survived the oral.system and was one of their 'successes'. I had a superior attitude towards other Deaf people who signed. When I went to Gallaudet, the Americans quashed this behaviour within minutes. I was made to feel that I was inferior because I couldn't sign. This was a big shock to me and made me feel very humble. In order to gain the respect of the students and to be accepted by them, I had to learn sign as quickly as possible.

There were twenty-five American students on the course between the ages of thirteen to seventeen. They were all from totally different parts of America and had varying educational backgrounds, hearing schools, deaf schools and integrated settings. What amazed me most was that they could all sign fluently and beautifully, which shamed me completely and made me embarrassed by my awkward attempts to sign. I had assumed that because I was brought up on spoken English that my written skills would be better than theirs due to the fact that their first language was ASL (American Sign Language). How mistaken could I be? One thirteen year-old boy who signed so skilfully, had stunning English which far surpassed mine. All my preconceived ideas were totally challenged and were quickly thrown out of the window. The month at Gallaudet was the most enriching and rewarding experience I've ever had in my life so far. I have so many wonderful memories of my time there. I learnt a huge amount about the Deaf world and about myself. The only way to describe the effect on me is that it was a like a final piece of jigsaw fitting into place. In my latter years I had always felt there was something missing in the core of me but I couldn't figure out what it was. I was a misfit. It was all so clear after that month. I had found my Deaf identity. I belonged.

Every day I attended lectures on different aspects of the Deaf world which included learning about the Milan Congress in 1880 (International Congress on Education of the Deaf) and the effect it had on the schools across America. Other lectures involved visiting professionals, some of whom told us about Martha's Vineyard, the island where Deaf and hearing people integrated to such an extent that it was difficult to distinguish one from the other. Deaf comedians showed us how Deaf humour was portrayed and had us in fits of laughter. Sociologists and psychologists from the University came and talked about Deaf culture and the Deaf community, identifying behaviour that is common and exclusive to the Deaf world.

After a day of lectures we spent two hours doing a Personal Discovery Programme which consisted of a series of physical and mental tasks which we had to solve with teamwork, co-operation and discipline, skills we would need throughout life. In the evenings, we would have various workshops with different people from the University. One, I remember, taught us not to be passive or aggressive but assertive. There were a lot of self-searching workshops designed to help you discover who you were as a person.

Luckily, my stay there coincided with the weeklong *Deaf Way* conference. This conference was held in a big hotel in Washington DC and was opened with an address from I. King Jordan, himself deaf, who is the President of Gallaudet. His speech was powerful and unforgettable and started off what was a fabulous week. There was so much to see and do. I attended lectures given by different people from all over the world, theatrical plays, signed poetry performances, art exhibitions of pottery, painting and photography. I saw Deaf comedians, beautiful dancers from India, stalls with crafts made by Deaf people from Peru, Africa, Mexico and so on...there was just so much to fit in. It was a fantastic experience seeing different Deaf people from different countries conversing with each other as if they had known each other all their lives. In the middle of the University's sports ground there was an almost circus-sized marquee, which was christened the International Deaf Club Tent. Here, scores of people gathered every night to talk the hours away.

I was very sad to leave at the end of the month as the experience had touched a deep chord within me. Coming from a totally hearing background it had been in a sense alien, but at the same time it felt so natural. I hardly used my voice that month due to chatting in ASL and this made me realise that no matter how good my speech, it is of no importance within Deaf community life. I had to change my priorities, my values and certainly my beliefs. Always having been in ordinary schools, I have never actually belonged to the Deaf community. Now I wanted to discover my roots by finding out more about what it means to me to be

Deaf and how it affects other people: it affects my sister in a totally different way to me. Discovering my identity would help me confront my
disability instead of hiding behind other people.

Gallaudet has a special place in my heart as it gave me a belief in
myself and the feeling that I, too, can achieve. During my stay there I
rarely came into contact with hearing people as the most of the profes-
sors were Deaf. Any hearing people I did meet within the University all
signed. I had access to information at all times as everything was geared
for Deaf people—phones, computers with modems, televisions, even
the local cinema showed films with subtitles. The cinema was full of
Deaf people, all signing. I think there is a greater awareness of deafness
in America. Gallaudet has a Deaf President. Nobody Deaf holds such
high office in educational establishments in this country. I feel Deaf
people are undermined here and it's a great waste of talent.

On arriving back from America, I was rather militant about the
rights of Deaf people, a lot more confident and, since I had a secure
idea of who I was, I was able to interact with hearing people a lot easier
since I stopped trying to be like them. As a result of the trip, I became
involved with the British Deaf community, learning BSL properly and
gaining the CACDP Stages I and II. Most of my friends are Deaf and I
can be myself with them as we share a common bond. It's difficult to
explain but they don't have high expectations of me and since the communication is so easy, the conversation just flows. If I was to sum up
my entrance into the Deaf community in a few words, I would say it
was like a 'coming home'.

My life now can only be described as a social whirl. The one thing I
enjoy about the Deaf World is that there is always something going on
at the weekends. It is not unusual for us to jump in a car in Birmingham
and go to a party in Newcastle. There are conferences, debates, rallies,
parties, discos going on all the time, especially sports discos, as there
is a lot of sport played in the Deaf world. Sport is a uniting factor as it
brings Deaf people together. Football, squash, tennis and cricket matches are played all around the country with discos in the evening. This
weekend there is a rally in Blackpool where Deaf people between the
ages of seventeen to thirty five meet every year for a weekend of socialising and meeting new people. A lot of the social life is centred around
the Deaf clubs, where the grassroots Deaf meet, and where you hear of

102 news and events to come. In some ways, the Deaf club is like a village hall and the centre of activity.

My quality of life has greatly improved and I'm very fortunate in having good friendships with hearing people as well as Deaf. In my university there are a number of Deaf students and I tend to socialise with them. My lectures are with hearing people and coupled with the help of an interpreter, I enjoy these very much.

Maybe if I hadn't gone to Gallaudet, it might have taken longer for me to get to where I am now but I am confident I would have got here in the end. As I said before, I had always felt there was something missing. Now I know what it is, the heart of me, my Deaf identity.

III MAKING LIFE CHOICES

Making Life Choices

This section focuses on the development of Deaf identity as the young person leaves school and mediates their sense of identity as both deaf and a student or worker in the settings of college, university and employment. The accounts by Candelaria Vilaescusa Pedroche, Chris Baxter and Raquel Rodrigo Canet emphasise the diversity of deaf people as they discuss the issues for each of them of late diagnosis of deafness, the effort involved in remediation and strategies to compensate for lack of hearing.

The importance referred to by Jennifer Dodds and Riki Kittel of being able to read is echoed by several of the contributors to this section who describe their skills in communication and the methods they use to access information and discussion. The commonality of experiences between Spain, Germany and Britain are of particular interest. Candelaria's college could be considered a model for inclusion as it was prepared to adapt the curriculum, but we should note that Candelaria experienced social isolation outside college. This might be construed as due to a lack of the deaf peers available to the British writers in the previous section, Jennifer Dodds, Teresa Waldron and Joanne Robinson (who has a Deaf sister), or to a more individual model of deafness in which deafness is viewed as a limitation. Katja Fischer argues for the need for youth provision to combat the type of social isolation experienced by Candelaria, to facilitate Deaf peer group support and contact with Deaf adults as role models. The identification of each writer in this section with other deaf people as friends, role models and potential life partners is a prominent feature. Raquel picks up the theme Hope Ahmed raised in the previous section, of the everyday battle deafness demands. Both Raquel and Candelaria point to their reliance on, and absolute necessity of, the provision of technological equipment and support services for students and in the work environment. Raquel, Chris and Candelaria raise issues about integration with their first and primary language being the spoken language of their country, and of the in-between position of someone not fully integrated into either community. These feelings can be contrasted with the discussion about the support provided by the Deaf community for Jennifer, Joanne and other writers in the previous section, and to the life long friendships established at the Royal Cross School. Teresa's lack of emphasis on these aspects of her social and community life suggest that her support is received from involvement with disabled people and the political work with other deaf people. The resolution of the integration debate raised here seems somewhat academic as in practice the writers are not torn by the choice of one community or the other but adopt a position of bilingualism and of biculturalism, living and working in both Deaf and hearing situations.

Volker Maaßen's account highlights the changing employment practices which are occurring all over Europe and demonstrates how job insecurity is affecting the Deaf community whilst also enabling individuals to change professions and to set up their own businesses. Volker's reference to his difficult relationship with the head of the regional Deaf association could be an indication of the effects of the paternalism Jennifer earlier referred to, or to an innate conservatism, internal oppression and resistance to change within the Deaf community. In Volker's references to the need and desire for solidarity within the Deaf community there is a sense too that the empowerment of the Deaf community is linked to the need to change the relationships with hearing people to reflect the kind of equal partnership that Volker has established in his business.

Stephen Robinson and Sue O'Rourke give an account of the changes that have been brought to bear on the services provided within the closed community of one of the three high security hospitals in England, Rampton Hospital in North Nottinghamshire. Unlike other Deaf people in the book who, it could be argued, have had more freedom to construct and choose the identity they portray, the patients' construction of identity has been imposed on them by the staff in the hospital, and by the wider community outside of the hospital who might stigmatise and dehumanise such patients as dangerous. Instead we could ask what happens to deaf children who grow up under oral/aural regimes,

108 and do not develop facility in spoken and written English whilst also being denied access to BSL? In addition to the identities we have ascribed to them, the Deaf patients at Rampton could also be viewed as childhood victims of a policy of denial to BSL, education and to appropriate Deaf role models. The additional service at Rampton, which is directed at the Deaf patients, attempts to remedy that policy of denial by providing appropriate language and communication together with positive Deaf role models to both patients and staff.

Deaf staff at the hospital have employment backgrounds similar to Volker's. Stephen's previous occupation was in engineering, as was Volker's. Both accounts demonstrate the development of professional working relationships between Deaf and hearing people, and also the eagerness of hearing people across Europe to learn sign languages both to communicate socially with Deaf people and to be in a position to make their services accessible.

One of the issues that Stephen and Sue raise is the lack of a medium secure unit for successfully rehabilitated Deaf patients to begin their journey out of the high security hospital system. Since the account was written, a medium secure facility has been opened at Bury, Lancashire.

Arthur Dimmock documents the history of Deaf sport and the role that Deaf entrepreneurs played in facilitating Deaf people. He points to the barrier to professional sport that coaching has become. Helga McGlip writes of her experience of amateur football and the relaxation that watching professional football provides, how she incorporates the identities of football player and Arsenal supporter with her Deaf identity, and how she manages communication in football settings, on and off the pitch, and within social and work-related situations. Katja Fischer tells us that in the German Democratic Republic deaf children were motivated through sports and mathematics to achieve. She, like Volker, refers to the need for Deaf people to pass the *Abitur* examination, the final examination at German secondary schools which qualifies a young person for entry to the university system.

Katja contrasts life in East Germany with life in the West. Young Deaf people seem to have had more access to the Deaf community from a young age facilitated by the Deaf teachers in schools, whereas there were no Deaf role models and no Deaf teachers in the UK and Spanish accounts. The Deaf teachers, like the hearing teacher described by Helga and other writers in the previous section, also denied the young people their dreams and ambitions for the future.

Access to the political debates and changes sweeping through Germany came via the availability of subtitled television. There were debates too about the status of sign language. Katja's growing politicisation, the increasing access to support services, and her awareness of the need for social workers and other professionals available to the Deaf community came together and facilitated access to University study and to work involving the provision of youth services to combat the type of isolation experienced by Candelaria.

The account by Katya Davidenko Leneshkina describes a previous period of political turmoil in the Soviet Union. The account begins during the Stalinist period in St Petersburg and continues through the Second World War with an account of the horrors of the Siege of Leningrad. She also refers to the famous art gallery in St Petersburg, the Hermitage. Katya is one of a large family, many of whose members are Deaf and she offers tantalising glimpses of life within the Russian Deaf community while detailing the struggle for economic and physical survival in conditions of starvation and malnutrition which often caused illnesses. Of the eleven children of the family, three of the survivors were Deaf. Within Russia, there is no tradition of fostering or adoption and Anya's response to a family crisis where there was insufficient income for food offers a different method of family support than we in the West might have expected.

The pioneer camp referred to is a political youth movement run by the local Communist Party and it is interesting to note that Deaf children could be accommodated within these camps when Deaf education in Russia, as in most countries, followed the system of segregation. Indeed, employment in the Soviet Union was also segregated and Deaf people formed a distinct workforce in the factories to which Katya refers. The enrolment of Katya and one of her siblings at the school for the hard of hearing despite, as she says, their use of sign language and profound deafness, indicates a higher level of facility with language.

110   Similarly profoundly or severely deaf children were not necessarily excluded from units for partially hearing children when these became available in Britain.

Mabel Davis is the first Deaf head teacher in Britain since the 1920s. She works at Heathlands School, a school attended by Asif Iqbal who writes in the final section of the book. Mabel starts her account from the perspective of an educationalist, examining the issues of integration for deaf children and pointing to a lack of emphasis on the social and emotional development of deaf children, factors implicit in the accounts that precede it, most obviously that by Candelaria. Mabel returns to this theme later in the paper when she discusses her experiences at Mary Hare Grammar School, integration as a Deaf adult and the lack of preparation for transition from school. Jennifer Dodds, Raquel and Candelaria express similar thoughts about the transition to Higher Education. Mabel also echoes Hope Ahmed's expression of the need for parents to be given access to information, and her awareness that it is often necessary for parents to strenuously assert their rights if they are to achieve what they consider to be the appropriate educational placement for their child.

Mabel writes of her personal experience of losing her hearing as a child and her process of changing identity. We, as Deaf people and hearing people working with Deaf people, speak of people as either deaf or hearing as if hearing people define themselves in those terms, whereas, in fact, hearing people do not consider themselves as having a hearing identity. Nor do hearing people consider themselves as belonging to a specific hearing culture, although reliance on hearing often is the means of access to those cultures. Raquel writes of her fear through the transition from her hearing state to her deaf state. Mabel describes an incident when she returned to her previous school as being a part of a process that enabled her to change her identity. She also refers to the importance of a peer group in the development of a positive identity and in this she mirrors the experiences of Raquel, Candelaria, Chris and Jennifer. The discovery that she wasn't the only deaf child was helpful to her and implies that Chris, Candelaria and Raquel would have been helped if they had met other deaf people at an earlier stage. Mabel stresses the positive nature of the special school in terms of a deaf child's mental health, although we can see from other accounts, particularly those of Katja and Jennifer, that mental health can also be undermined within special schools.

Without doubt, Mabel would have been the subject of integration if she had been a child today, and perhaps she would have suffered the same stresses as Joanne, however we would hope that standards in special schools have risen. Katja refers to poor standards of education throughout Europe, but in the GDR the lack of access to *Abitur* does suggests a particular lack of emphasis on academic attainment. Although Jennifer's account does not focus on educational standards in her description of how she coped when all information was delivered in spoken English, it is clear that her full academic progress was hindered.

The Hang Glider

by Dorothy Miles

Here are my wings;
And there, at the edge of nothing,
    wait the winds
to bear my weight.
My wings,
so huge and strong,
built with my life in mind…

I have made other wings before,
   test-tried,
      wrong-broken,
         cast aside—
I searched, and asked, and saw,
        and built again…
and here I stand.

Take up my courage
   with my pack,
and forward go—

    NO TURNING BACK!
(The wings won't turn).

The cliff is high,
   and far way down
     the sea;
I'd hate to drown!

But they are watching me.

I have seen others do it—
    step off and fly—
so why can't I?

Suppose…
    suppose the winds might die,
and I
    Step off and dive
                and dive
                    and dive…

The winds won't die!
Experience tells me that
Courage
and faith in my experience,
that's all I need.

Here are my wings…
Here are my wings!

A Thirst for Communication

Candelaria Villaescusa Pedroche

Childhood—School

I was born in 1976, the first of three children. Everyone in my family is hearing except me. When I was born nobody suspected I was deaf. My parents began to notice there was something wrong when I didn't react to noises in the street and at home. My father remembers how I would ignore a train going past, even if we were walking right beside it. I went to a lot of doctors, but they didn't detect my deafness until I was nearly four. Whilst my brother Luis, who was born a year after me, was learning new words I couldn't even speak, I just made senseless noises, I was immersed in silence. They finally diagnosed the reason for my inability to speak as profound bilateral neurosensory deafness caused by a medicine. So I've been deaf since I was very small, probably since the first year of my life.

Despite becoming deaf at a very early age I look back on my childhood with a feeling of happiness; I was unaware of my deafness and always protected by the love of my family but I was also happy due to my extroverted and mischievous character.

After the diagnosis it was recommended to my parents that I should wear hearing-aids. Although I was deaf in my right ear, I retained some hearing in my left, so I started to use hearing-aids just before beginning kindergarten, at around four years old.

My parents wanted me to learn to speak and communicate with other children, to read and write properly, and because of this they thought it best to place me in a public [state] school with hearing children. Therefore, my education was based on verbal communication and developing lip-reading skills. I was lucky, as the headmaster was a supporter of a new integration law for children with special needs and so accepted my admission as a student. I was the only deaf child at the school.

The interest my parents took meant that they dedicated a lot of 115
time to me outside school. Every day via lip-reading they taught me
new words and I would repeat them, although at the start I didn't quite
understand their meaning. When I went to see a psychologist she said
that I had 'echolitis': I limited myself to merely repeating the words that
were said to me without understanding their meaning. With the effort
of my parents, slowly but surely and with patience, the day arrived
when I could understand the meaning of words. My mother remembers that one day she asked me, whilst pointing at a ball, 'what's this?'
and I answered 'what's this?' I didn't understand that each question
had an answer until one day at last, after my mother said 'Me: What's
this?'—'You: A ball', as if a light came on in my mind, I understood
that if she asked 'what's this' and pointed, I had to say ball. After that
day learning was a lot easier for me and what I'd missed in almost four
years, I learnt in the next three. I was like a sponge that absorbed everything I was taught. I enjoyed learning and discovering new things. I
never tired of asking about things around me. A new world appeared
before my eyes: a world of words that makes us feel part of society. My
brother, who I have always been close to, also helped me to pronounce
words despite his young age.

I had a lot of support, not only from my parents but also from a private speech therapist who gave me after-school classes for three years,
and a pre-school teacher who gave me revision classes at school but out
of school hours.

In terms of language, the most intense learning period was from four
to seven years old, although I've never stopped learning new things as
the learning process for a deaf child is a very long one. I remember that
at primary school I would often take refuge in the library, as I loved to
read from a very young age. By practising reading I found that my vocabulary grew and my reading comprehension improved. To be a good
student required understanding as well as large doses of motivation,
willpower and perseverance.

I played with the other children at school although I didn't always
understand what they were saying but even still, the language of play is
universal. My relationship with my classmates and my teachers was very
good, and I went through primary school free from problems. I was a
responsible and hard working girl and with the help of my hearing-aids

and thanks to the immeasurable support of my parents and teachers in lessons, I achieved good grades.

Adolescence—College

Having completed my basic education I decided to study for an advanced level exam at a public college in my town. The way I looked at it, if it didn't go well I could always do something else but I wouldn't lose anything in trying. Before starting I felt both hopeful and nervous, although I never felt scared of embarking on this new stage. I've always been the sort of person that adapts well and quickly to changes.

During this period the support faded away. I carried on wearing hearing-aids but didn't receive any help from private revision teachers or any other professional. There was an average of thirty-five students in the class and I always sat in the front row. The teachers knew that I lip-read and if I didn't understand something I would raise my query in class. I never stopped showing an interest in what they were saying and I loved to study.

I didn't have any major problems as the teachers based their lectures on textbooks and it was sufficient to study the texts they said would be included, as preparation for the exams.

Some changes had to be made to subjects such as music. One part of the exam was to listen to a melody and distinguish which instruments were playing. In my case the teacher decided that that part could be resolved with an essay on 'The History of Music'.

I have never taken advantage of my deafness to avoid learning. The college said that I could be excused from English and Valencian language classes but I decided to take them and not give in. Therefore, in addition to attending college, my brother and I also joined an English academy that had native teachers. I went to this academy for eight years and I even passed the first-year English exam in the Official Languages School. How did I manage it? With a great deal of will power. To improve my pronunciation in English, my teachers at the academy would write the word on the blackboard as it would be pronounced in Spanish. For instance, to learn how to say 'house' they would write 'jaus'. I'm aware that I can't pronounce English perfectly but I think it's a great achievement that my English teachers understood me when I spoke to them in English.

My social life at that time was pretty much restricted to college. During that period I hardly left the house, my free time was taken up with my family and studying. I had good relationships with my teachers and spoke to almost all of my classmates although I lost much of what was said in group situations, especially at break times. They never laughed at me or excluded me for being deaf but all the same I wasn't part of a group that I could go out at weekends with. I took refuge in my studies and although it didn't affect me badly, I sometimes came to feel a kind of complex about being deaf.

I completed my secondary education with excellent grades and when it came to sitting the selection exams necessary to go to university, all I asked was to be sat in the front row to better understand the comments of the teachers about the exercises in the exam. I didn't think it was necessary to ask for any other kind of special conditions and I sat the exams in the same amount of time as anyone else.

University

Encouraged by my success at secondary level I began university with more assurance and self-confidence. Through personal experience I think the way in which you begin any new stage of your life will determine what follows. Belief in yourself is the first secret to success.

I began a degree in Biological Science at the University of Valencia. At that time, in 1994, there was still no legislation to help disabled university students. I remember the first day of class as if it were yesterday: What could I do? I told all of my teachers about my limitation so that it would be taken into account. I sat in the front row and tried to follow the teachers' lectures solely by lip-reading. To begin with I copied the notes of a classmate who sat next to me, but after a while I got the feeling that it bothered him, and also a lot of the time I couldn't understand his handwriting.

Because of this I stopped taking notes and decided to ask classmates at the end of lectures for their notes to photocopy and take home with me to study. I limited myself to copying the notes the lecturers made on the blackboard. I was never absent from class and I tried to follow and understand the teachers' explanations, raising queries both in class and in tutorials. Despite my efforts with lip-reading it was inevitable that I would lose a lot of information in the theoretical classes, although how

118   much information I lost depended on the style and consideration of the teacher I was with.

Unfortunately, preparation for most of the exams meant studying the lecture notes. Therefore, especially during the first year, I referenced bibliographies and the books mentioned by lecturers at the beginning of the class. This was the only way for me to continue with my studies. I knew that I was losing a lot of time by writing the notes out again, summarising them and then drawing diagrams of the information I found in books, but in the end it was worth the effort, even if I had to try twice as hard as my classmates.

A few things changed in my third year. For the first time I received a form in the enrolment envelope telling me I could register as a person with a disability, if I wished to do so. I did and thanks to that form I made contact with a service at my university, created in the previous year, to support university students with disabilities. This service offered technical help during periods of academic activity and I requested a FM transmitter. I had never used one before and although I wasn't used to such apparatus, it was a positive experience. With the transmitter I was no longer bothered by noises in the classroom and only 'captured' the teacher's voice. At the start I found it difficult because I was used to focussing on lip-reading to 'listen' and understand what the teacher said. I did notice that some lecturers found wearing the transmitter a bit uncomfortable.

In addition to this I also received notebooks with duplicate [carbon-copy] sheets. I got these from the service and gave them to my classmates. At the end of sessions I could just leave the lecture room with the notes of a classmate, without needing to do photocopies and waste time.

Of course, I've had problems in specific situations. If overhead transparencies were used and the lights were turned off to see them better I could no longer follow the lecturer. I was left uninformed with video documentaries or videos about experimental procedures for laboratory practicals. Obviously, none of the videos carried subtitles. In lectures, when classmates asked questions or had debates I lost all the information because I was sitting in the front row. The same thing happened when the lecturer walked down the aisle whilst speaking. This posed no problem for my hearing classmates, but for a person like me with a hearing loss, very normal behaviour during a university lecture can turn into a huge communication barrier. At times I lost a lot of information, but I carried on and didn't throw in the towel because what really mattered was what I studied for the exam.

Nevertheless, I can't complain as I finished my degree successfully and I think I adapted well. In general the lecturers were good, most of them were very nice and ready to help me if I had a problem, although each of them had their own particular lecturing style which would either help or hinder my understanding accordingly. However, I think the most important thing for them to see was that, despite my difficulties, I was really motivated and interested with a desire to work, something which I think I always showed them.

I always felt like I was just another student and I sat the exams the same as everyone else without any kind of special circumstances. Only my hearing-aids, classmates and will power helped me. With regards to my classmates there were never any problems, especially from the second year on when we got to know each other better. This inspired confidence on both sides but I have always been a very sociable person who likes to relate to people.

After university

When I finished my studies in biological sciences I became involved in various activities. I took part in a course on Environmental Education, I learnt about Information Technology, I got my driving licence and I took a teaching adaptation course that allows me to try for a biological sciences secondary school teaching place in the future.

In addition to this I enrolled to undertake a doctorate in the Teacher Training School in the programme of 'Research of Experimental and Social Sciences Didactics'. This was a new experience, the group was a lot smaller for the doctorate than before which made me feel more comfortable. The classes took place in a relaxed atmosphere and I followed what was going on much better.

I've fitted in well with the development of my third year studies and I still juggle them with other activities. In 2000 I won a year's scholarship from the Valencian Government, which I'm still enjoying now and allows me to work in the Sea Fishing section of the Local Ministry for Agriculture, Fisheries and Food. I have a very good relationship with my work colleagues, there's a brilliant atmosphere and I have no trouble in

120 communicating with them. All I had to do was explain to them at the start how they should approach me and how best to speak to me so that I'm able to understand what they say. I feel extremely integrated as one of them, without any kind of difference.

As you can see, I'm a great believer in gaining extra training prior to work, I think it's very important to specialise in order to find a good job. I'll never stop learning new things even if they have nothing to do with what I've studied throughout my career because I think it's essential to have a global view of life.

In terms of the future it's very important to me to find a job that motivates me and gives me financial security. If possible, I'd like to have a job related to the environment or teaching. In this way, I do think that my deafness will have a part to play in me finding a job, because many companies aren't equipped to have a person with a hearing loss work for them. Fortunately things are changing, above all thanks to new technologies that break communication barriers but there are still a lot of changes to be made in society. This means that deaf people must continue to fight.

One of the hardest things that a deaf person faces when trying to find a job is the need to show that deafness is not an impediment to doing the job effectively. The exception is those tasks that can't be carried out due to the limitation of deafness, a telephone operator for example. We also find communication barriers in job interviews; many businesspeople are surprised simply to find a deaf person with a university degree because they wrongly believe that we're not capable enough to study at university.

Some of the hearing people I've met never imagined that a deaf person could communicate just as well with hearing people as deaf people. I've had to explain that a deaf person doesn't have to be dumb, they just communicate in a different way, with sign language or with lip-reading as in my case. A lot of people still don't know what deafness is and associate it directly with problems of social isolation because they assume that a deaf person is someone who can't be sociable, he/she is a solitary person that is easily excluded. How wrong can they be! If they only knew the thirst for communication that deaf people have.

Being a deaf person doesn't prevent me from fully developing as such, as a person in any aspect of life. Despite having limitations we can always profit from our abilities.

Despite my deafness I accept myself as I am. I've never had a complex about being deaf, I've always felt part of society but I am also aware that I'll never be like a hearing person. I don't think you should be discouraged when faced with communication barriers, I don't think that deafness is an impediment to one's happiness.

I feel identified as a deaf person, but at the same time I feel perfectly integrated with hearing people. An experience that influenced my life as a deaf person was contacting the Deaf community five years ago for the first time. I also joined a course on 'Communication in Sign Language' organised by the Valencian Association of Deaf People. This marked my approach to sign language. Although I had no prior knowledge of it I soon decided to learn it as a priority in order to be able to communicate with other deaf people. I've noticed that deaf people who, for various reasons (family, education, level of deafness, personality) have no knowledge of sign language and then discover it, have to make a huge effort to learn it. They find it hard to take on a new language, a visual language with its own vocabulary and grammatical structure. Nevertheless, I was able to learn to communicate perfectly well in sign language. Most deaf people I know communicate in sign language and now I'm happier to be able to communicate using it.

Now I get along well with both speech and sign language. In the same way I feel comfortable with hearing and deaf people although my strongest friendship ties are with deaf people. To share an experience, to know we don't hear makes us more united and although each deaf person is different, it's nice to know other people face more or less the same issues as you. You can understand them easily and you feel equally understood.

Therefore, and with regard to partnerships, I've only had one stable relationship with a boy that was also deaf. Although that relationship ended because we didn't get on as a couple, my view is that I'd rather go out with a deaf person because communication is vital when it comes to living together. That doesn't mean to say that I wouldn't go out with a hearing person if I felt that he truly loved me and accepted my deafness. I suppose that if a hearing boy really falls in love with a deaf girl her deafness wouldn't matter to him, but you can't forget that staying together in this situation requires a continuous effort on both sides, greater than

122   normal, for mutual understanding. In any case, when it comes to this I'm a realist and I think it's very unlikely that I'd fall for a hearing boy due to my deafness. I've had experiences of being around hearing boys that I thought I got on well with but I don't think they got over the 'what will they think?' syndrome. It's very easy to say, ' I wouldn't have a problem with going out with a deaf person, because it's what's on the inside that counts', but in the moment of truth very few people dare to do what they say, true? I know lots of deaf boys but so far I haven't found one that I could have a relationship with. As well as deafness, I'd like to share a cultural level similar to my own that will improve the understanding between us both, although at the end of the day what's important is to feel mutual love and respect.

In short, my relationships include friendships with the hearing people in my town and the university but as time goes by, I find I have more and more deaf friends that I've gradually met through deaf people's associations or outside of these. I now know that if I'm ever a mother, my child, regardless of whether they're deaf or hearing, will have a bilingual education because I don't want them to feel excluded from any social setting, or that they're not able to understand and communicate, as has happened to me many times.

Diary of a Twilight Dweller

Chris Baxter

I started to write this article as a deafened person but in the process I have realised that the term is probably not the right one for me. People write of 'losing' their hearing; I never lost mine, it just seems I discovered over time that lots of it, those bits that constitute 'normal' hearing, weren't there!

When preparing to write this piece I read in the book *Being Deaf* Maggie Woolley's excellent piece 'Acquired Deafness, acquired oppression' which looks at 'achieving' deafness, as I prefer to call it (some are born Deaf others have deafness thrust upon them, others achieve deafness). There are some similarities in the way we identify ourselves as Deaf through use and promotion of sign language and respect for Deaf culture and community. But the sense of 'loss' for me is now far outweighed by the benefits of being Deaf. I'll try and explain why that is, and for that we need a short history of this twilight dweller...

Looking back on my school years, painful though they were (aren't everyone's?), I was often the class clown with a highly developed sense of humour: my father despaired that I could remember jokes better than my eight times table. Incidentally it is interesting to note that my father was deaf from his early years probably due to what we know now as glue ear, his formative years at school until the age of nine were severely disrupted by his deafness and his education never really recovered. My father has a highly developed sense of humour also; perhaps it is genetic, more likely it is a coping strategy.

Humour has always served me as a coping strategy, a way of gaining acceptance, of 'fitting in'; the need to 'fit in' in human society being an incredibly powerful driving force. This keen sense of humour overspilled with quite disastrous results into my education, hence school was followed by futureless underemployment rather than further and higher education.

At work my popularity hinged on my being the joker with the

124 quickest quip. Usually the first to make a witty comment, whether or not it was related to the current topic of conversation didn't matter, that I should not be exposed as not quite understanding what was going or the exact words people used was far more important to me. But I never suspected I was deaf, I just assumed I was stupid.

So eventually, bored to tears with work and what it had to offer I finally got back into education and went on to do a degree, still joking my way through, I was, without exception, the first one asleep in lectures when the lights dimmed and the lecturer moved out of view. I was also easily bored by the lengthy rambling discussions and lectures. The reason for all this was of course due to being an intelligent deaf person who hadn't a clue what was being said to me unless the speaker was facing me and talking straight to me. I read voraciously through my childhood, and still do given the chance. I believe much of my knowledge was gained in this way, again a useful technique when you are not hearing clearly or 'as others do'.

Pop songs were always interesting when they were rendered by me with unusual lyrics which nobody else seemed to recognise, I really should have realised, but I had good pitch and could sing and play instruments in tune, even doing complicated tests and passing them and playing in the school orchestra and appearing at the Fairfield Halls, Croydon at the tender age of eleven, how could anyone have realised I was deaf?

When I think about it, the sleeping during lectures was really the key, I remember feeling desperately tired and angry sometimes that I hadn't managed to stay awake, I was so tired.

When people try to understand me and my journey into 'Deaf', both Deaf and hearing people are alike as they try to understand it in terms of loss, in the way Maggie describes. This is probably because until recently I used the sign 'deafened' when asked if I was Deaf or hearing. Lack of appropriate diagnosis had led me to believe this was the case.

Although I haven't felt grief and loss as such, I have felt anger and frustration but these feelings were linked to the treatment I have received as a Deaf person, emotions I think all Deaf people will recognise. Loss of respect for me as an individual, the way I can see people 'downgrade' me when they are told I am Deaf, they either avoid me or want to adopt me as their 'marvellous' Deaf person—see also tragic and brave heroes among disabled people for more examples of this phenomenon. For tragic, tune in to any Children in Need or other appeal on the TV or look at the advertising used by charities. For 'brave deaf heroes' see profoundly deaf percussionist Evelyn Glennie, Deafblind Powerwaterbike rider/speed king Graham Hicks and anyone else undertaking what others in society might consider 'impossible' tasks given the nature of their impairment and 'triumphing against all odds' despite it.

Other 'losses' are the inability to live a flexible and spontaneous life. Deafness as such isn't a loss, it is a reduction in choice brought about by living in a society that really doesn't cater for any of us who are 'different'. When considering 'choice' and 'adaptation' in this way I find it useful to recite my mantra regarding communication methods. If you want to communicate with me you can do it through speech in a suitable environment where with my residual hearing and lip-reading skills we'll probably be OK. You can communicate with me in BSL, SSE, Makaton even. You can write to me in English. We could even laboriously communicate through fingerspelling alone (although I may fall asleep) or Deaf Blind manual alphabet. In my younger (and cerebrally brighter) days you could have written to me in Braille and Moon and I would still understand you. Now, if we can't communicate who's fault is it? I really don't accept it is mine. I have fulfilled the need society places on me to 'adapt' to 'fit in', I have been 'reasonable'—to paraphrase the Disability Discrimination Act. When will others show the same 'reasonableness' to me? If the communication method and environment aren't suitable I am disabled.

Instances where I am 'disabled' in the work place, for example, are the recent trend of mixing food with meetings. Breakfast meetings, the latest way of cramming your day as full as possible with work, these and working lunches, if they are with hearing people, are a nightmare, often organised at the last minute, too late to get an interpreter. The prospect of lip-reading through all that scrambled egg or smoked salmon is really very unappetising. At least I can eat and sign with other Deaf people, but we all need to make sure the food is cold before we start, because it sure will be by the time we finish!

For me, communication with Deaf people is always relaxed. Even if we don't completely understand each other it is never too much effort to assist with comprehension. Struggling to hear or lip-read is never fun.

The loss of opportunity to take full part is to be mourned, but it isn't the fault of deafness. It is the lack of care or planning on behalf of the organisers. With other Deaf people I can have meetings in the noisiest locations so long as they are adequately lit, but if we were to invite a non-signing hearing person into this arena and they would struggle even with a voice over. Now is it their fault for being hearing or is the problem the poor choice of location for the meeting? Is the building with steps inaccessible to the wheelchair user because she is a wheelchair user or because there are steps?

In Maggie's article she discusses how she came to recognise herself as a Deaf person. I would concur with this 'revelation' but it didn't happen for me until I went to train as an adult tutor. There were two Deaf BSL tutors on the same course, they looked relaxed and happy receiving the information via an interpreter whilst I struggled to lip-read and to take a full part. Faced with my model of being deaf or theirs, the choice was obvious and easy. To go back a little… I first discovered the audiological fact of my deafness in my early twenties and I cried, wept buckets in fact. I discovered my Deaf deafness in my early thirties and have never looked back. I am faced with disbelief fairly regularly which can be wearing. From hearing people who hear my voice, unaffected by being deaf, and who might see me managing one to one conversations, the usual questions are:

'You say you are deaf—I never realised', (that bit's OK) followed swiftly by the intrusive delve into my medical details thus, 'how deaf are you'? My response to this is usually to point to myself and say 'this deaf'. Sometimes people ask this expecting a percentage. 'How much can you hear?' My usual response: 'pardon?' (Well, they started it!)

'You're deaf, how do you manage?' I would like some suggestions for a standard response to this one.

'You're deaf—how do you hear me?'—again difficult to respond to I am tempted to lie about the hairs in my nostrils vibrating and sending signals to my brain replacing the scilla in my cochlea, but all too often I am accused of having a chip on my shoulder and taking it out on poor unsuspecting hearies. I haven't, I'm just having fun.

From Deaf people I get an entirely different response. Deaf people are rarely as nosey, or at least are not so personally intrusive as hearing people, although they usually ask very direct questions, which I prefer every

time. I have found mostly acceptance from Deaf people who are curious
AS to why I seem to have made a choice to be Deaf. I hope this article
goes some way to help and explain the reason, but it is difficult because I
didn't go to a Deaf school or even a PHU (Partially Hearing Unit). I can't
claim membership of the Deaf Ex Mainstreamers although in essence
I was a deaf mainstreamer. Nobody knew I was deaf (least of all me). I
don't go to the Deaf club, I don't go to any club, rarely even to pubs these
days but I believe I am involved with the Deaf community and spending
time with Deaf people feels like coming home.

I resent and utterly reject the medical model notion that Deaf people are damaged and need a cure, but I would uphold the individual's
right to choose when it comes to audiological medicine, so long as that
choice is fully informed and researched.

The future for Deaf people does not lie in medical research in my
humble, considered opinion, rather in the emancipation of our people
from the tyranny of the hearing world, the need to conform and to be
normal. I am one of the medical world's mysteries. Nothing can be done
to restore my hearing (should I want them to!) and nothing is known
about why I am deaf, despite ten or more years of hearing tests, tinnitus
tests, blood tests, full medical history consideration. I am DEAF and that
is fine by me. Every time someone tries to find a reason for my deafness
my confidence is rocked, as if it is something that requires justification
to make it real; meningitis, medical mishap, genetics etc. Every time I
am told that 'nothing can be done' (and at the time of writing this includes digital hearing-aids) I presume I am expected to feel something,
grief, loss. I don't. I have on more than one occasion had to deal with
the professional's sense of failure more than my own feelings!

I am proud to be Deaf, I am proud to share a language, sign language. Even though I may mangle it at times, I consider it mine. I am
grateful to be accompanied in the oppression.

I cannot be proud to have a hearing loss (now where did I put it?) or
impairment (makes it sound so painful); I can't live my life apologising
for being me, being Deaf. No change that. I *won't* live my life apologising
for being me, being Deaf.

The Transformation from Hearing to Deaf and my acceptance of Being Deaf

Raquel Rodrigo Canet

I was born hearing and at approximately nine years old I became deaf. At home they noticed that I was becoming more vague, quieter and more introverted. I turned the television up louder and was scared of the telephone. They took me to the doctor. I remember that they carried out a lot of tests on me during that time. Every time they did a test on me a knot would tighten in my stomach from nerves, and I still feel the same way today: the possibility of losing all my hearing scares me. I am profoundly deaf but still retain some hearing and I can wear hearing-aids, which is why I intend to keep the little hearing I have left.

I remember it as if it were yesterday, the first time they told me I had to wear hearing-aids. I felt myself dying. My only thought was that I didn't want to be disabled, I wanted to be normal, to hear, I wanted to be the best, to be happy. The same questions circled my brain again and again, tormented me: what am I? Who am I? Am I deaf or hearing? Why has this happened to me? Why? Why? And I couldn't find an answer.

I took me almost a year to accept my new situation. I drowned myself in writing a lot. I needed to exorcise my anger, my pain. I shut myself away from the outside world because I didn't want my parents to see me cry or suffer. One night I wrote a letter, one of those letters you write because you need to let out that internal hurricane, that tempest that oppresses and drowns you, that sucks away all of your energy and upsets you. It was one of those letters scribbled in bad handwriting that, once the anger has gone, you rip up into a thousand pieces, scared that someone might know the real you. Luckily that letter was never destroyed. My mother kept it for ten years and now I keep it, with affection, because in some way it symbolises the first time I realised I was a deaf person.

For many years I thought it wasn't fair that I should lose my hearing because of a medicine, but accordingly I have become a better person. I have come to understand that there are a lot of things in life that don't have a reason, a motive or a just cause and that it's not worth going over, tormenting yourself again and again; you just have to accept it. But although this is difficult, the moment comes when you take it on board and realise you must live with it, it happened to you and you should carry on and fight. Deafness is an on-going fight and whoever says it's not is lying and doesn't want to recognise it. Information doesn't come to you, you have to go looking for it.

My academic development

At school my teacher didn't realise what was going on. Every time I think about that stage in my life I feel angry, I've often asked myself why he didn't pay more attention to me, why didn't he detect my deafness sooner when it was so evident. I had a hard time. It was a very difficult and delicate period and I promised myself that if I were ever a teacher I'd never let anything like that happen again, as early detection can save a lot of suffering.

Physical education was true torment. I was always last to follow the teacher's instructions and I spoke very loudly when doing calculations without realising it. I was never in time with the rest of the class during recitals, I was slower and reading always drew attention to me because I never knew where we were on the page. It was a very stressful situation to be in. When they told me I was deaf and gave me hearing-aids to wear I covered them up with my hair so that no one would see them, especially my classmates and the other children. I didn't want them to laugh at me. I sat in the front row and only the teacher knew of my deafness. I didn't tell anyone else. I remember feeling envious of a three year old girl once: she listened to her parents calling her, laughed at what they were saying and I remembered with nostalgia that I used to be able to do that.

I carried on in the same vein at secondary school: I sat in the front row and only told my teachers and those closest to me. I preferred to go unnoticed. It was easy as no one but the teacher spoke. I wanted to prove to myself that, although I was deaf, I could go far. I wanted to show that I could get to the same places as a hearing person and even go beyond that. I couldn't see the danger in that logic.

I got to university and it was here that a profound change happened in my life. I was studying for the teaching diploma in Special Needs Education and I realised that I no longer controlled the situation, as there were more than eighty people in the class. I carried on sitting in the front row and took my own notes but checked these against photocopies of my classmates' notes. The problem that I increasingly faced was in the open debates where people participated a lot. I came to the conclusion that it wasn't enough to just tell the lecturers, the whole class should be aware. I would have to ask them to stand up so that I could read their lips. In this way I went from a conformist position when watching videos, films and during conversations, to a re-vindicated position, demanding to receive complete information. I therefore requested summaries of videos and bibliographies to complete the information I had and to fill in the gaps.

Something I remember that has been engraved in my memory was when I was awarded a distinction for my course, a prize that is given to the two people with the best academic records of the year. That represented a big achievement for me; all of my effort, all those hours and nerves were rewarded with something that I never thought I'd have. It was one of the most wonderful moments of my life.

The assessment that helped me

In the last year of my degree I received an assessment from an educational psychologist for the first time. Until then I hadn't wanted to ask anyone for help, I wanted to do it all by myself. My big ambition since childhood was to become a University professor and even to do a Masters in speech therapy. Every time I look back on that now I'm aware of how naïve I was, I realise that the demands would have gone beyond me and I would have just drowned. In pursuit of this goal, all I did was study and study, I dedicated my life only to studying, everything else was unimportant to me, it could all wait. Many people told me that I should work to live and not live to work, but I just made 'deaf sounds' to those comments and didn't stop studying. I wanted to go far, for people to feel proud of me. Now I realise that that behaviour showed that I didn't accept my deafness, I didn't want to see my limitations, I wasn't really aware of where I could get to.

Receiving the assessment opened my eyes to a lot of things. On the one hand, I had a chance to try a FM transmitter, of which I had no prior knowledge. They did a test on the transmitter and the results were optimal. Unfortunately, I couldn't make full use of it as I was doing a work placement at a special education school and the conditions weren't wholly appropriate. But on the other hand, I received guidance on how to improve my academic training, through sign language and the Internet. These two points were fundamental for me as thanks to them I got my first job.

My first job

For five months I worked as a basic training teacher and as co-ordinator of a work placement workshop in which I taught classes using sign and oral language to six deaf women, all of different ages and levels of education. It was there that I came to know the gaps that other deaf people have, I discovered the very low reading comprehension levels that many deaf people have. I remember that it had a big impact on me, as before then I thought that all deafness was like mine, that to be deaf wasn't a big deal. It was a very enriching period of my life, that I have fond memories of as it was my first experience of work.

When I finished work I experienced the crisis that almost everyone goes through when they complete their degree: finding a job. I signed up with lots of employment agencies, sent out my CV and didn't find anything. I asked myself what the point of studying was if in the end finding a job was such a difficult task. Luckily I got the job I'm in today, in which I feel fulfilled and very comfortable.

About my current job, reflections

I've been working in the University Assessment Centre for Students with Disabilities at the University of Valencia since 1998, which is a service for the attention and assessment of students that present any type of disability in their higher education. There are two of us working there, a full time psychologist and myself carrying out support work on a part time basis. Working here has made me realise the importance for disabled people of having an identity. On many occasions, particularly with deaf people, I've been aware that I've served as a role model, an incentive to continue studying. This is very important because in many cases disabled people abandon their studies due to the tremendous effort that it imposes on them and the daily battle it represents to them.

The truth is that I've learnt a lot during this time, in particular thanks to my work colleague who has always shown her support and has taught me the necessary strategies to provide a better response in the service I offer. I've learnt social skills, to know who and how to be, to know how to better weigh my abilities against my limitations, to be more of a realist and somewhat more mature. I've been lucky as not all deaf people have an appropriate role model at work. Now I see the same conduct in some deaf people as I used to have: not respecting the turn of speech, not controlling the tone of voice, slamming doors: small details that are obstructions to integration.

In my work I've also encountered some of my limitations: listening on the telephone, especially if there are background noises, having conversations with disabled students that have distorted speech or people that speak in different languages, and I still have trouble in meetings or group conversations. Some of these barriers have been overcome by a series of modifications that have been set up in my work place. Firstly, they gave me a special telephone that omits background noises and at the same time they put thick windows into all the walls that whilst muffling background noise also help me to control my visual surroundings. The support I've received and keep receiving from my classmates has also been very important; they are aware of my deafness, they vocalise for me, face me and explain things at a slower pace. I'm in a job that after two years I command well: I feel like a fish in water. I'm happy because I think it's a job that suits me well. But I'd be lying if I denied that a terrible fear comes over me when I think I might become completely deaf: what would happen to my job, to my life?

My second degree

Currently I combine work with other studies. I'm in the last year of an Educational Psychology degree. Here I've been able to use the transmitter in optimal conditions. The lecturer wears the FM transmitter and thanks to this I can take notes with confidence. Therefore, the classes are really useful to me, I'm not taking up an idle seat but rather I enjoy learning and attending classes every day. Nevertheless, the moment a debate starts up I become anxious. Frequently I sense that someone is talking, I try to find the person and pray they'll stand up but then other classmates start to talk and when I manage to find the person that's talking they've finished and someone else has begun. Its very difficult for me to follow the leading thread of a topic. My classmates are far away and this prevents me from lip-reading, and on top of this there's background noise which makes it very hard for me to make use of auditory information. I often ask a classmate to tell me what's being said but what a person has taken ten minutes to say is explained to me in two words. If we add together all of those lost minutes, lost hours: the amount of information that escapes me is astounding. I feel as if I receive information in pieces and those pieces I lose are all gaps, gaps that I need to fill in with a lot of reading and questions in order to really understand things.

As a result of this I sometimes lose the strength and will to carry on because all of my efforts are useless: I can't control the situation, on the contrary it's the situation that controls me. Hearing-aids, lip-reading, the transmitter, asking people to stand up—none of this helps me at moments like these. My classmates will laugh at or dispute someone's comment but I'm lost, I don't know what's going on and so I opt for one of two things: I ask a classmate or I smile and resign myself to not knowing.

About sign language

I've been sharing my life with deaf people since I was nineteen. I've gone from rejecting deafness, to acknowledging it in part, to using it in many cases as a flag that identifies me as a person.

Recently I was asked a question that made me think a lot: 'Do I feel integrated in society?' I've asked myself that question at many points in my life. I think it's easier to integrate when you're a child because the key to integration at that stage is play. You play, run and jump with other children. But as you grow up language plays a more vital role in your life; when the need to communicate is evident, integration turns into something more complex and difficult.

I feel it's really necessary for me to be amongst deaf people because it helps me to form my identity. They are people with whom I share the same limitations, the same communication barriers (radio, television, cinema, music, videos, etc). Independent of the language we use, oral or gestural, the barriers are similar. We should make use of the services and technologies of assistance that make up for and help us to balance out our opportunities in relation to everyone else. If many of these re-sources didn't exist I would certainly feel less integrated, less informed,

134 less independent and most importantly, less happy.

Although the existence of common aspects with deaf people is a fact, I should also point out that amongst deaf people, especially with deaf people that use sign language, I also don't feel totally integrated. Although my level of sign language is perfectly acceptable it's not that of a native user, and therefore I sometimes also lose part of the information from deaf people. Oral language is easier for me as I possess a greater vocabulary and can express exactly what I want to say, with tact, subtly, without offending anyone and even use irony. I can't do this in sign language because I don't possess sufficient mastery of the vocabulary. On the other hand, there are moments amongst deaf people when I feel hearing because I act as an interpreter, as an intermediary between both worlds. I help deaf and hearing people communicate with each other. In this sense many deaf people consider me to be more hearing than deaf, because I wear hearing-aids, speak on the telephone and communicate with hearing people. They say, luckily less and less now, that people with hypoacusia (partial deafness) are like hearing people, and that's not true: I have fewer problems and communication barriers, I don't dispute that, but I still have limitations that I can't prevent.

I certainly feel more hearing than deaf. My friends are hearing, everyone in my family is hearing, my work colleagues and classmates are hearing. I spend 75% of my life with hearing people. I feel hearing because my maternal language is oral language and not sign language, because the last six years of my life can't compete with the previous 25. I feel hearing because I'm more comfortable with oral language, where I can express exactly what I'm feeling, because I can translate ideas and my deepest thoughts into words.

Certainly, I feel integrated in the society that I find myself most immersed in, but at times I feel displaced, separated and pulled to another world, the world of deaf people. My big dilemma, since I met deaf people at nineteen years old was, what was I, deaf or hearing? I didn't feel totally identified in either world, I found myself between two situations and throughout the years it has been one of my biggest worries. Today I'm happy because I've discovered that I don't have to choose, I want both worlds, I want them both to unite, I'm an advocate of bi-lingualism and if I ever marry a profoundly deaf person and have children, I will educate them with a bilingual focus. I hope I'm able to educate them as my parents educated me: they, with little education, have provided me with and given me good role models, as well as self-confidence and drive, without which I might not be here today, sitting in front of the computer writing these words.

About tomorrow

The truth is that if I could be born again and someone told me I could choose the life I wanted, despite of everything that's happened, I would choose to be deaf again. I'm convinced that having the opportunity to live through an experience like this has helped me to improve my professional abilities, it has been easier to empathise, not only with deaf people but also those with any kind of disability. I see things through two different eyes: those of a professional and those of a person with a disability.

I recognise that it's a blessing for deaf people to live in the twenty-first century. I've often imagined living in older times when they used to carry out atrocities on people with disabilities, an age when ignorance reigned and there was a lack of education and information, and where the absence of resources and an adequate response was startling. With relief I see that we're on our way to a better world, where there's respect for that which is different, for the individuality of each person and the right of the individual to be a person that demands real responses to their needs. I imagine that by following this ideology, the path of integration will be much easier for the deaf people of tomorrow.

Making a Business of Sign Language

Volker A. Maaßen with Gisela Binczyk

My name is Volker A. Maaßen, and I was born in 1954. Like my parents, I am deaf from birth. I have been using sign language from early childhood since this was our natural way of communicating at home. Of course, when I was a small boy, I was not aware of the fact that DGS (German Sign Language) is a language. The question simply did not arise: sign language was the way to express myself and talk to others. Of course, at times problems in communication with hearing people did occur, but this seemed normal and gave me no reason to worry. My wife is deaf and we have a daughter who is deaf, too. Thus, in my own family, too, we communicate in DGS all day long.

I have spent all my life in Cologne. I went to the Cologne deaf school for ten years, then started a vocational training course as an engineering draughtsman. This training lasted for three and a half years. I passed the exams and continued working as a draughtsman. I became first interested in sign language when the 'blue' sign books appeared.[1] It was at that time that I was asked whether I was interested in participating in a sign language project as a volunteer, and it was only then that I came to realise that sign language has a grammar. And so, after a while, I was asked to work as a lecturer in a regional project called MOVESDO, a training program for sign language interpreters. At first, this was a completely new and strange idea for me. Of course, I knew DGS, but I had no idea whether I was able to teach DGS. I was afraid that I would not be able to cope with such a task. I was really torn, but then I thought, OK, I could give it a try, and I wrote my application and handed it in. About two weeks later, I had a reply that invited me to come to Essen for an interview. Everything was explained in great detail to me then, for instance, what I would have to do and what my workplace would be like and so on. I realised that this job was completely different from anything I had done before, and I was curious to try it out. On this same day, I met Peter Rapp for the first time, too, who was to become my colleague as well as my friend, my companion, and my business partner today, which, of course, we did not know then. I told him that I was toying with the idea of joining the project as a lecturer. He had applied for the project, too, but did not know, then, whether he would be taken on.

When it became clear that I really had the job, I began to think about it a lot and for a long time. Of course, I had to talk to my wife, because this workplace would change our private life, too. I would have to travel to Essen all the time, some eighty kilometres away from Cologne, and I would have to work on weekends, too, since the training project was organised as a part-time programme. Also, I was expected to take part in seminars myself, and all in all I would have to be very flexible. The project was limited to an initial four years, and my contract would be restricted to that period of time. So, what I did next was see my boss and talk to him about this new opportunity available to me. He told me that he really wanted me to stay in his company but that, if I really wished to accept this offer, I should go ahead. I then asked him if he could give me leave of absence for those four years, but he said that this was impossible for a private company. But he went on to suggest that he would re-employ me after the four years were over, and this made my decision somewhat easier. Eventually, I handed in my notice for my old job as a draughtsman and accepted the post in the project.

Before I started working in my new job, I went on holiday with my family. When I was on holiday, thoughts about the project kept revolving in my mind. After the holiday I had my first working day, and so I drove to Essen. I then met Peter again there. We had truly become colleagues now. To start with, everything was shown to us and we had our own desks. It was very strange to have a desk of my own that was completely empty apart from a few pens and pencils in the upper drawer. My first task consisted in getting acquainted with the exact course of the project. Next I had to spend some six months sitting in on classes and meetings at the Centre for Sign Language in Hamburg. Being there, we had daily lessons on the basic skills of teaching. We often had the opportunity to ask the lecturers questions and discuss various problems with them. This was a very strenuous time for me, because I kept going back to Cologne on weekends during all that time. I had a hard time getting to know the various methods of sign language teaching, which was still in its infancy then. Everything was completely new to me, and the day of my first teaching lesson was drawing nearer.

Back in Essen, I was presented with the curriculum for the lessons. Reading it through I began to feel that I would not be able to teach in this way. Peter and I then tried to work out how this curriculum could be put into practice. In the beginning, this was difficult but in time it improved, it was a good time for us. Of course, as in any model project, some things went wrong but there were also moments of success. We were often arguing with our boss, the head of the regional Deaf association. He kept disagreeing with the views that we, and the research team from Cologne University that was a partner in the project, held with regard to teaching methods and the overall curriculum. The main problem was that he had been chosen to be responsible for the task even though he was not fully familiar with the work. It was often tiresome to explain things to him, and I would have liked him to interfere less with my work.

After about three quarters of the project time passed, I started thinking about what to do after the four years. Applications for continued funding of the project had been submitted, but as yet it was uncertain whether the project would continue. I did not like the uncertainty of having to work in this manner for any length of time. If a follow-up project was granted for another two or four years, this would mean that in another three to five years we would be in the same situation of not knowing what would happen next. Would we be granted yet further funding? On the other hand, I felt positive about wanting to keep working in the area of sign language since I was really enjoying it. I wasn't much into research, but was more interested in the learners and wanted to teach DGS to many more people. Peter wanted to go to university after the four years in the project. That was fine for him, since he had *Abitur* [2] and was still young, but it was no good for me.

A hearing researcher in the project had the same problem. She did not want to have to hope and worry every two or four years about her future. We often discussed various options. She, too, could have gone back to university but she did not want to do that anymore. One day we met up with a good friend of ours and shared our thoughts about what to do. Suddenly, the two women came up with the idea of starting a business. At first, I did not get the idea and asked how this was meant. They told me that we should set up a company that includes a language school and an interpreting service. I liked the idea. When I asked about

the necessary finances, I was told that we would not need much money 139
to begin with. This was a very strange feeling for me: My own company!
I had only ever been working an employee, but now I would become
my own boss. Well, we had to draw up a number of contracts, but having signed these our company was born. Now we had a new problem:
What should we call the company? There were so many options: 'Language School for Sign Language'? But it was not just a language school,
but an interpreting service, too. So we needed a name that could stand
for both areas and would mean something to others. Then, one of the
women suggested the name 'LOOR ENS'. 'LOOR ENS'? I had understood
the signs, but did not get the words. LOOR ENS? What does that mean?
Then they explained to me that this was a phrase from the Cologne
dialect of spoken German, in standard German it means something like
'have a look', 'see here'! Well, that suited me fine! Our company was all
about seeing, not hearing, and it was a Cologne company, of course! It
did occur to us that people from Hamburg, Berlin or Munich would not
understand the phrase, but the matter was settled and LOOR ENS became the name of our company.

Of course, there was a lot to do, we had to look for office space and
teaching rooms, print business cards, get our company registered with
the trade inspectorate and tax office, and so on. When I had the first
business cards made I gave one to Peter. He was truly baffled and said:
'Oh god, you haven't started a business, have you?' 'Well, so what?', was
all I could answer. Later I went to the secretary of the regional Deaf
association and showed him my business card, too. He was shocked,
became very upset and demanded that I should support the training
project. For me, it was a matter of principle that I would carry on supporting the project until the four years were over. The secretary and
others in the association were then concerned that I might make use of
their curriculum, but I reassured them that I was going to develop my
own new teaching strategy. There was criticism from many sides. Other
colleagues, for instance, accused me of a lack of solidarity. And even
my parents were critical, worrying that I was taking a risk and might
not be able to draw my pension when I retired. I relieved some of their
worries by telling them that I could still look for a job in my old profession as a draughtsman if all else failed. Others yet again told me that I
would need to persuade various institutions to consent before starting a

business. But I told them that someone who wants to open up a baker's shop does not go round to ask all the other bakers if he is allowed to set up a new baker's. He simply does it.

Thus, when the project was over, we began to advertise our language school and sent out information to various institutions. In return we registered some four or five students, and I was quite taken aback, realising that there would not be any profit after paying out all the expenses such as the rent, etc. But my partners managed to convince me that we would make it in time. And indeed, after some time there were so many registrations that I could not teach all the classes by myself. It was then that I thought of Peter. I asked him if he was interested in working with us on a fee basis. As it happened, his university plans were not working out very well since no one would pay for his interpreters, and so he soon began to work with us. I explained my teaching approach to him, and he added new ideas of his own. More and more people registered for our classes so that soon we did not have enough space any more. We needed larger offices and teaching rooms, and after a while we found the right place. All we had to do now was decorate the rooms.

The number of our customers kept growing, and now there was the new problem that some of the customers were not interested in ordinary classes but, for instance, wanted to learn signs for specific professional or other contexts. Then there were deaf children who wanted to learn from us but who needed teaching methods completely different from the ones we used with our adult customers. The demand increased so dramatically and in such a diverse way that Peter and I were not any longer able to do all the teaching. And so, yet again, we took on someone new in the company. This new colleague is hearing, and he specialises in working with children. He teaches classes in DGS, Signed German and written German, as well as giving tuition in all the school subjects. Thus, deaf children can have private tuition in the same manner as it has always been available to hearing children. This addition to our company really took a great load off Peter and me.

We have developed what we believe to be a well organised company. LOOR ENS has three departments. First, there is the interpreting service. All the colleagues working in this department are interpreters. They organise their workload for themselves and independently of the other departments. The second area is the language school run by myself and Peter, and the third department is the newest, the 'learning club' (*Lerntreff*). All the colleagues working for LOOR ENS had initially been business partners. But since in the workload of all departments and the number of tasks have grown so much, we now have an additional employee working in each department. The interpreting service has taken on a new interpreter, the language school employs a Deaf DGS-teacher, and there is a new Deaf educator working for the learning club. All the post are regular work placements, not job creation schemes, and all the employees have contracts for an indefinite period. There is still too much work to do, and we are thinking of taking on even more employees in the different departments.

Often the question of solidarity with other Deaf people is raised. My position on this question is this: solidarity is very important, of course. My whole family is deaf, and we feel solidarity with the deaf community. I need deaf culture, and I am in favour of the recognition of sign language, too. But, in the world of business, one has also to think of business success. For me and my partners, the company LOOR ENS is a way of making one's living, and we have a responsibility for our employees, too. In business, too much solidarity is injurious to the interests of the company. For instance, sometimes there are customers who want to learn Signed German. One such customer registered for a course with us, even though he lived quite far away. When I suggested to him that he might find some other opportunity to learn Signed German closer to his home, he told me that in his area only DGS was offered. We were severely criticised by other deaf people as lacking solidarity because we offer classes in Signed German, too. But it is simply a matter of respecting the demands of the customer, and if there are customers who want to learn Signed German, this is what we teach. Often these customers have not understood the difference between DGS and Signed German, and I can demonstrate this in the classroom. After a while, the customers generally decide to switch to DGS. Similarly, I think deaf people should stop saying that we do not need hearing people, or that we can achieve everything without any help from the hearing world. Really, this is no more than a dream! I have been part of setting up 'LOOR ENS', but I must say that we could not have done this if there had not been any hearing people. There are so many things to be organised on the telephone, such as fixing dates with customers or the tax consultant,

142   and as a Deaf person I simply cannot do this. To be true, there is now a project called TeleSign[3] that enables Deaf people to make phone calls and thus contributes to their independence, but back when we started there was nothing like that. TeleSign is an important development for us Deaf people, and I am happy that something like this exists now since it is a step in the right direction.

It has meant a lot of hard work. In our line of business, it is anything but a matter of course that we can spend our evenings and weekends at home. And I much appreciate the support of my wife and my daughter as well as the partners and spouses of my colleagues, who have always shown so much understanding for our work and have put up with great deal of inconvenience because of our working hours. However, if I was asked today if I would take the same decisions again as when we started LOOR ENS, I would clearly answer: Yes! I greatly enjoy the way I work.

Notes

1   The first volume of the *Gebärden-Lexikon*, a collection of signs used in the German Deaf community, was published in 1987, the fourth and final volume was completed in 1994 (edited by Günter Maisch and Fritz-H. Wisch, Hamburg: *Hörgeschädigte Kinder*). The collection came to be known as *Die Blauen Bücher*, the blue books; it was intended mainly for educational settings and is still widely used by parents and more open-minded teachers of the deaf.

2   The final examination at German secondary schools that qualifies for entry to the university system.

3   TeleSign is a funded project that aims at establishing a relay service in Germany on the basis of using visual telephones that enable deaf callers to use sign language interpreters to communicate with hearing people.

Being Deaf at Rampton Special Hospital

Stephen Robinson and Sue O'Rourke

Rampton is a special hospital which provides mental health services in conditions of maximum security to people who have committed serious criminal offences making them a 'grave and immediate risk' should they be in the community. In 1987 a project was established to research the needs of patients with communication problems at Rampton Hospital. A pilot was run jointly by a sign language tutor and a Deaf patient. This taught the basics of sign language to staff and patients and was the beginning of the development of a specific service for Deaf patients. In 1989 a Deaf sign language demonstrator, Janet Goodwill, was appointed. She and a colleague, Rae Than, wrote in the book *Being Deaf* of her experiences as the sole Deaf person working in this highly unusual environment. Janet was based in the Further Education Department of the hospital and in a short time made a huge difference to the lives of both staff and patients, not least in heightening awareness of just how much inequality existed between the provision of services to Deaf and hearing patients.

This was only the beginning and much has changed since then. In 1989, Janet Goodwill and Rae Than wrote that the most significant changes were:

1   The development of a professional interpreting service for the Deaf patients leading to improvements in communication.
2   The appointment of a sign language demonstrator enabling on-site tuition in British Sign Language (BSL).
3   The secondment of a teacher to University to study a post-graduate Diploma in Deaf Education.

These developments were important first steps in promoting an equality of access to services at Rampton Hospital. In the last twelve years the interpreter service has expanded and grown in terms of hours and the development of expertise. We now have a contract for thirty-two hours

144   interpreting per week. This service is well respected and well used. The continuity of using the same individual interpreter for much of the patient-related work over the years has meant she has developed considerable skill and expertise in this highly specialised area of interpreting. Other interpreters are now able to work more confidently at Rampton Hospital with her support and supervision.

Demand to learn BSL is always high. Tuition is offered to Deaf patients and staff. We have recently secured funds to employ an additional BSL tutor to teach a group of hearing patients to sign. This is not only meeting a demand from hearing patients but will also improve the social environment of the Deaf patients.

The Education Department continues to develop skills in working with Deaf patients, offering a range of classes, either specialised or integrated and is constantly striving to offer the same opportunities for learning to the Deaf patients as are afforded to their hearing peers.

However, it is important to remember that the primary reason for Rampton's existence is to provide mental health services in conditions of maximum security to people who have committed serious offences making them a 'grave and immediate risk' should they be in the community. The aim of assessment and treatment is not only to improve the quality of life for the patient, but also to address reasons for offending and to lower risk. If Deaf patients were to participate in this process and eventually be discharged safely into the community further steps were necessary. From 1989 to the present there has been a gradual acceptance of the need to bring specialist skills into the clinical arena as well as the educational areas of the hospital. Janet Goodwill and Rae Than highlighted the misunderstanding which took place between Deaf patients and hearing staff, even when the staff have some skill in BSL. The arrival of Janet illustrated the way in which a Deaf professional could pick up the nuances of communication which are so vital in the assessment and treatment process, as well as in an educational setting.

In 1991, Stephen Robinson joined Janet Goodwill on a part-time basis and later became the full-time sign language demonstrator when Janet left her post. Still based in the education department, Stephen found himself developing a broader clinical role as staff became increasingly aware of Deaf issues and the need to improve clinical services to Deaf patients.

As for many other Deaf professionals, venturing into the world of   145
mental health came as something of a culture shock to him. From the
hearing perspective, the presence of a Deaf worker challenged long
established ways of working, often resulting in staff feeling deskilled.
Working together sensitively has enabled Deaf and hearing team members to appreciate cultural differences and to realise the need for creative
staff roles. Ultimately this has resulted in Stephen's post being unique as
there is no 'fit' with the established NHS job descriptions and titles. We
have therefore called his post 'Deaf Services Development Worker and
Advisor'. We would advocate for the creation of similar posts in settings where hearing culture and ways have to be radically changed in
order to meet the needs of Deaf service users.

—I worked in engineering as a toolmaker before coming to Rampton
Hospital. I had experience as the BSL tutor of an evening class and was
looking forward to developing this. I was new to an educational setting
and to mental health, so I was nervous and excited on taking up my appointment. Although employed as a sign language demonstrator within
the education department, I soon realised that the Deaf patients saw
me as a role model and wanted to talk to me about their problems and
frustrations in a way that they perhaps did not want to with the hearing
staff. At first this was difficult as my official role was as a teacher and I
was unsure whether I should be used in this way. It became obvious that
I was being given valuable information which needed to be fed back to
the clinical teams. Over time I became a link person to the wards en-
suring that information I received was not lost. Nursing staff began to
appreciate this and realised that I could clarify issues and enhance communication. I was asked to do more of this based on the wards and this
was negotiated with the education department. An important part of
my role was building up a sense of trust between the hearing staff and
myself.

As they realised that I would feed back information to them, they became more comfortable with my role and asked me to help them communicate clearly when they were talking to Deaf patients.

Over time, I have become more confident and more assertive in different settings. My new job title of 'Deaf Services Development Worker

146   and Advisor' reflects the diversity of my responsibilities. My role is now primarily assisting clinical staff in the assessment and treatment of the Deaf patients. Although I do not have a mental health qualification, I am clear that my role adds information and improves the reliability of the assessment process, even when the hearing professional has a good level of skill in BSL. I know the Deaf patients well, their background and in particular their idiosyncratic forms of sign. As a native BSL user, I can pick up on slight changes in communication style, in facial expression and manner of signing and feed this into the assessment. My being there during ward rounds and meetings can empower the patients to express themselves and changes the power balance in the assessment.

Some of the patients at Rampton Hospital have, unfortunately, not had access to sign language until a late age. Some of them have a mental illness which interferes with their way of signing or of their understanding, others have a learning disability. As a Deaf person I can think of creative and visual ways of assessing and treating from a Deaf perspective. We use drawing, role play and reconstructions of real events in BSL in order to deliver treatments. We use group work in addition to direct work with individuals.

On a day to day basis, it is important to have a Deaf role model to illustrate to Deaf patients appropriate problem solving skills, how to cope with difficult relationships and how to relate to hearing staff when communication is difficult and frustrating.

Rampton is a large organisation through which we aim to spread Deaf awareness and basic BSL as widely as possible. Our success in achieving this is due to the interest of staff across the spectrum of professional groups represented at Rampton. The hospital induction programme includes a brief session of Deaf awareness and this stimulates many men and women of all ages and backgrounds to seek out more information. Reception and security staff, secretarial staff and patient escorts are all represented in BSL classes and there is always a waiting list. The commitment of the staff means that both Deaf visitors and Deaf patients can have pleasant basic conversations around the hospital. Those directly involved in work with Deaf patients are encouraged to progress through CACDP Stages I and II. Priority is given to clinical staff in day to day contact with patients; this includes nursing staff, doctors, occupational therapists, social work and psychology staff. Pressures of work and staffing difficulties often mean that staff attend courses in their own time but there are now over seventy staff with BSL Stage I, and many with Stage II.

As well as ongoing BSL training, the Deaf service runs a Deaf Awareness week two or three times a year. This provides basic training for a large number of staff throughout the hospital and places are always in demand.

—There is a second Deaf member of staff. While I work full-time, primarily in a clinical role, my colleague Jackie Fletcher works part-time in the education department. In order to give the Deaf patients some contact with the Deaf community and the outside world, the fortnightly Deaf club continues on a Thursday evening. We have trained a number of volunteers over the years and have now eight Deaf people who regularly come in to the hospital for the Deaf club. Their commitment to travelling to Rampton and spending time with these patients makes a huge difference to their quality of life and is much appreciated.

Deaf and hearing people working together can be tricky, and of course it is frustrating at times, but I feel that generally the hearing staff at Rampton Hospital have a very positive attitude towards deafness and BSL, an attitude which is improving all the time as the level of Deaf awareness increases. It has taken many years of patience and understanding and an ability to resolve differences in a non- confrontational way, but now I feel that hearing staff see me as a vital part of the clinical team. This is seen most obviously in an awareness by staff of their limitations. In the past, staff with the CACDP Stage I award may have tried to communicate an important piece of information without assistance. This is unlikely to happen these days: hearing staff are very likely to ask me to be involved in order to clarify communication and also to improve their own skill.

As for the future, although much has been done there is much left to do. At the time of writing this there is a commitment by the hospital to open a single ward as a Deaf Unit by the end of 2001. This has been a long time coming and is a considerable achievement, reflecting the greater awareness of Deaf issues particularly by managers within the hospital. Currently the eight Deaf patients at Rampton Hospital are on two wards, an admission ward and a rehabilitation unit. In the past, the Deaf patients were on four wards, which was inefficient in terms of staffing and diluted the Deaf patients' level in terms of the cultural and language environment. With the opening of a Deaf unit catering from admission to discharge, we aim to continue to develop our assessment and treatment from a Deaf perspective. We also have the opportunity to train and employ more Deaf staff and have made a commitment to offering specialist placements to Deaf nursing students from the Salford University Course, the first course in the United Kingdom to train qualified nurses who are Deaf. We have already begun to use video to communicate care plans and other information to Deaf patients. With the opening of a Deaf unit, we would hope to expand this provision. There are eight Deaf patients at Rampton Hospital and two Deaf staff and the expertise in both mental health and deafness, and in forensic assessment and treatment, are beginning to be recognised nationally. Stephen is proud to be asked to represent Rampton Hospital at various courses and conferences and to share some of his expertise, particularly in promoting the role of Deaf professionals in forensic mental health and deafness. Since Rae Than and Janet Goodwill wrote about the early developments of the Deaf service in Rampton, much has changed. However, we have a long way to go in continuing to adapt treatments and therapies for Deaf people and in providing a service from a Deaf perspective.

When the Deaf patients make progress and are no longer considered a risk, there is a huge problem as there is no specialist medium secure provision for Deaf patients. Whilst there exist options at discharge for hearing patients, regional secure units, private institutions with some level of security, even going back to prison, there is no equivalent specialist resource for Deaf people in this situation. We hope that this is shortly to be resolved as there is a growing awareness nationally of unmet need in relation to forensic mental health and deafness. Following the publication of the Daniel Joseph homicide enquiry, there was a national strategy for Deafness and Mental Health commissioned by the

Government. At the time of writing (June 2001), we are awaiting con- sultation on the strategy so whether the new strategy will address these areas of unmet needs and begin to provide true equality of access in culturally and linguistically appropriate settings, is yet to be seen.

A Brief History of Deaf Sport

Arthur Dimmock

Most deaf people are able bodied and there is nothing to stop them participating in competitive sport but since coaching had became an important aspect in almost all forms of sport barriers were set up. This was the consequence of communication problems as coaches need to give instructions by oral means, which is a dissuasion to many deaf enthusiasts, however talented. With the coach in the saddle, everything is heavily stacked against these people. It was ages since a deaf footballer was invited to sign professional forms in the Football League, which meant that a number of good footballers ended their careers with clubs outside the league. Despite what many deaf people call rank discrimination some managed to distinguish themselves in fields other than football.

Historically, sport originated in Ancient Greece and their sporting events were termed Olympic Games, that originated in 776BC. The blind poet, Homer, recorded what was called the heroic games in the Iliad and Odyssey but the heroes thus named are mythological figures such as Ajax, fleet of foot, the other Ajax, of great strength. Athletes from all parts of Greece came to the games, traditionally staged at Olympia, Western Peloponnese. Many hailed from Sparta where the worship of muscle was encouraged. One may wonder if any deaf athlete took part in the games but Sparta had a policy of hurling children even robust ones, found to be deaf, from the Taygete Cliff to certain death so it is highly unlikely that any deaf man from this part of Greece became an Olympian athlete. Even when Rome reigned supreme, and the gladiatorial games were daily events there was no record of any deaf participant taking place. Only Quintus Pedius, a talented deaf artist, was mentioned in its history but he died in his late teens.

In 19th century Britain sports events were reported but mostly fragmentary as the old missions that staged the few events were bent on the spiritual welfare of its charges so that pecuniary contributions from the public could be enhanced. In 1858, however, the man who was to change the scene was born in the Camden area, North London. Becoming totally deaf at the age of eleven, he was already adequately educated so did not need any further schooling, Arthur James Wilson, sank his head in books and by the time he was fourteen he wrote an excellent article for *A Magazine Intended Chiefly for the Deaf and Dumb*, and later several more for *The Deaf and Dumb Magazine*. At fifteen he worked as a wood engraver but had to give up through eye strain. Before the end of his teens he was engaged in the making of bicycles in what seemed to be a smithy. Cycling at the time was gaining popularity and he was bitten. He organised tough bicycle races, which meant pedalling to the top of Box Hill in Surrey. Few managed to complete the distance. He heard about a race in Ireland so he challenged the champion, R. J. Mecredy and won. The men were seated on a strange contraption with two large wheels at their side and a small front wheel for steering.

Mecredy, who edited the Irish Cyclist with his brother, noted Wilson's talent as a writer and when he split with his brother he made Wilson his partner. He wrote under the pen-name of Fæd which is 'deaf' spelt backwards. In 1889 the pneumatic tyre was invented and the Pneumatic Tyre Company based at Dublin was looking for a general manager to expand business. Wilson applied and got the job, despite what Mecredy called a 'terrible handicap'. Before the turn of the century Wilson and his new wife moved to London and established a workshop in Farringdon Street, employing thirty hands. Later he moved to larger premises in Clerkenwell Road and traded under Dunlop Pneumatic Tyre Company, employing two hundred people. Wilson thus became a rich man and during the First World War he organised and paid for thousands of war wounded to attend various entertainment and sporting events, and even hired the Albert Memorial Hall for their enjoyment. Wilson even managed to get King George V and Queen Mary interested in cycling as an exercise and they allowed him to show them how to ride bicycles, and Wilson was thanked for his efforts.

He founded a retirement home at Sydenham, South London, for employees of the motor and cycle trade who fell on hard times and even provided their orphaned children with shelter and education. In 1918 he founded the Federation of London Deaf Clubs (FLDC) which became the largest sporting organisation in Britain. It involved interclub match-

152   es between London's seven major clubs. The practice enabled some deaf billiards players to become proficient, notably Maxwell Fry and John Arnold, whose recurring century breaks were the talk of the London sports scene. In the late twenties and early thirties the Anerley School for the Deaf for boys, near where the old Crystal Palace was before flames razed it to the ground, gave intensive training in athletics to all the boys, which was undertaken by the headmaster, Mr Stannard, who was an accomplished athletic coach. Some went to achieve honours; one was Herve Vassall who won a gold medal for the pole vault during the London IGD in 1935.

The world's first cycle race originated at Paris in 1868 and, a few years later cycling was seen to be popular among several deaf sportsmen, and in 1895 a race from Paris to La Varenne-Chennevieres, a distance of fifty kilometres was held. The winner, Henri Mercier, covered the distance in 1 hour 38 minutes despite several punctures, a cantankerous machine and cobbled roads. A year later Rene Hirsch was the only deaf cyclist to engage in a 100-kilometre race. He finished 86th out of 201 competitors. Early in the 20th century, France had some sort of club or association for deaf cyclists. They met at weekends and indulged in touring spins in the country, mostly around Paris, which had the largest population of deaf people.

Then Eugene Rubens-Alcais appeared on the scene. He was born in 1884 at Saint-Jean-du-Gard near Nimes and came to Paris where employment was plentiful. He had a wide interest in cycling and founded the first properly established cycling club. German deaf people heard about the club and tried to establish one in Berlin but the police issued a proclamation that deaf people were not allowed to ride bicycles. The mind of Rubens-Alcais switched to alternative sports, such as athletics and tennis. In the early 1920's he met Antoine Dresse, a deaf Belgian banker, and they both discussed the possibility of an international body to organise sport for the deaf, and in 1923 they founded the Comité International des Sports Silencieux. Rubens-Alcais became the acting President and Dresse the general secretary. The first International Games of the Deaf was held in Paris. Participating nations, including France, hailed from Britain, Belgium, Holland, Hungary, Italy, Poland, Rumania and Czechoslovakia. The events consisted of athletics, cycling, and football, swimming and shooting. The FLDC, with competitors gathered from Britain and Ireland, came under Rev. Vernon Jones, a partially deaf man, and A. J. Wilson. Britain won the silver medal at football. The next IGD was held at Amsterdam in 1928. The FLDC under the same leaders won the gold medal at football. Over the years more nations participated and more sport was added to the list. Women's events commenced in 1931.

Football has been a major attraction to the Deaf. The first all-deaf football team was formed in Glasgow in 1871, known as the Glasgow Deaf Football Club and reputed to be the oldest in the world. It was established by pupils of the Glasgow Institution for the Deaf and Dumb. Matches were played at the nearby Queen's Park ground before it became Hampden Park. The first all-deaf match was held in 1889 at Falkirk between Glasgow and Edinburgh in the presence of 2,000 spectators. Edinburgh won by 3 to 1 and received a handsome cup. About the same time, and for the next few years, most cities in Britain had their Deaf Football teams. Even most Schools for the Deaf had their own teams. The Newcastle school once owned four football pitches and the game was an almost daily occupation.

The first team played against hearing school teams and always won, thanks to daily practice. One of their players, William Readman, signed professional forms for Wolverhampton Wanderers in 1933 but he was rarely in the first team so he was transferred to Blyth Spartans where he ended his career. There were some deaf professionals in the Football League; namely Billy Nesbitt who won a Championship and a FA Cup winners medals with Burnley around the period of the First World War. James McLean was on Cardiff City's books in the 1920s but he rarely made first team appearances.

The most outstanding player was Cliff (Boy) Bastin. A schoolboy prodigy, Cliff Bastin's name was paramount in football supporters' discussions of the 1930's. *The Arbiter* rated Bastin as 'one of the most brilliant footballers of modern times'. Cliff's career began while playing for Exeter schools and his prodigious skills were soon to be seen when he was selected to play for England Schoolboys versus Wales when only fourteen years of age. Soon after he joined the local side, Exeter City, and made his league debut when he was fifteen. Cliff scored six goals in seventeen league games, as a seventeen-year-old. Herbert Chapman signed him for Arsenal in 1929 for £2,000. He appeared as an inside

154 right but later he converted to his famous left wing position. By the end of his initial season at the club Cliff featured in 21 league games and scored seven times in the 1929/30 season and was the youngest player to appear in an F.A. Cup Final, when Arsenal beat Huddersfield.

When the team won the league championship in the next season Bastin's partnership with the legendary Alex James on the left flank started to flourish. Not only was he ever present, the youngest, at the age of eighteen or nineteen years old, to be so for the club. He contributed no less than 28 league goals, including a hat trick against Derby County. In 1931/2 he won the first of his twenty-one England Caps when he was only nineteen years old. He became the youngest player ever to win an England Cap, League Championship and F.A Cup medal in one season and became known as Boy Bastin because he had done everything in the game while still a boy. In the 1932/3 Bastin set a record, which undoubtedly will stand for all time, when he scored a staggering 33 league goals. No other winger in history of the game, before or since, has come remotely close to equalling this total.

The reason that Bastin was so deadly was that, unlike any other winger, he stood at least ten yards in from the touch line so that his alert football brain could thrive on the brilliance of James threading through defence-splitting passes with his lethal shooting finishing the job. It became abundantly clear that he was having problems with his hearing at the time. He and James used a kind of sign language on the field but this type of silent communication was of their own making. Herbert Chapman, the man who was his mentor and whom he idolised, died in 1934. Nevertheless, he bagged 20 goals in 36 league appearances in that year. Arsenal dropped to the sixth place in the 1935/6 season.

This was partly due to the fact that the new manager, George Allison, was in a quandary as to with whom to replace Alex James when unavailable and Bastin played in an alien position, as inside forward. However, his contribution in helping Arsenal to win the F.A Cup against Sheffield United was immense, scoring six times in seven ties. The 1936/7 season must have seemed strange to Bastin as it was the first time in eight seasons that he was not involved in domestic honours. It was through being switched from position to position, but in the next season he was back to his original position and scored fifteen times in 38 league appearances.

On the 4th February 1939 he scored his 150th league goal. During the war he was exempt from active service owing to his deafness. After the war at the age of 34 he played in a further six league games before a leg injury took its toll and he retired from football in 1947. His club record of 178 first team goals stood for years 50 before Ian Wright broke the record in 1997. Cliff Bastin is not only a legend in Arsenal's history but will be remembered as a football immortal. He was never booked, let alone sent off. He died in 1991 aged 79 at Exeter where he ran the Horse and Groom pub for twenty years before retiring. Raymond Drake who played for Stockport County during the mid-fifties is assumed to be the last profoundly deaf professional to be involved in the league. No more appeared. Rodney Marsh and Jimmy Case were England internationals but they are just hard of hearing or slightly deaf.

Deaf women's football teams cropped up in various cities where there were Deaf clubs. The first one appeared about 1967 in Liverpool. Towards the end of the twentieth century deaf football teams declined, this is believed to have been caused by oral and mainstream education tending to reduce the numbers in the Deaf community and deplete club membership. Snubbed deaf footballers, showing promise, might do well in countries such as Israel or Turkey, where an avalanche of support comes from most quarters even from coaches without adequate manual communication skills using basic gestures.

Stories about prize-fighters are aired over and over again but, beyond the nostalgia, was a brutal sport, and promoters were greedy men bent on making money for themselves and sharing little with the fighters.

The most prominent was James (Deaf) Burke. In his childhood he was, what was then known as, 'a gutter urchin', but a veteran pugilist, Joe Parrish, rescued him and trained him. He was a mere 12st. 6lbs., 5'8" in height but he proved a match for any man, bigger or heavier. When the British champion, Jim Ward, retired the chief contender was the Irish champion Simon Bryne who found himself, much to his annoyance, matched against this 'deaf and dumb' upstart. Fearful punishment was sustained in the early stages of the contest. Burke's arms were black and blue through stopping the Irish man's savage blows and Bryne's fists swelled to double size. Bryne took it all and was in a dreadful state. At the 99th round Burke, who was kept going on brandy, managed to summon up the last of his strength and caught his rival full on the face.

Bryne collapsed in a heap and had to be taken home unconscious. He was in a coma for three days before dying. 'The Deaf Un' was the new champion and was soon on his way to America with Parrish. He was matched against Samuel O'Rouke in New Orleans for a purse of $1,000. The opponent, a friend of Bryne, was much bigger but Burke found that he knew little of ring craft and was able to punch him at will. However, angry spectators invaded the ring and Burke had to fight half a dozen to save himself from getting stabbed. Someone slipped a bowie knife into his hand and he managed to escape on horseback but failed to collect the prize.

Returning to England things appeared to change as people's attitude towards him became unpleasant, apparently the result of Bryne's death, even though Burke had heroically saved a woman and four children from a blazing house. He lost his last match against Bold Bendigo on a foul. He succumbed to hard drinking and returned to the 'gutter' where he was found dead in 1845 at the age of thirty-six.

World-class boxing was not confined to Burke alone. Italy produced Mario d'Agate, quoted in boxing journals as the Deaf Mute boxer. Because of his deafness he was refused a licence but after years struggling he finally got it and was a veteran when he won the World Bantamweight Championship against the legendary Robert Cohen in 1955. He battered his opponent into submission in the sixth round. He held the title for a year before losing to Alphonse Halimi on points in a disputed contest. Mario soon retired and became a successful businessman.

The fighting game among the Deaf was not confined to boxing. Another Italian, Ignazio Fabra, funded and coached by a government agency, won the world flyweight title in the Greco-Roman Wrestling Championship in 1955. Other wrestlers who reached prominence were Harry Kendall, who was selected to represent Britain in the 1960 Rome Olympic Games, Mike Eagles and Alan Kilby. Kendall and Kilby became widely known through their appearances on the television.

Lester Piggott, the jockey, was found to have a hearing problem so he was sent to the Gorleston School for the Deaf in Norfolk. A speech impediment is a notable part of his identity and this has led to him being a man of a few words. However, since winning twenty-six horseracing classics, he is regarded by some experts of the turf as the greatest jockey of all times.

Deaf racing cyclists seemed to have been helped along by their club and members. The register of cycling records gives a glowing manifestation of an Essex club, Becontree Wheelers, and its team trio, Clarke, Eshouse and Fell, who during the post war years broke national records in numbers far exceeding anything in club history. Nonnan (Nobby) Clarke, the deaf rider, was an integral part of the team.

His finest performance was winning the five-mile invitation at the old Paddington track in 1944 in which the nation's top sprinters took part and Clarke's win gained him the Best All-Rounder trophy. He collected gold medals in the 1949 IGD at Copenhagen and 1953 at Brussels where he finished the 100-kilometre course ten minutes ahead of the Italian champion C. Carzaniga who took the silver.

Another prominent deaf cyclist was Malcolm Johnson of Rotherham who was the nation's fastest roadman recording 52 minutes 25 seconds for the twenty-five miles course in the 1960s. Johnson, like Clarke, collected gold medals at Washington, 1965 and Belgrade 1969 International Games. Clarke, along with another Deaf racing cyclist, Peter Stovold of Fulham Wheelers, managed to recruit a number of Deaf riders in the early 1950s in view of forming a Deaf Cyclists Club but they were given scant help from coaches and officials so the project floundered. After Clarke's early demise and Johnson's retirement, Stan Gilbert emerged. He belonged to Cambridge Town and County Cycling Club and was their champion for a number of years. Despite his deafness he was made club captain and his most impressive performance was covering 432 miles in a 24-hour road race.

Everyone knows that the Tour de France is the world's toughest cycle race. Riders spend nearly a month around the whole country, struggling up mountains and speeding dangerously downhill. The only Deaf rider to enter the contest in 1949 was Jacques Geus, a Belgian. He managed to finish the tour and was placed a respectable 27th out of nearly one hundred riders. The winner was Fausto Coppi, the great Italian termed *le campanissimo*.

Other distinguished Deaf sportspeople who represented their countries in the Olympics proper were Gerhard Sperling, the East Germany walker, R. Windbrake, the West Germany runner, the Russian hurdler, Viatcheslav Skomorokhov, swimmers, Jeff Float (USA) and the Australian woman, C. Fitzpatrick. Skomorokhov was placed fifth in the 400m

158   hurdles during the 1968 Olympic Games at Mexico City. The winner was Britain's David Hemery who broke the world record for the event. In the 1980s the Russian, who after retirement became an athletic coach on government pay, was brutally murdered, believed to be at the hands of the Russian Mafia. During the 2000 Games at Sydney, Australia, Terence Parkin, a twenty-year-old South African, won the silver for the 200 metres breaststroke, timing 2 minutes 12.50 seconds.

Others who aspired to reach a stage worthy of national or international acclaim were Mike Hawthorne, a gymnast who had won several medals in local contests but had to wait until he was a veteran to win a silver for floor tumbling in a national contest for veterans. Another was Hitesh Lakhani who is probably the only deaf snooker player to make the maximum break of 147. He managed to become a professional but had difficulty in getting sponsorship and nothing more was heard of him for some years.

The Deaf of America have been striving for years to get their most successful baseball player voted into the Great Baseball Hall of Fame. William Ellsworth (Dummy) Hoy was the first disabled man to succeed as a professional in major leagues. His rise to stardom began in 1886 and for fifteen years he was outstanding and much applauded when playing for such prestigious clubs as Cincinnati, Washington and the Chicago White Sox. Being profoundly deaf and without speech, he used signs to communicate with team mates and this enabled him to make history of inventing the hand signs that are now widely used by umpires in all baseball games. A prominent sports writer claimed that that Hoy's 2,054 hits in 1,798 games was better than quite a few 'immortals' now enshrined in the Hall of Fame but Hoy was always outvoted or ignored over the years. It appears the baseball hegemony felt that, because of the 'dummy' tag, the inclusion of a deaf man might blemish the roll of illustrious names enshrined in the Hall of Fame. Hoy died in 1961 just six months short of his 100th birthday.

Deaf sports people, even if talented in their specialist area, continue to be ignored. Sadly, Terence Parkin's Olympic success recently did not get the usual hullabaloo, reserved for well-known stars. Some otherwise much needed publicity would have gladdened the hearts of Deaf people and their hearing supporters.

Football in my Blood

Helga McGilp, with Martin Atherton

Sport, and football in particular, has always played an important part in the life of Helga McGilp. Here, she discusses some of her experiences as both a watcher and player of football, and the way her involvement in the game has impacted on her relationships with both deaf and hearing people.

—I come from Aberdeen originally, and I was born deaf into a deaf family. My mother and father are both deaf, and I have four sisters who are all deaf. My family has three generations of deafness; my mother's parents were deaf, my father's parents are deaf too; my aunties and uncles are all deaf. From 2 years old until I was 11, I went to Aberdeen School for the Deaf. From 11 to 17, I went to Mary Hare Grammar School—that is an oral school—and then I moved to London. I have lived there for several years now. I see myself as culturally Deaf, but I also see myself as being flexible with communication. It depends who I am with—whether they use speech or sign, I can change and adapt. I try to be flexible.

Watching football as a Deaf person

I started watching Aberdeen when I was about eight or nine years old. Aberdeen School for the Deaf and Aberdeen Football Club were near each other, about five minutes walk, that's all. School used to start at ten o'clock, so I used to set off maybe quarter of an hour early, and go to the ground, because I knew the players would be arriving for training. I used to collect their autographs—I met all the players. I remember I met Alex Ferguson once—he was the Aberdeen manager at that time. He gave me his autograph and I dropped it, and he picked it up for me. I used to mix with all the famous players then. I always used to be late for school be-cause of collecting autographs. I used to collect the same ones over and over again, I remember once Neill Cooper asked me, 'Why do you keep asking for autographs?' I had pages and pages of them at home!

I used to watch Aberdeen's home matches, every two weeks. I remember my mother used to give me three or four pounds to go. I asked my father to come with me, but he was a Rangers supporter, so I went on my own and I used to sit in the stand behind the goal. Those were good years for Aberdeen, they won the European Cup Winners Cup in 1983, versus Real Madrid. Aberdeen played really well in the 1980s—'83, '84, '85—but now they have gone down. I supported Aberdeen until I went to Mary Hare School, and every time I went home in the holidays, I would go and watch a match. Nowadays, I live in London and I started watching Arsenal a few years ago. I started going there because my home is only about ten minutes walk from the ground, and now I watch their home games.

The reason I watch Arsenal is because it helps me to switch off. My job is very pressurised, so going to football helps me to switch my brain off. Other people—deaf and hearing—maybe they relax by listening to music, or going to the pub or a disco. I relax by going to watch football. Going to a match and spending a couple of hours watching football means I can go home feeling relaxed—it has given me the chance to switch off.

Playing football as a Deaf person

When I was attending Aberdeen Deaf School, I used to organise lots of football. I used to organise the other children into teams. My mother and father are both keen outdoor bowlers, and my mother used to win lots of trophies. I remember when I was about eight or nine, I picked one of her trophies to take to school. At lunchtime or break time I would ask the other children if they would like to win it in a football competition. We used to play with 10 or 15 a side. I would pick two captains and get them to pick the teams. This went on for two or three years until I went to Mary Hare—there was nothing there, it was really quiet! After a while, I started to join in with the boys' games, and I learnt a lot from them. When I was about fourteen, I became more interested in tennis and other sport.

A few years ago, I started playing football again, and I joined a hearing women's football team. Really, I hoped to set up a Deaf women's football team in London, but there weren't enough players for a full team. There were about five came to practise, but the number used to go up and down. So I decided to join a hearing team, and try to get the other [Deaf women] to join as well. We could learn from the hearing players, and then go back and set up our own Deaf team. Four or five of them joined, but gradually dropped out, and I was the only one left in the hearing team. It is called Hackney Women's FC, and I was there for about two years. We trained every Wednesday and played a match every Sunday against London hearing clubs.

Of course, playing with hearing footballers meant there was a communication barrier. For example, before the whistle blew to start the match, we would all gather in a huddle, and everyone had to say something. Sometimes, someone would say something funny and everyone would start to laugh, but when it was my turn to comment, I didn't know what to say, because everything had gone straight over my head. One person in the team, the captain, she took her Stage I [sign language exam] and went on to take her Stage II—that was nice, because she started to learn to sign to help me get involved with the team.

The attitude of my hearing team-mates was fine. Every Wednesday—I was a student at University at the time—I would go straight to training. When training finished, we didn't bother getting changed, we all went straight to the pub, to have a pint, play pool. At the end of the night, when they were all drunk, they would start singing. That's been really part of my culture—drinking, playing pool—but at the time it was good. Every Wednesday night, because I was in the pub with hearing friends, conversation was superficial, but we had a laugh. My Deaf friends knew I went to the pub with hearing friends every week and they always knew they could find me there. Sometimes I would be invited to a party—they would mime 'Want to come to a party?' and I would gesture 'Yeah, great'—but there wasn't really much communication. Really, I wasn't involved in any conversations or anything. When I arrived at the pub, I would go straight to the pool table. That way, we didn't need to try and communicate. If there wasn't a pool table, we would have had to sit around and talk. Sometimes, I would ask my Deaf friends to come and meet me at the pub, to act as support. Also, every Wednesday you would see the same faces, and they would invite you to have a drink or a game of pool, so that helped. Slowly things improved;

for example when the match finished, the others would gesture something, like 'good game' or something.

As for training, really I taught myself to play from being about eight years old. I played at school, at home—I remember at home, the goals didn't face each other, they were offset—the garden was very long and I learnt to play there. Also I used to go and watch Aberdeen playing, I learnt their skills. At Mary Hare, playing with the boys taught me how to play football. After school, the women's hearing team helped me to improve—they were at a high standard, that's why I joined. Earlier, when we had tried to set up a Deaf women's team, they were not at so high a level, and I found that frustrating. The hearing team were better, and I found that more of a challenge. I felt I could learn more from them. Also, we had one or two qualified football coaches who used to come along and that helped as well.

Communication wasn't really a problem, as the coaching was visual—they used to show us how to dribble or whatever. If I wasn't sure, I would ask someone else to show me. I preferred to watch first, to see what I should be doing, before I tried it myself. The others used to check that I understood what I should be doing, and helped me that way.

Every Sunday, before the match, when the referee arrived, the captain and I would go to the ref, and she would explain that I was deaf. If the referee was behind me and blew the whistle, I wouldn't know, so it would be better if the ref. was in front. Sometimes my forwards would nod to let me know when to play the ball. If I was upfield, I might not realise I was offside, and carry on to try and score. Maybe the other side's goalkeeper would know I was deaf and wave to let me know, or a defender would grab my arm. Of course, there was a communication barrier again.

I remember one incident when the whistle was blown but I carried on playing, and the referee got angry and called me over. The other team's captain and my captain came over and explained that I was deaf and couldn't hear the whistle, and so he let me off. Sometimes if I committed a foul, the referee would tell me off, and then just let me go. I think I may have got away with some things because I was deaf! If something happened because of a lack of communication, or the other team were angry with me—maybe I had fouled someone, and they were shouting at me—my team mates would all come up and protect me.

The attitude of the other teams varied—some weren't bothered that I was deaf, others were like 'Wow, you're deaf?' Some people would patronise me if I missed something, maybe laugh at me. If they teased me, I would just ignore it. I never cared about the other team's attitude, all I was bothered about was my team's attitude and having their support. They always wanted me to give them sign names or to teach them simple signs—but it wasn't a problem for me, because I enjoyed playing the game.

I remember when I was about ten or eleven, a teacher asked me, 'What do you want to be in the future?' I said I wanted to play professional football for Aberdeen, with number 9 on my back. When she told I couldn't do, because I was a girl and I was deaf, I was heartbroken. From about eight or nine, it was my dream, but I didn't realise that it was impossible, I didn't understand why. I've met other young deaf people who want to be professionals, and they get really frustrated.

Football can be important for social life

I think football is important for personal development; for example, part of my job at one time involved interviewing people, asking them about their experiences with social workers, were they happy with them, etc. This involved going to their homes, maybe visiting a man the same age as me, or boys of thirteen, fourteen years old. When they invited me into their homes, I used to look around for something about football, to talk about and use it as an icebreaker. If I saw a football trophy or a football scarf, I would ask them if they supported that team, tell them about my football interests, and we would maybe talk for ten minutes just about football. When we finished, and it was time to interview them, they were relaxed about it, because talking about football had broken the ice.

Also, if I meet a new deaf person, someone that I don't know, I will bring up football to try and establish a link with them. Football helps bonding between us. Sometimes, people I know might see me and say, 'Arsenal lost, Man Utd. won 5–0', and we have a bond between us through that. That is why I think football is very important to me. It's the same as when I was doing interviews, talking about football is a good icebreaker.

I think football is important for social life too. I remember being with a group of friends back in Euro '96—some of my friends weren't

164 very interested in football, but I had agreed to go to the pub to watch England against Scotland. I told my friends and asked them if they wanted to come with me and have a drink. Some other friends asked us where we were going, and when we told them we were going to the pub to watch the football, they decided to come along, even though they weren't interested in football. They wanted to learn about football, so that they could be a part of the group—they didn't want to be left out. They obviously didn't know the rules of football, and they would say something that made us laugh. That's when I realised that they had come along so that they wouldn't be left out of the group. In Euro '96, the group would pair up, to take turns to pay for the food and drinks, so football can be important for social life as well. It also helps to build new friendships.

I remember watching the England Deaf team playing football once. There was a difference between the hearing and Deaf spectators—the hearing fans were shouting to pass the ball, shoot, whatever, whereas the Deaf fans were gesturing and pointing. Also some of the Deaf players were trying to fool the players or the referee, I saw a lot of that there. Hearing players use their voices more, whereas Deaf players are more visual.

Whilst I was watching that match, it was hard to concentrate, because there were Deaf people all around me in the stand, and because they were signing to me, I kept missing things that happened on the pitch. When I am with hearing people, for example at Arsenal, people are talking, and that isn't a distraction, I can just watch the match. But when I am in a Deaf crowd, there are lots of distractions, people signing, or waving and tapping you on the shoulder to attract your attention. I prefer to be left alone to concentrate on the game. Also, if the match is a bit boring, I might start a conversation with someone, and then miss something exciting when it happens! So, it is different to hearing football.

At Arsenal, there are different types of fans as well. Behind the goals, they are noisier, and shout and jump around more—they do the same on the sides near the pitch. At the back, people are more serious when they watch the game. I prefer to sit on the side to watch the game. When Arsenal score, I jump up and cheer, but in the lower stands, they will jump around, wave their scarves, shout and taunt the opposition fans. I wouldn't like to sit there, I prefer to sit and watch the match quietly. It's interesting, at Wembley, they have seats near the pitch that are low, and you can't see the pitch properly, especially when people start standing up and jumping around. It's interesting to think why people choose to go there. They must go there for the atmosphere, for the singing and to taunt the opposition.

Maybe if I was watching a Deaf match I would be more lively, but when I go to watch Arsenal, that is serious. I want to watch the game, not jump around—it is the game that interests me. I remember one match when I went behind the goals, instead of my usual place on the side, and it was really noisy. I had to turn my hearing-aids off. It was so noisy I just couldn't concentrate on the game. I will never go there again. I prefer being sat high up on the side, where I can see the game and concentrate.

I go the match by myself, and I sit amongst hearing people. Sometimes in a match, I feel like turning to the person next to me and saying something. If I had a Deaf friend there, I could say, 'He's rubbish' or 'That was a foul, he should be booked' or whatever. It was the same at Aberdeen. I used to ask my father to come with me, but he would say, 'I'm a Rangers supporter, I'm not interested in Aberdeen', and so I had to go on my own. When I am watching Arsenal, I wish I could go with a Deaf friend sometimes.

That's why, if there is a match on Sky TV, I might ask a deaf friend to meet me in the pub, to watch the match. Then we can watch the match together and discuss what is going on. I would love to be able to do the same at a match, but it isn't possible. Getting a ticket for Arsenal now is really difficult—you need to buy a season ticket, or book a couple of months in advance, so it is really difficult to ask a friend to come with me.

I remember when Liverpool were playing Arsenal at home—my oldest friend supports Liverpool, and she asked if I would buy a ticket for her. The tickets went on sale about two months before the match, at 9.30 in the morning. I went down to get one after work, at about four or five o'clock, but when I got there, they told me they had sold out. I said, 'I thought you had loads of tickets?' and they told they had had plenty that morning, but they had all gone in one day. It's the same all the time now, trying to get tickets for Arsenal. My nephew is twelve, and I have

166   the same problem getting tickets for him. His mother—my sister—she doesn't let him go to the matches on his own. I remember when I was eight or nine, my mother used to send me off to Aberdeen on my own, it was safe. Also, I liked the chance to do something on my own. My mother would give me some money, and I would go to the match, get a seat, buy a programme and read it, then go home—it helped me try to be independent. Sometimes, I think football can help children learn how to be independent.

   I have another Deaf friend who goes to Arsenal; he sits downstairs, and I sit on the top tier. We normally meet about one hour before the game for a drink and a chat about the match, then we go to the ground together. He has supported Arsenal for twenty to twenty-five years, and is a regular season ticket holder. Really, his whole world revolves around Arsenal. I met him one night and he told me he had gone home and cried the week before, because Arsenal lost. He told me he wanted to marry his girlfriend, but she had to choose between Arsenal and him. But I told him, 'Carry on going, get the best of both worlds'. I met his girlfriend and explained how they could have the best of worlds. It's a real problem, because I know his world would collapse if he couldn't go to watch Arsenal.

   My life is simple—football helps me to relax. I know some people say I am mad, but I'm not bothered!

Katya's Story

Katya Davidenko Lepeshkina

From August 1941 until January 1944, the Germans blockaded Leningrad
(now St Petersburg) and it was cut off from the rest of the country. The
only supply line lay across the thirty miles of Lake Ladoga, to the north
east of the city. Food shortage were acute, electrical supplies were cut
off, and temperatures could drop as low as -40°C. During the 900 days
of the Siege of Leningrad, one third of the population died, mostly of
starvation.

I was born in Leningrad (now St Petersburg) in 1923. I was one of a large
family, there were eleven children but two died in infancy. My mother,
Maria Ottovna Everete, was a native Estonian, had been born to a well
off family in Narva; she was one of thirteen children. My mother was
hearing but I know my mother's sister was deaf, and also that there
were a number of other deaf members of the family.

My mother married Alexander Lepeshkin from Tver and they moved
to Leningrad where they opened a bakery in Vasilievsky Ostrov. The
business flourished and they were said to make the best bread in the
area. They were comfortably off and even after the Communist revolution in 1917 they were able to keep their bakery. They had a big apartment in Vasilievsky Ostrov. As well as myself, two other children in the
family were deaf, Marina and Vova.

However, the peace of our family life was disturbed, when during the
Stalin era my father was arrested and put in prison. Later he was sent to a
concentration camp, and he was exiled to Siberia. Although he was able
to come back to Leningrad in 1938, he died of tuberculosis very soon after his return. The life of my family changed dramatically after my father
was arrested. We had to move out of our nice apartment on Vasilievsky
Ostrov, into one room in a block on the same street. The room was quite

large, about thirty metres square, but small for my mother, Maria, and her nine children. My eldest sister Valya was not allowed to enter higher education because she was a daughter of the 'people's enemy'. Neither she nor I could get work for the same reason and with so little money coming in, the family had not even enough money to buy food.

At one time my mother became so desperate because she could not feed all her children. After everyone had gone to bed at night she turned on the gas from the stove in the room hoping they would all be gassed and no one (including herself) would wake up in the morning. However, when we were all sleeping, my mother's younger sister, Anya, came to visit us. She smelled gas, switched off the stove, opened all the windows and pulled my mother and all of us children out of the room. Although some of us felt quite ill, she saved all our lives. After this, she took a different child every week to stay with her own family to help my mother.

Life was still difficult, but eventually my mother was able to find a job in a biological laboratory. She stole mice and frogs from the place of work and brought them home to cook for the family. Her salary was very low. We all went to school but could not eat there, as we had to pay for school meals and there was no money for that.

Marina went to the school for the deaf on Giorokhovago. This was the first Russian school for the deaf and had been opened in 1810. My brother Vova and I went to the school for hard of hearing children, although we were both very deaf and always used sign language.

When World War II began, most of the family was in Leningrad. My deaf brother Vova had luckily been sent to a pioneer camp and survived the war in Zlatoust near Chelyabinsk and they still have very good links with Chelyabinsk Deaf Community.

It is impossible to describe the horrors of life in Leningrad during the siege, November 1941 to March 1942 were the worst months. Maria became very ill (she had dropsy). She went into hospital, but the hospital was destroyed by a German bomb. The rest died of hunger, first Valya and Boris, then Marina, Ellya and Luda.

Valya had married a hearing man and they lived separately from our family. They had a deaf son Boris but all three died in the siege. Marina had married the deaf son of a famous art collector, Dudin. Some of the paintings in the Hermitage came from the collection of Dudin. Although Marina also died in the siege, luckily their hearing son had

FAMILY TREE

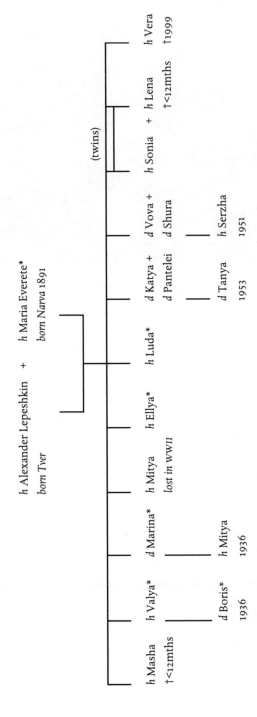

h Alexander Lepeshkin + h Maria Everete*
born Tver   *born Narva 1891*

(twins)

h Masha   h Valya*   d Marina*   h Mitya   h Ellya*   h Luda*   d Katya +   d Vova +   h Sonia + h Lena   h Vera
†<12mths   lost in WWII   d Pantelei   d Shura   †<12mths   †1999

               d Boris*   h Mitya   d Tanya   h Serzha
               1936   1936   1953   1951

key Children are listed from oldest (Masha) to youngest (Vera).

       h hearing
       d deaf
       † died

Memorial to those who died in Siege in Leningrad, situated on the outskirts of the city.

been sent to summer camp before the siege; he was then placed in a children's home, so he survived.

The survivors, Sonia, Vera and I had to wrap the bodies of our brothers and sisters when they died and push them outside the entrance to the apartment block. A special lorry collected bodies every morning from outside the apartments. I became very ill and close to death but I was discovered by some people from the Leningrad Deaf Society. They said they would try and get me out of Leningrad but I did not want to leave my flat and my sisters. Finally they persuaded me to join a group of Deaf people. The only way out of Leningrad was on a boat crossing Ladoga Lake. There were about thirty Deaf people in our boat. Many boats tried to cross the Ladoga and we were part of a long line of boats crossing the lake. The line was bombed by the Germans. Somehow, I did not feel any emotion. I was lying in the bottom of the boat but felt no fear at all. All the other boats with sick people on them, children as well as adults, sank but I could not do anything for them. Somehow, the boat with thirty Deaf people managed to cross the lake.

When we got to the other side, I was sent to Barnaul, Altai, by train. The trip in the train took nearly two months. I could not eat at all, my

The building which includes the Davidenko house. Three families shared one apartment, including sharing the kitchen.

body would not accept food. We were not allowed to sleep and my friends had to keep me awake, as if I slept, it would mean death for me.

When I arrived in Barnaul I weighed 38 kg. I was sent to live with a Deaf family in a small town, Rubtsovsk near Barnaul. The family did not want me living with them. They thought I was an old useless woman of sixty when in fact I was only nineteen years old. However, I could read and write well unlike the family, all of whom were illiterate. I was able to help them with reading and writing and, because I was relatively well educated, I was able to get a job as a storekeeper. However, all the time I was there, I suffered from stomach problems and scurvy.

When the war was over, my dream was to return to Leningrad, to my family. The local Deaf community in Bernaul did not want me to go. I had become quite important to Deaf people there and helped at the special factory for Deaf workers. By this time I had a good place to live there.

I knew our old room in Leningrad had been taken over by someone else, and also it was difficult to get a pass to Leningrad. Then in the autumn of 1945 a friend of mine, Maria Rezvan, who was a member of the National Deaf Association and had been living in Moscow for a long time, organised an official letter for me which allowed me to go to Leningrad.

When I reached Leningrad I had to begin again from scratch. I started off by sewing for a living and managed to get a room in a hostel. I found Sonia and Vera again and we were able to organise for Vova to move back to Leningrad. He started working in a metal workshop.

Eventually I was able to get a room of my own in a shared apartment. Vova moved in with me until he married Shura, an illiterate deaf woman from the country. In 1951 their son, Serzha, was born.

Then I met Pantelei Davidenko, a gifted deaf artist, who made postcards and sold them in different towns. He had been born in Krasnador and had completed his education there. When I met him he had already been married four times. We began to live together and in 1953 our daughter Tanya was born, she was also deaf. Pantelei was not there very much of the time, he travelled around a great deal.

In 1958, he finally persuaded me to move to Moscow. I did not like the idea but in the end I agreed. Firstly we lived in a tiny room in the north region of Moscow, Vokovskaya. The room was five metres square and that was for four people, Pantelei, myself, Tanya, then 5 years old, and Pantelei's 15-year-old hearing son by his second marriage. Pantelei's third wife lived in the room next door.

I started working in a factory, again doing sewing and I have worked there ever since. Pantelei left me soon after we came to Moscow. Since then, the two of us, Tanya and I, have lived together. We have a dog and two cats. Every day I cook up basic food and go to feed the stray dogs in various parts of Moscow, although really I cannot afford it as my wages, together with my salary, do not really give me enough to live on. I belong to the Deaf club in Moscow, and am active in the group for older people there.

Tanya is also an active member of the Deaf community in Moscow. She worked in the Moscow Bilingual School from its very beginning, and now she works at the new Moscow Centre for Deaf Studies and Bilingual Education. She is one of the foremost teachers of Russian Sign Language in Russia. She also carries out research into Russian Sign Language and has visited many different countries, including the UK, to discuss issues with colleagues and present her findings at conferences.

Children of a Lesser State

Katja Fischer

I was born in the German Democratic Republic (GDR) in 1973, and I lived in the GDR until the *Wende*, i.e. the historic changes of 1989. My deafness (prelingual) was caused by meningitis when I was one year old. Whenever life in the GDR is discussed, people who have not grown up in the GDR and never went there or paid only brief visits, ask if it was very hard to live under such circumstances. Similarly, hearing people keep asking us deaf people if it is very hard to have to live without hearing. Certainly, there are different opinions on this point, but usually Deaf people say that we are used to being deaf and don't know any different, even if sometimes we wish we could hear to make life a little easier. This is exactly how I felt about life in the GDR. I grew up there and was used to the fact that I did not have the same freedom to travel as people living in Western Europe, that clothes and cars were not as varied and colourful, or that exotic fruit was hard to get. There were only two types of cars, and to get one you had to wait for at least ten years. At times, I would have liked to wear the fancy things available in the West instead of the boring clothing, so uniform and colourless, that we had to put up with. Bananas were a rarity, and if any were available at all, we had to queue for them patiently. Here, being deaf was an advantage: we Deaf people showed our 'severely handicapped' passes and simply passed the queue.

It was the declared aim of the GDR to provide a good education, sports and employment for everyone. Among the great things that existed only in the GDR, were the so-called *Spartakiad*, a sports tournament, and the annual Mathematics Olympics, a competition for the best deaf pupils of all ages from schools all over the GDR. On such occasions, there was signing everywhere, contacts were renewed or newly established. The Deaf community was alive long before one reached adulthood. Since nearly every one wanted to take part in these events, deaf pupils were greatly motivated to do sports or develop their math-

174 ematical skills. The best national athletes were later sent to international competitions in various countries. Who would not want to go and see some new part of the world! It was common for deaf schools to visit the local Deaf association and establish contacts when pupils reached the age of *Jugendweihe* [1] and celebrate their initiation to adulthood by singing songs in praise of the GDR. Whenever there was a celebration or party in the local Deaf club, many Deaf youngsters would go there and join in. There was a lot of partying, and it was always crowded. Everyone was expected to treat others to drinks. Money was not important—there was not much to buy in the GDR anyway!

As far as education is concerned, 'we', i.e. Deaf people in the GDR, used to say that those in the West have everything but know much less. They cannot even cook, we used to think, since hot meals can be bought pre-cooked in supermarkets over there. A friend of mine escaped to the West, and she wrote to me and told me that school was boring and that she felt she was not learning anything. Today we know that neither side, East or West, provided an adequate educational system for deaf people. There was however, a difference in the way young Deaf people were supported. In the West, better ways existed to encourage individual deaf pupils to make their way into higher education. To this day and all over Germany, however, schools still refuse to use sign language and concentrate on lip-reading and speaking skills, sometimes using signs to support spoken language. What was missing in the GDR was the chance for qualified deaf pupils to make their way to *Abitur* (the qualification necessary for entering university), or even enter a university, as was possible for hard-of-hearing people. In the Leipzig deaf school that I went to as a boarding pupil for 13 years, from Kindergarten to graduation, there were two teachers for the deaf who were themselves Deaf. One of them was a sports teacher; the other was in charge of handicrafts and technical drawing. We were always glad to be with those teachers, because they would always have some news to share with us. The handicrafts teacher was a representative of the GDR's Deaf sports association, and he was internationally active. He sometimes told us about new developments in the Deaf world. Communication with those two teachers was relaxed and informative. Without being aware of it, we identified with the Deaf teachers because we shared the same language. Of course, we did not know anything then about the fine distinctions between sign language, signed German, and Sign Supported German.

We kept, of course, asking him how he, as a Deaf person, had managed to become a teacher. He told us that he was an exception and that we should simply accept the fact that Deaf people in general could not become teachers. Today I wonder whether this was his honest opinion or whether he had been influenced by his hearing colleagues. Whenever we were talking—and, indeed, in school it was rather more talking than signing—about jobs to be dreamt of but not to be found on the list of the some fifteen different professions available in the vocational training schools for Deaf people in the GDR, our hearing teachers would say: 'You cannot hear, so how can you communicate with hearing people or use the telephone? It is simply impossible. You are Deaf, and it is a fact that there is only a limited choice of professions suitable for you'. It comes as no surprise that my first choice of a dream job was to become an old age pensioner! What's the point of starting a career if you cannot decide about it yourself? At some point, after visiting various workshops and having been through a number of practical placements, dental technology seemed like a possible choice as a profession. At that time, in the GDR, dental technology was 'studied', as it was called, in theory and practice at a vocational school for the rehabilitation of 'hearing-impaired' people. Well, I thought, studying is what I have always wanted to do. Everyone in my family went to university to study, so why not me, too?

I had only just started 'studying', i.e. vocational training as a dental technician, when the big political changes, the *Wende*, began. When I had been at the Leipzig school, my teacher used to tell us secretly about disputes and rows between demonstrators and the police in the city centre of Leipzig. But this was in 1988, at a time when protests and demonstrations were not the big media event they were to become. There were elections in the GDR. In Plauen, my hometown in the south of the GDR, the GDR-government achieved its worst results, because many people did not vote or voted against the government. More and more people started to take part in demonstrations. I followed these events mostly in the media, it was only later that I took part in demonstrations myself, too. I was lucky to own a television that could receive teletext subtitles. My grandpa had organized this for me, using West German currency, and for me, this had been the greatest gift because it enabled

176 me to follow films or the news, reading subtitles.

The evening of November 9, 1989, I spent with most of my fellow students in front of my television in the student residence hall, when I happened to read some strange subtitles announcing something to do with leaving the country. Oh no, I thought, not this topic again—there has been too much of this in the news lately. And so, it was only the next day that I, just like everyone else around me, learnt that the Berlin Wall had come down and that we were free to travel to the West as we pleased. It was simply incredible, I thought I was dreaming. The school went on strike, there were hardly any lessons at all, and there was only one topic. It was an historic moment. Still, I saw the West only after another six weeks because no one in my family much liked the idea of having to wait in long lines of cars or travelling in overcrowded trains. The Wall was gone, but for me personally many things stayed the same, apart from the fact that now I had the Deutschmark, hard currency, to buy almost anything and go wherever I liked.

I was bored stiff by the four years of training as a dental technician, it was no different from school. Hardly any signs were used, and everything was taught very methodically, disregarding individual preferences and teaching everyone in the same manner regardless of how great individual differences in knowledge and competence might be. However, my true horror only began when I got to my first practical placement in a dental technology laboratory outside the school. It was like jumping into cold water: communicating with a world I knew very little about was too much for me. There were misunderstandings all the time. Still, after this first practical period, it took another six years before I decided I had had enough of dental technology. I used to refer to it as 'this bloody job', because I did not enjoy it at all, it was all manual labour and it left my brain untouched. Then, through general reforms in the public health service, work pressure increased. People were thinking twice about paying larger contributions to get their sparkling new 'third teeth', and only the best technicians could survive in the dental laboratories. At the same time, the political changes taught me many new things. For instance, I learnt that Deaf people can actually study properly and work in the professions of their dreams! Also there were great debates going on in Germany about sign language, which was supposed to be an independent language that Deaf people should be proud of. But not everyone was of the same opinion.

I used to attend meetings fairly regularly, and I was working actively in the local Deaf association in Plauen as well as in the youth section of the regional Deaf association of Saxony. These activities strengthened my conviction that at some point I must follow my dreams and study to be able to work with Deaf people. I always enjoyed giving advice to and supporting Deaf people who had questions or problems at work. I had experienced myself that not knowing about things means being stuck and getting into trouble. For instance, I never knew that there was such a thing as the 'Hauptfürsorgestelle', an authority that provides means to support disabled people at their work place through paying for interpreters or buying relevant equipment. I had seen enough to know what it was like to be without professional support. When I had problems in my job, there was no professional help available and my problems got worse and worse. Another time my friend sent me a frantic fax, saying that her boyfriend, who had indicated that he might jump from a bridge, had simply disappeared. We went to the police and told them all we knew. It turned out that the police found the man just in time, right next to the bridge. Or again, a Deaf youngster whose parents were divorced. His mother had a drinking problem, and he kept being tempted by drugs. All of these problems have their root in a situation where for all of us, myself, the man and his girlfriend, as well as the youngster, professional help is unavailable or inaccessible because we are deaf. And these are only a few of the many problems Deaf people face in Germany because of the almost complete lack of professionals that have the language, experience and cultural knowledge to really help us.

It was as if a little note had fallen from heaven. There was this piece of paper with the address of the PotsMods-Project at the University of Applied Sciences in Potsdam, designed to enable Deaf students to take part in a diploma programme in social work. Someone had left the note lying about at my birthday party. Clearing up afterwards, I had picked it up and kept it. Notions such as 'social work' or 'social education work' seemed fairly strange to me. It was only later that my mother told me what kind of profession this was. This was my turning point. I had come a long way, but now, at the age of twenty-three, I could at last follow the dream I had cherished for so long and study, and what is more, learn the profession I really desired. It was unbelievable! I wanted to

178 go straight up to my old teachers and show them what had become of me, a Deaf person! I had never been this happy in my old job. Through studying I acquired not only the skills to be a social worker but learnt so much more about things that before no one had taken care to properly explain to me: how to work in teams, psychology, communication skills, how to use an interpreter, Deaf culture, dealing with hearing people, or coping with conflicts are things that come to mind, but the list contains many more things that one needs to know to lead a meaningful life.

Unfortunately, not many Deaf people in Germany are able to study at a university, since most of them have either learnt a profession and are thus not entitled to interpreting services[2] or lack the necessary qualifications such as *Abitur*. Now, since I was very lucky to be able to take part in the PotsMods-Project, something other Deaf people can only dream of, I would like to give to others some of the things I received myself. To this end, I have taken up voluntary work again and have become actively involved in the Berlin Deaf association as well as in youth work. In the Deaf association, I have been elected vice chairperson, and we are striving for reforms and setting new aims. One of my big aims is to develop attractive provision for young Deaf people. Berlin is a big city with thousands of activities for young people, but none of these address the needs of Deaf youngsters.

Three times I organized and took part in holiday trips integrating deaf and hearing children aged from ten to thirteen years. One deaf eleven-year-old complained to me that he was always bored during the holidays or in his spare time after school. This started me thinking about setting up a youth centre. I pursued the idea, and after much preparation, in February 2000 I was able to open up the Berlin youth centre for the Deaf and hearing-impaired. Specifically, we want to give young Deaf people a chance to meet Deaf adults with whom they may identify. Unfortunately, in the schools there are almost no Deaf adults who might serve as role models. Our centre is independent of the schools and offers leisure time as well as learning activities. In 2001, we organized the first holiday trip for Deaf young people from Berlin. Meanwhile, after graduating from the University of Applied Sciences in Potsdam, the youth project has become the centre of my professional activities, and I work as a coordinator and head of the project team.

Graduating from university in 2001 finished an important chapter 179
in my life. After four years of studying, I was among five Deaf students
who were awarded a diploma and honoured with a distinction for excel-
lence in our diploma theses. This had been studying in the true sense of
the word: whereas in many institutions that specialise in the vocational
training of disabled people, Deaf learners are served with watered-down
theories and simplified knowledge, here we had been on equal terms
with our hearing fellow students, with allowances only made for our
true disadvantages such as accessing lectures through interpreters, receiving copies of notes made by other students, or being allowed extra
time in exams. It was thus enormously rewarding to receive our diplo-
mas. As yet, this has only been possible for a few of us. But times are
changing, and more Deaf people will have similar opportunities. At last,
in the summer of 2001, a law was passed in Germany that will change
the lives of Deaf people and may enable more Deaf people to go to university and study if they so wish. It may thus be appropriate to conclude
by quoting an optimistic saying: 'Where there's a will, there's a way'.

Notes

1 *Jugendweihe* is a ceremony in which fourteen-year-olds are given
   adult status. As an alternative to the Christian ceremony of
   confirmation, it was widely practised in the GDR.

2 Provision of means to finance interpreting and other support
   services for deaf students at German universities hinges on the
   interpretation of the term *Eingliederung* (roughly, 'integration') in
   relevant social laws. More often than not, deaf people are considered 'integrated' once they have successfully completed a first vocational training. Since very few deaf people in Germany reach the
   qualification necessary for entering university (*Abitur*) without first
   completing a vocational training, the question of how to finance
   support services at universities has become a major issue. The effect
   of new legislation introduced in 2001 and alluded to at the end of
   this contribution remains to be seen, though it is to be feared that
   it will not be as clear-cut as, understandably, the author seems to
   hope.

Integration from Strength

Mabel Davis

The need for a flexible variety of provision is nowhere more obvious than in the education of deaf children. Whatever the other disabilities or learning difficulties of hearing children may be, they do have access to what is being said. Placing a deaf child in a mainstream classroom does not always mean that integration is taking place. It is true to say that the majority of hearing-impaired children are successfully integrated for a variety of reasons. The range of degrees of hearing-impairment is wide but not necessarily linked to educational needs. For example, there are profoundly deaf children coping well in mainstream and others with only a moderate hearing loss who still require the support of a special school. It is a very complex field which demands a high level of specialism and resources, all of which is a huge topic in itself.

Sufficient to say that currently there seem to be no measurements in place to assess the social and emotional progress of deaf children in mainstream schools and their quality of life in, outside and after school. From our experience at Heathlands School we do know that children continue to be referred to us after being allowed to fail in a mainstream setting while transfers from our school to mainstream schools is on the basis of success. In terms of numbers, there are far more transfers from the mainstream schools to us. The saddest aspect of this is the sheer frustration experienced by deaf children who use sign language to access the curriculum in mainstream schools. Often they are given no sign support at all. Even when the need is recognised and they are given a communicator this is not the whole answer as that communicator often becomes their sole means of access and this generates an unacceptable level of dependency on a single adult. It also gets in the way of direct contact between teacher and child. Unless the mainstream teacher and other pupils in the class receive deaf awareness training and sign language lessons on a regular basis, the deaf child will have a restricted channel of access to the curriculum. Such training has both cost and time implications that need to be considered. There is also the fact that the deaf child will be unable to develop social skills through interaction with a peer group in the classroom and in the playground. Communicators are often counter-productive in this respect as well as impeding the development of independent learning skills. It is hardly surprising that such arrangements tend to have the effect of creating emotional disturbance which can lead to behaviour difficulties. It is then up to the special school to restore their confidence, give them pride in their Deaf identities as members of the Deaf community, provide them with a Deaf peer group and, through a communication-rich environment, foster their progress towards achievement.

If mainstream schools were suitable for all deaf children we would not be having to remedy the damage they do. Parents would not have had to go through such stress and effort to get their children into a type of provision more suited to their needs. Many parents have wept to find that our school existed at all as their local education authorities had given them no such information. Most parents have found out that there was an alternative from other parents of deaf children, or through the voluntary organisations such as the National Deaf Children's Society or the British Deaf Association, or through watching a chance documentary on TV. We should be questioning to what extent parents are being given unbiased advice as to the range of provision that does exist and to which they have a right of access as equal partners in the decisions made about their children's education. So many placements seem to be fund led rather than needs led and this tendency needs to be strongly challenged.

A personal perspective

There can be few headteachers who can claim to have been an actual consumer of special school provision as I can, but the fact that I have managed to reach the top of my profession can only be a credit to the special schools I attended. The fact that I am the only Deaf headteacher in the country may be revealing in its implications about how deaf children are being taught. Questions need to be asked about why I am the only one. Why are there so few deaf teachers? Why indeed are deaf people so underrepresented in the professions as a whole and what is being done about it? How, in short, do we fit into this inclusive ethos

182 and is social inclusion in our best interests? Perhaps if I give you some
insight into my own personal experience you may be in a position to
draw your own conclusions. Certainly it may help explain the direction
I have taken professionally and the vision I have to ensure that deaf
children achieve and achieve significantly.

In 1952 there was an epidemic of tuberculosis in Ayrshire, a dairy
farming county. At seven years old, I lost my hearing as a result of the
treatment with streptomycin which destroyed the auditory nerves in
both ears. Overnight, I lost my hearing totally. I woke up one morning and thought it was very quiet. I also thought people were acting
strangely, tiptoeing about and whispering to each other so I couldn't
hear them, I found it annoying. When it persisted, I tried to work it out.
The only time there was such a hush on the ward was when the doctor
was due to make his rounds. I remember thinking that that wasn't the
explanation because he had been round the other day and he worked
alternate days. Suddenly I got a shock to find a nurse by my bed. I had
not heard her approach and when I tried to ask her how she got there I
couldn't hear my own voice. Even then, it simply did not occur to me
for some time that there was something wrong with me and that everyone and everything else was as before. Perhaps that was nature's safety
mechanism in operation because the psychological effects of losing
one's hearing are, needless to say, quite fearsome.

When I came out of hospital I did not return to my public school
down the road. Instead I was taken to a school miles away from home.
No one told me why. I distinctly remember walking into a classroom
where there were only a handful of children—and it hit me that they
were deaf too. I was just so relieved and very happy to find I was not
alone. I turned to my mother and said 'I'm not the only deaf girl in the
world'. How else could I ever have known this? My introduction to special schools was therefore a very positive one. I had identified with a
deaf peer group and felt immediately that I belonged. This aspect of any
child's social and emotional development is not to be underestimated.
But with deaf children it is so much more than that as it involves being part of a cultural and linguistic group which makes it essential for
mental health as well. In that context, segregation was not a bad word
at all. If this had happened today support would be provided to enable
me to remain in my local school but no one really knows how that may

have worked out. I am just very glad I was able to join the Deaf world and through that network of support to be in a position later to make choices on my own terms.

Progress

Back then, the only problem with the special school was that the work was so simple it seemed like being on one long holiday, that is where some special schools fell down in the past. They really were not up to scratch and such schools deserved to be closed down when the time came. Perhaps we should now be defining the role of a special school in the new millennium. We need to send out a strong and positive message of our value and of our success. We should not agree just to be seen in the role of supporting mainstream schools, as the Government seems to want, but as a valid, viable and essential provision in our own right. We need to get through to people like the Minister for Education and other influential ex-special school pupils, and make them understand that the old and negative experiences of the special schools they attended is in the past and should not be allowed to cloud the future.

Obviously, for me the special school experience was a positive one, but even then I harboured some doubts. I got so bored that one day, instead of catching the bus to the special school, I walked down the road to my old school and went and sat at my old desk. It must have caused quite a commotion, but during that short time with my hearing peers I came to realise that I couldn't follow the lessons. I was there in the class, I knew the children and the teachers, I was still the same person with the same level of intelligence that I had been before, but I was lost. When my mother, called in by the poor headmaster, came to fetch me home she asked me why I had done this. I was very young, only nine years old and I wasn't really sure myself, but one thing I did know. There was something I had needed to find out for myself and only then could I begin to accept my deafness and move forward.

A couple of years after that experience, I won a place at the famous grammar school for deaf children in Newbury, a school that is still going strong today. It challenged me intellectually and allowed me to grow up as a normal child where deafness was not an issue. We were all deaf together, so we were able to develop on a level playing field. If I had gone to a mainstream school, even with the best support, I would

184 always have been the odd one out. I would be the last to find out anything, unable to participate in the free and easy exchange of children's
chatter which would have forced me to become a social misfit rather
than the confident, self-assured person I became. I know this for a fact
because I remain isolated even amongst my colleagues who are the
most Deaf aware group I have experienced. Anywhere I go in the hearing community, my experience is the same. I can take it, but who has
the right to expect this of a child?

The dilemma

In spite of the fact that I owe so much to that segregated school, there
was one aspect that let me down badly. It was so exclusive that it did
not really prepare me for life in a hearing society. There needed to
be some transition preparation and that never happened. When I left
school the isolation was often hard to bear. Deafness is an invisible disability and one that often evokes impatience and embarrassment rather
than sympathy. The sheer effort of communication is often tiring on
both sides so the easy option is to avoid it altogether or restrict it to basics and superficial niceties. The only thing that keeps most profoundly
deaf people sane is the lifelong friends we made at boarding school who
share the same experiences.

They are the ones who offer access to a Deaf society where we can
truly relax and be ourselves. We can group and campaign for educational and employment resources that will improve the quality of our
lives as Deaf people in a hearing society. Fortunately no Government or
education lobby can force us away from a congregation of our choice
once we have left school. The Deaf community is a vibrant group of
people who will fight fiercely to protect our schools, our community,
our language and our culture for our children and their future.

The way forward

The idea for a way forward is therefore to promote access to what, at
Heathlands School we think of as 'the best of both worlds', an ethos
based on respect for, and acceptance of, differences. We are a special
school where deaf children are given full access to the curriculum
through sign language. The standard of teaching and the quality of
learning is such that pupils are not only meeting but exceeding Gov-

ernment targets in Maths and Science at Key Stage 2 and are even now
breaking into the five passes in the A–C categories in the GCSE (General
Certificate of Secondary Education) exams. Socially and emotionally
they have access to both a Deaf peer group and a hearing peer group
but from a position of strength…their strength. They are therefore able
to develop a positive self-identity as young people with a valuable contribution to make to a hearing society in which they have none but the
normal fears, shared by all.

The strategies used within this all-age school vary in the Primary and
Secondary sectors but the principles are the same. Parallel to having the
support of qualified teachers of the deaf, speech and language therapists
and audiologists, the pupils are also given access to integration opportunities through our partnership arrangements. These include partnerships with local nurseries, with seven local primary schools, with one
secondary comprehensive and with one other secondary special school
with a curriculum suited to children with moderate learning difficulties.
The benefits of such partnerships are immeasurable on both sides.

Two major issues are currently proving a challenge to deaf education and to special schools in particular. One is the subject of cochlear
implants and the other is inclusion. There are links between the two as
an increasing number of young children are being implanted. (In some
areas of Britain the implant rate in young children under five is one hundred percent). Our integration programmes are therefore becoming of
vital importance and there are implications as to how such programmes
should be funded in the light of the Government's inclusion policy. In
order to ensure that we continue to be able to offer our pupils the benefit
of access to both special and mainstream opportunities we may need to
think in terms of expanding our integration programme by increasing
the number of integration teachers and opportunities for integration at
all levels. This will become a priority for long-term strategic planning.

Reverse integration is also organised at Heathlands School because
successful inclusion is a two way street. Mainstream children need to
enjoy the positive experience of a special school environment too.
Deaf awareness training is offered by our staff to the local authority
mainstream staff for inservice training (INSET). Curricular activities, for
example in PSHE (Physical, Social and Health Education) involves the
teaching of sign language to mainstream pupils as well as extra-cur-

186 ricular sign language clubs during the lunch break and in the evenings. Secondary students on both our school roll and on the roll of the mainstream school take the CACDP (Council for the Advancement of Communication with Deaf People, the examination Board for BSL exams) sign language exams each year and gain qualifications to pursue paths as interpreters should they so wish. Even if they do not, their knowledge, experience and attitudes contribute to the more effective inclusion of deaf children and deaf people within the wider community than the forced implementation of a political ideology could ever achieve.

Conclusion

To conclude, by all means let us promote inclusion but not as a blanket measure. Let's ensure that it goes beyond the physical aspect of access and really does meet the academic, social and emotional needs of our children as well. Special schools are in the very best position to safeguard the interests of the most vulnerable children in our society. If we value the work that we do, our commitment and expertise will be respected and sought after. We need to develop ourselves as regional resource centres as well as promoting the twenty-four hour curriculum of residential schools. We are needed more than ever now by the mainstream schools. The onus is on us as to how things progress and what shape inclusion takes. We can be empowered and proactive in fostering co-operative partnerships, but I issue one word of warning. It is essential that the headteacher of the special school retains full control of the management of their own school together with equal control of the partnership arrangements. That way funding is targeted to support special needs and the relevant training needs of staff are met. There are other important reasons for maintaining this control, but that is another story for another day.

IV   A QUESTION OF IDENTITY?

A Question of Identity?

Amparo Minguet Soto's experience of losing her hearing resonates with the accounts given in the previous section by Raquel and Mabel. Being on the receiving end of pity strikes a chord with Joanne's earlier account of being the subject of someone else's good deed for the day. The word 'deaf' was taboo as Amparo's state of 'not hearing well' was individualised. Although Amparo did not have Mabel's experience of attending a Deaf school, she shares the experience of others, Teresa, Helga, Volker, and those who attended the Royal Cross School, in having contact with a teacher with a positive and encouraging attitude. She also had the ability to read, as did Piers, Jennifer and Candelaria. Amparo also identifies a sense of isolation in her social life that Candelaria experienced, and the instinctive need for a peer group as discussed by Mabel. Like Joanne, she attended a sign language course with her mother, and the contact with other Deaf people enabled her to make a psychological adjustment, to develop an ease with her Deaf identity, and to find ease in communication, enabling her to realise the considerable stress of oral communication when a more natural alternative is offered.

Amparo stresses, as Joanne did, the importance of international exchange. She points to the need for sign language to have a status which facilitates the professionalisation of the role of the interpreter, raising it from its roots in charity. José Antonio Libros Solaz also reinforces this point. Amparo and Asif Iqbal point to the poor level of educational attainment within the Deaf community, hiding the potential within the community from itself, as well as from the wider community.

Amparo outlines the process of radicalisation, and describes the efforts to educate the wider community through theatre as part of the pathway that led her to becoming a teacher, a role in which she hopes that she can promote diversity and social change whilst having the confidence as a Deaf teacher to control the communication environment.

José and Asif also discuss the need to control the communication environment within the home when the family has both hearing and Deaf members, and the parents and children do not understand each other's languages. José was not successful in his attempts to persuade his family to sign as his family place a low status on sign language, refusing to acknowledge that it is equivalent to spoken language. However, now living independently with access to a professional interpreter, he can assert his right to access to information and take on the responsibilities expected of him within his local community. Asif was more successful in taking control of communication within the family environment, and he gives us some insight into the bilingual life that he and his Deaf sister experience.

The cultural meaning of deafness is highlighted when the diagnosis is given to parents with a different cultural experience. The issue of lack of information highlighted in earlier sections by Hope and by Mabel is heightened in relation to second language users. Asif's description of having a language and a religion imposed on him without the context of deafness being understood makes us question the experiences Amparo and others relate, of English and Castilian Spanish being imposed on deaf children through speech, and to wish that more of the writers had described their experiences of contact with Christianity. José describes how, at his Deaf school, sign language was frowned upon, except in the teaching and celebration of religion when oral methods of communication were discarded.

Andrew Charles writes of his experience of abuse, racism and cruelty at his Deaf school. He also discusses the legacy of his education: the development of communication, culture and a life-long peer group as well as academic education and training for employment. He also describes the emotions engendered when he was abandoned by his birth mother, his re-connection with her and her rejection of him. Through the accounts of José and Andrew we gain some insight into the isolation and fear of children, their disempowerment and the strength of them as individuals in their determination to survive emotionally and economically as Deaf adults.

Asif points out for us other cultural factors: the importance of access to films, differences for men and for women, his advocacy for his sister,

192 the impact on his life of meeting with a Deaf family was similar to the effect Jennifer described at the start of the book. Asif could be described as having a triple or four-fold identity. There are the identities Asif ascribes himself (Deaf, British, Asian) and the identities that are imposed upon him (immigrant, Moslem, deaf). These constructions ignore the diversity within Asian communities, and his identity as a man both in Asian and in white British society. Given the importance that most of the writers have ascribed to the role of the peer group in building identity, one is left to wonder about the lack of focus on the construction of gender identities within the Deaf community and the unexplored issues of diversity for Deaf Asians.

José was educated at the Valencia Deaf school where the methods of instruction in the late 1970s seem to have been the same as those described as used at the Royal Cross School before 1945, but unlike the Royal School, the nuns also used physical torture on the youngest children. Andrew Charles' experience of abuse was even more horrific. As the children at Valencia grew older, they had access to Deaf teachers, but the locus of power, as in the German school described by Katja in the previous section, remained firmly with the hearing hierarchy.

Many of the writers throughout the book have stressed the importance of technology. José here outlines the different technological devices that he uses. Along with the technical developments that have brought information technology and reliance on computers, there have also been improvements in hearing-aids and the development of cochlear implant devices. José discusses his use of hearing-aids over the years and his changed attitude to listening to speech. He does not tell us if he intends to try to develop his own speech. Jennifer was quite clear: speech is not natural to her and she chooses not to use it. Piers' contract with the hospital meant that he felt obliged to use speech with bus drivers, and with teachers at Mary Hare.

Gloria Pullen returns to some of the themes raised in the first section of the book in her argument against the medical model of deafness. She demonstrates how to survive as a culturally Deaf adult in the world of work and wishes that parents of deaf children had an easier route to gaining a more positive model of deafness, as provided by the Deaf community. In the account she gives of her voluntary work in Uganda, a change in the status of local Deaf people can be seen as communication develops. Gloria also describes her own position as a Deaf parent of a Deaf child, and some of the difficulties the family experienced because of the imposition of the 'medical model' upon their lives. Gloria, like Katja and the writers from Rampton Hospital in the previous section, and Amparo and José in this section, demonstrate and discuss positive and equal Deaf/hearing working relationships based on BSL.

As Joanne describes, at Gallaudet University lack of deaf teachers and professionals is not an issue as it is in most of the other accounts in the section. However, there had never been a Deaf President at the University in its 124 year history as the only university for Deaf people in existence in the world. The role of the President is equivalent to a chief executive or in British University terms, of a Vice-Chancellor, and this position became vacant at Gallaudet in 1988. The suitability of Deaf people to be at the head of the organisation was questioned and a hearing person who was not a sign language user, and who had little knowledge of Deaf culture, was selected. The students, having signalled their desire for a Deaf President, collectively refused to accept the decision, disrupting the University in their campaign for the decision to be overturned. Here I. King Jordan, one of the deaf candidates for the post, gives his account of the selection process. We also include an interview he gave ten years later which reflects on the changes over the decade of his leadership.

This was the first time that militancy amongst Deaf people had become an international issue. The effects on mainstream America cannot be overstated: there was an enormous amount of press coverage, which brought the issues of the oppression of the Deaf community into the public domain. Many hearing people, including those in positions of power and authority in political and academic life, took up the cause of Deaf people. As Asif notes in his account, at the 1994 Gallaudet Commencement President Clinton attended, spoke and demonstrated his knowledge of American Sign Language.

It is important to note that this campaign was not about the selection of a particular hearing academic over a Deaf one, but was about hearing/deaf power balances and that it had an effect, not only across America as King describes, but in Britain too where between 1992 and

194   1995 three major deaf organisations appointed Deaf Chief Executives following decades of leadership provided by hearing people. King makes the important point that there had to be a genuine change of attitude by the Board. If the Board's support was superficial, then his job would become untenable. The appointment of King was a success for the Deaf community and for deaf status. He recounts many examples of Deaf people gaining promotion but he also points up the negative side: the propensity within the Deaf community to criticise and to engage in what is known within the Deaf community as 'back-stabbing'.

The use of computer technology maintains and increases the pressure on Deaf people to develop literacy skills. When reflecting on the changes in the student body, King highlights the extremes: the lack of motivation of many deaf students on the one hand and on the other, the change of focus of graduates away from work within the Deaf community to high status jobs in mainstream professions. Jennifer has described the situation of an increasing number of Deaf graduates in Britain who are seeking to work in the Deaf community, and this is reflected in many of the accounts in this book from mainland Europe where Deaf people are working to provide support services to Deaf people and to teach sign language to hearing people. It is interesting to speculate whether the next stage of development will see an increased confidence within European Deaf communities facilitating a parallel movement of Deaf professionals into mainstream careers.

Don't Look

by Eudora Antiaudio

It always happens
You're on the tube home
Minding your own business
Sitting alone
And then the doors open
And two Deafies get on

Don't look!
Whatever you do
Don't let your eyes follow their flow
We always assume
Everyone's hearing
What would they do
If they knew what you saw?

'I'm divorcing my husband, I've decided.'
The woman signed to her companion
With a swift look around the carriage
She decided it was safe to go on:
'He's been having a fling with his student,
Well, I've had enough of it all.
My Herbert can take all his belongings
Cos I ain't living with him in this hell.
And when I find that woman
She'll wish she'd never met him at all!'

196 My Herbert?!
Oh God, so that's what his wife looks like.
You think, as you vanish in terror at the next stop
Covering your tracks
With a heart beating fast.

So don't look!
Whatever you do
You might learn something
You never wanted to know!

Dean or Deaf

I. King Jordan

People who don't know about DPN (the 1988 *Deaf President Now* campaign at Gallaudet University) always assume that I was very active and had some kind of leadership role during DPN. That is absolutely not true. I was a candidate for the position of President, but I wasn't really involved in the activities of DPN *per sé*. Because I was a candidate, I did not think it was appropriate for me to get involved. So at the beginning, I actually stayed away from Gallaudet.

Saturday, March 5

I had my final interview on Saturday, March 5. Earlier, six semi-finalists had all-day interviews on campus with different constituency groups. From those interviews, they narrowed it down to three finalists. Those three finalists were interviewed on Saturday and Sunday, March 5 and 6. They didn't tell me where this final interview would be. There was almost a paranoia from the board that there would be interference in the process if people found out. Instead of my going to the interview, they sent a car to my home. It was very secretive.
The interview was held in a lower level conference room at a downtown hotel. It was a long, narrow room with pillars, terrible for visual communication. The interview was long—almost three hours. I thought I did very well. In fact, I went home and told my wife that I thought they would offer me the job.

Sunday, March 6

On Sunday, Phil Bravin, who was chair of the search committee, called me on the TTY, and his conversation was very short, almost curt. I talked to him later, so I know that it was a very difficult phone call for him to make. I said, 'This is King. GA'. He said, 'Good afternoon, this is Phil. I want to let you know that the board has appointed Elisabeth Zinser as the seventh President of Gallaudet. GA'. I was stunned. I said something like, 'Thank you'. What else could I say? And he said 'Okay, bye. SK'. That was the whole conversation. Linda and I were home alone at that point. I didn't watch TV—that was before captioning, so I didn't watch the news on TV. If I had, I would have known that the students protested Sunday night, but honestly, I had no idea. So Sunday, at dinner, we talked about the decision of the board. We figured I gave it my best shot, and the board decided on somebody else. In sports, you compete as hard as you can. If you win, you don't gloat; you congratulate the competition. If you lose, you don't get bitter; you say, 'Well, I tried my best'. That basically is what I was trying to do then.

Monday, March 7–Tuesday, March 8

Monday morning I got up, got ready for work the way I always did, and drove into Gallaudet. As I parked in the Sixth Street lot across from Gallaudet, I looked over at all the students at the Sixth Street gate. Just as I got out of my car a friend, Joe Fritsch—at that time athletic trainer at Gallaudet—drove by. He said, 'Gee hi. You don't want to go over there right now'. So I got in his truck, and we went out and had breakfast on Capitol Hill. He explained everything that had been happening—the march to the Mayflower Hotel, how the students had closed the campus. After breakfast, he dropped me off, and I came in the front gate. As I walked in, the students moved back. Everyone was cheering. Then local TV people came running up and stuck microphones in my face, wanting to interview me. It was still very new to me—I was a Dean, trying to go to my office and see if I could find the provost to find out what was going on and what my responsibilities were. I think I said something to the students like, 'Please don't damage the University', or 'Don't hurt anybody'. That's all I said.

Well, I couldn't find the provost, Catherine Ingold. My office was empty. No classes were going on. So I started talking to people, trying to find out what was happening. There was no help from the Dean-level administrators.

Not much else happened. The next day, my staff came to work, and my office—the Dean's office in the College of Arts and Sciences—was open. But many of the buildings were closed. I watched one really interesting thing. The students had locked the Edward Miner Gallaudet building with a large u-shaped bicycle lock. The Physical Plant Department came with a torch to cut it off. Those locks are really strong. While they were cutting it off, the students lined up with bicycle locks. So they cut one off, and the next student in line put a new lock on. The workers looked back, saw all those locks, and gave up. For years you could still see the marks on the door.

Wednesday, March 9

I got a phone call from Catherine Ingold, my boss, who wanted to meet with me. Students would not allow her to come onto campus so I suggested that we meet at a restaurant on Capitol Hill, the *Hawk and Dove*. It was there that she told me that the chair of the board, Jane Bassett Spilman, was in the city and that the board wanted to meet with me. So I went over to the public relations firm where the board had gathered. Again, the whole set-up was very secretive. I was put in one room with nobody there. Jane Spilman would come in and talk to me, and then she would leave, and somebody else would come in and talk to me, and that person would leave. They were seeking my help to quell the protest and to make a positive resolution to what was happening. At that time, I was probably ready to help them—I still had the attitude that I was a Dean, an officer of the University, and I wanted to be a good sport.

They had flown in Elisabeth Zinser from North Carolina and wanted me to arrange a meeting between her and the student leaders. So I called DPN headquarters. The board and Zinser wanted to meet on campus, but the students wouldn't hear of it. So we agreed to meet at a motel nearby. Zinser was very pleasant and very persuasive. She told the students that she wanted very much to work with them, to help them end this in a way that would lead to positive changes for the University. She said she didn't see herself staying as President for a long time, just long enough to help Gallaudet train more deaf people to assume leadership positions. But for every point she made, the students would make counterpoints. It was almost as if they'd had training—they just kept repeating their demands again and again: 'I'm sorry, we don't disrespect you as an individual, but there is no way that we will ever accept you as our President. The four demands are…' They were very rational, very thoughtful, very nice to her. She kept trying and trying to insist on some concession or compromise from them. They wouldn't even talk about compromise—they just kept repeating the four demands. So we left the meeting and got into a car. Zinser and I were in the back seat. She was making a lot of phone calls. At the time, I didn't know what was happening—remember, I'm a deaf guy sitting in the back seat and she's talking into a phone. Later I learned that she was calling educators that she knew, asking for advice on what to do. And the advice she was getting was, 'Stand firm. The board has the authority here, and you can't capitulate to the student demands'.

I thought we were going back to campus, but instead we went to the National Press Club for a press conference. I also was not aware that I was going up on stage until I was called. Just before I went up, I was told that Harvey Corson, the other finalist, had formally supported the board's decision to appoint Zinser and urged the students not to support the protest (it wasn't true; later I talked to Harvey Corson, and he told me he hadn't said that. But it's what I was told). So I went up on the podium. I was thrust into the lights and the cameras—a new experience for me anyway—and was asked, 'What are you going to do, Dean Jordan?' I remember saying that the board has the authority to determine who the President will be, and that as an officer of the University, I supported that authority. While I was saying that, Mary Lou Novitsky and a camera crew from *Deaf Mosaic* were in front of the podium, only 10 or 15 feet away. I was looking right in her eyes. She stood there and started shaking her head. You could see it really hurt her. I was touched—her facial expression and her emotional reaction had a lot of influence on me. After the press conference, I was driven back to campus. Someone told me the faculty were meeting, so I walked over to Elstad Auditorium to see what was happening. The meeting was just ending, so I went backstage. Harvey Goodstein, one of the really strong leaders of DPN, was there. Already, word was out about the press conference. Harvey came up to me. He said something like, 'I know what you said at the press conference, and I really disagree with you. I respect your position, I respect your right to say what you want, but I need to let you know that I disagree with you, and I'm not stopping'. I expected him to be angry with me and maybe he was. But when we finished, he hugged me. That also had a lot of impact on me. So I left campus and went home. I was very emotional then. Linda and I had a long conversation. Finally we agreed that whatever happened, I probably wouldn't be a very good Dean anymore. That's when we said, 'I'll be Dean for as long as they decide I can stay Dean, but I'll be deaf for the rest of my life. So maybe it's time to start thinking and behaving like a deaf person instead of like a Dean person'.

Late that night, Pete Merrill called me. (Dr Edward C. Merrill Jr., fourth President of Gallaudet) He said he was following everything that was happening, that he had recommended when he left Gallaudet that the President who succeeded him should be a deaf person, and that if they didn't appoint a Deaf President now, then they would never appoint one. Then he said something like, 'Stop trying to analyze all of the facts here, and listen to your heart. Do what your heart tells you to do'.

That really sealed it for me. I decided that I would go back to campus and support what the students were doing. At that point I realized the depth of feeling and the amount of involvement—that it wasn't just radical deaf people saying this, it was all deaf people—oral, hard of hearing, signing, Cued Speech, and then it was people who weren't deaf, it was people all over the country. In front of the main entrance to campus, they had signs that said, 'Honk for a Deaf President'. Everybody who passed Gallaudet honked. Everybody wanted a Deaf President.

Thursday, March 10

The next day, I came on to campus with a written statement supporting what the students were doing. I had called the DPN council, and they were happy that I was going to do that. They called a press conference on the steps of Chapel Hall. Greg Hlibok, President of the Student Body Government, spoke for a while, and then I spoke. Linda held a paper I read from. I read my statement, and the press all came up and interviewed me. Several TV trucks were parked on campus. As soon as I was finished with the press conference, they started taking turns interviewing me. One even asked me to climb up on to the roof of the truck!

Again I left campus. So I wasn't on campus and didn't participate in the march to the Capitol the next day. I thought I had shot myself in the foot in terms of any possibility of ever becoming President of Gallaudet. The board would have to be angry at my reversal and my announcement supporting the students and all four of their demands. I had a really hard time with that after I became President because there were some board members who were absolutely convinced that my reversal was self-serving—and that I had used the leverage of the protest to get

202 the job. But honestly, I never thought I would be chosen as President.

In fact, that came up again and again in TV interviews, with Greg and with me. The TV people kept using my name because I was there. And every time they would use it, Greg would say, 'We're not talking about an individual. We're talking about a Deaf President'. And I would say the same thing. If this protest were about one individual, it would never have happened. The Deaf Community is still made up of so many constituencies and interest groups that if an individual had been identified, then I very much doubt that there would have been the kind of unity and co-operation that there was during the week. The whole time everyone worked together, and that's because there was a very common goal: a Deaf President.

Sunday, March 13

I had long-term plans for a friend to visit from California, so Sunday afternoon I drove up to Baltimore-Washington International Airport to pick him up. Right after I left, Phil Bravin called my house and told Linda only that it was very important that I call him. I knew that Zinser had resigned the previous Friday but, again, I never thought I would be the person they selected as President. So on this afternoon I was just King Jordan, driving to the airport to pick up a friend. I parked my car and went into the airport. After my friend arrived, we were walking back to my car. He's a hearing guy, and he said, 'They're paging you'. So we went to a phone and he called to find out what the page was. They said, 'You have an urgent message from your wife'. I was really worried. Why would my wife call me? She never does that. We called home, and the message was just to call Phil Bravin. So I said, 'Okay, I'll call him when I get home'. It was starting to get dark as we drove home. The board must have been wondering, 'Where's King Jordan? What's going on here?' So I called Phil on the TTY. It was a very different phone conversation this time. He was talkative and friendly, and he offered me the job.

Before I called, we sat around the kitchen table, my wife and friend and I, saying, 'Just suppose they offer me the job? What do I do? The President must have the support of the board. I've had a very good ten years only because I've had the full and enthusiastic support of the board if I didn't have that, I would have lasted six months.' I was thinking, 'Suppose I take the job and the board doesn't like me and doesn't want me to succeed? Then I can't possibly succeed'.

I had that conversation with Phil. He assured me that significant changes had already happened with the board—that the board was committed to becoming a deaf majority, that he was now Chair and would personally pledge his support for me. So I said, 'Okay, with that, I gratefully accept the job'.

I drove to the Embassy Row Hotel. My wife, my friend from California and I drove in one car, and my kids drove in a second car. We knew that I was going to get caught up in all the events after the press conference naming me President, and the kids had school the next day. As it turned out, they came with us to celebrate anyway. When we arrived at the hotel, the first person I met was Sandy Sanderson, a deaf board member from Utah. He ran across the lobby and gave me a really hard hug. He was really delighted. Then Frank Sullivan came up and hugged me. We all went up to a room upstairs where the representative of the public relations firm that had been working with the board had drafted a statement for me to make. The press had been waiting for a long time. Everyone was rushing to get downstairs quickly before the press left. So I rushed downstairs with this statement I had never seen before. It was a very good statement, but in retrospect I should have insisted that I take five minutes and put the statement in my words. It said something about how an idea can become reality—but I was nervous and reading it for the first time, so I said 'realty'.

My wife has never let me forget that—nor has my friend from California! After that press conference we all drove back to Gallaudet. There was a big celebration going on in the Abbey in the Ely Center. They had a huge projector screen TV set up with a little stage in front of it. When I got there, they rushed me up on the stage. It just so happened that at that very moment the evening news was on. As I got up on the stage, there on the TV was me giving that statement. Wow! The Abbey went crazy. Reporters who are supposed to maintain objectivity were hugging me. I saw reporters crying. A lot of people were crying. My kids were there celebrating with everybody. It was a very positive and celebratory evening.

The View from the President's Office:
In an interview Dr Jordan talks about where he's been and where Gallaudet is going

Questions by Vickie Walter

Q You have been President of Gallaudet University for almost ten years now. How has this affected your life personally? In what ways has your life changed?

A Ahhh. I could talk all day and still not hit everything. Before I applied for the job, my family went away for the weekend to discuss applying for the presidency. We spent the weekend at a rustic Potomac Appalachian Trail Club cabin, talking about what it would mean if I became President, how it would change our lives. My daughter, Heidi, at the time was a sophomore, and my son was a senior. What would they do about high school? But we all decided, go for it and apply for the position, even though we knew there would be changes. But we had no idea what the changes would really be like.

   The first year of my presidency was like a blur. I travelled a lot. Everywhere I went, people talked about how they supported what was happening. It wasn't a protest that was negative, it was a demand for what was right. That was a great thing. If my children had been younger, I wouldn't have remained President. I would have had to step down because I really cheated my family very badly. I worked long, long hours and I travelled. In the past, we had a 'carved in stone' time for dinner. Holidays and sports were very important. My kids were on cross country and indoor track teams, and I'd go to their meets. I think I saw one track meet after I became President—and to do that, I had a driver drive me to Springbrook High. I worked in the back seat, and then I got out and ran to watch the mile race my son was in. Then got back in the car and drove back to Gallaudet. But my kids were old enough that it didn't hurt too much.

Today, 10 years after DPN, people still recognize me. I have become a public figure. Once, Linda and I took a vacation at a very remote island just so we could get away. At the first evening's dinner, a young boy of about 8–10 walked up to our table and said, 'Aren't you the first Deaf President?' Just this weekend my truck broke down. A nice man stopped to offer help and when he looked at me said, 'Oh, you're the President of Gallaudet!' I have a thousand examples of that.

I have two roles in my position. One is chief executive officer of the University. Sometimes that's really demanding and very pressure-packed. The second role is that I'm still seen as a role model for deaf people, children especially. I am paid to manage Gallaudet, but I probably spend as much time and energy being that model. Also, I am very open to public criticism. Every decision I make—for example, the decision to sign and voice at the same time—is second-guessed and criticized, often very publicly. And a final change I must mention is that my life has been enriched more than I can ever say. I cannot think of any single job that would be more perfect for me. I love what I do and look forward to coming to work every day. It is an honour and a privilege to represent deaf people and Gallaudet, and I hope to do so for a long time.

Q   You were a faculty member at Gallaudet for a long time, and then Dean of the College of Arts and Sciences. Did becoming President change your view of the University?

A   The view of the University from my office is very different from the view of the University from any other chair or office. I know what the people in Congress and in the Department of Education want and expect. I know what the budget situation is and is going to become. I know what I have to say to potential donors, recruits, and parents. I think of myself as a good teacher, and I had great relationships with my students. I did that job well. But when I was a faculty person, I didn't know those things; I didn't really care about them. Somebody has to pay attention to the questions of are there enough parking places, can we afford to give an increase to the staff people who work at Gallaudet and how about renovating the dorm next summer will that happen? The view is absolutely different.

Q   How do you think that Gallaudet changed as an institution during the past ten years?

A Two changes. One is very visible. We have changed the learning environment much for the better. The buildings have been renovated and upgraded and the grounds improved a lot. It is a beautiful place to work, and I believe very strongly that working in a positive environment leads to better work. Second, I like to think there is more sense of community. The students have been empowered, deaf faculty and staff have been empowered, and deaf people know that any leadership position is open to them. There have been some major changes in the curriculum, but I think the biggest change in the academic part of the community is that the students have different goals, different expectations. Before, the large majority of people went into the helping professions—teachers or counsellors or house parents. There is nothing wrong with that; they are fine occupations, but that was pretty much it. There were few people who majored in chemistry or biology or business. They didn't want to become doctors or dentists or lawyers. Now, many students have graduated from law school. Students now are becoming engineers or physicians. They take pre-med courses through the Consortium of Universities of the Metropolitan Washington Area. They are becoming entrepreneurs; the largest majors are now in business areas. Students expect that when they finish our accounting curriculum and after some work experience, they will be able to sit for and pass the CPA exam. They expect to become CPAs or MBAS. The workforce is welcoming deaf people when it didn't used to do that, so students are majoring in different things. I think that is very, very positive.

Q What do you consider your biggest accomplishments during the past decade?

A Helping to de-stigmatize deafness. A decade ago, people looked at deaf individuals as sad and handicapped. Today, many more people look at us as individuals who communicate differently but are just as able as others. I have greatly increased the circle of friends that Gallaudet has. We now have a Board of Associates with almost fifty members made up of some of the country's more important and influential leaders. This was for sure not true a decade ago. Look at the Congressional Basketball Game, for example. We have many friends in Congress. Fifty members of Congress attended the game.

Q   Have you had any disappointments during this time?

A   The single biggest disappointment is when a highly able student does not succeed. We see Honours students arrive at Gallaudet and then not study and not succeed. It tears at my heart to see this. Underachievement of students who stay is a related disappointment. We have so many really able students who just 'get by'. I would give anything to know how to motivate them to achieve up to their potential.

Q   DPN (the 1988 *Deaf President Now* Campaign) is seen as a milestone not only at Gallaudet but in the lives of deaf people throughout the nation and even the world. How has DPN affected the lives of deaf people?

A   Two ways. First, it has opened the eyes of people who are not deaf. People out there now look at us differently. This affects the lives of deaf people in that hearing people respond to them differently—more positively. Second, it has changed the way we think about ourselves. It used to be that we accepted limitations that had been imposed on us. Deaf people couldn't do this and couldn't do that. Now deaf people aspire to do many, many things they never aspired to before. I truly believe that the slogan 'Deaf people can do anything but hear' is widespread and believed!

Q   If DPN had not happened, where do you think Gallaudet would be today?

A   We would not have nearly as many friends as we do. We would not have been able to make the physical renovations because we would not have been able to raise as much money. We would probably be a quiet little liberal arts university in Washington DC, that nobody outside deafness knew about.

Q   As a result of DPN and the passage of the Americans with Disabilities Act and other laws, deaf people have higher expectations than they did in the past. Are all of those expectations being realised? And if not, what still needs to change for deaf people to become full participants in society?

A   Of course, not all expectations are being realized, but there are a whole lot of success stories that can be traced directly to DPN. One of the best stories I heard was very shortly after DPN. A young deaf man's deaf father had worked for the same firm for about thirty years. He had been passed over for promotion many, many times. Same old story—you can't use the phone, how will you communicate with those you supervise, etc. When the CEO saw what happened with DPN, he called the guy in and promoted him on the spot. He apologized for lacking confidence in him and said he had learned a lot! One of the great pleasures that comes with this job is being able to travel and meet so many young deaf children. Young deaf kids really have different aspirations than they used to. They still look up to what 'Deaf President Now' means. Yesterday I was walking to a meeting, and three young boys from Kendall School happened to be walking down the sidewalk. They stopped and talked to me. It was very casual, very informal, and it was clear to me that they were delighted to have bumped into me. I knew they were going to go back to school and brag about how they had just talked to the Deaf President.

In my travels, I talk with kids who tell me they want to be President, and I say, 'Good for you! You can be President. You can be a university President, and you can be a President of a big corporation'. And they can! They will do great things—there will be lots more lawyers, dentists, doctors, business people. All is not perfect—there are still examples where people don't get the opportunities they should. As I said way back when, DPN will lead to new opportunities, but it takes a long time for attitudes to change. There is still a tendency to judge someone on the basis of his or her speech. But more and more deaf people are working where they didn't used to, and the more this happens, the more hearing people are exposed to 'normal' deaf people, the more they will realize that we are just like them. Then attitudes will really begin to change. But it is much, much better than it was! It's a different world now than it was before DPN.

Q How are changes in the nation and the world affecting Gallaudet University today?

A The biggest change in the nation is the opportunities provided by ADA (Americans with Disabilities Act). DPN changed the way we think about ourselves. ADA opens up new opportunities for deaf people. Gallaudet is right there in the middle with the wonderful opportunity (and awesome responsibility) to prepare these high aspiring deaf people to capitalise on these new opportunities. Also a big change is the rapid and extracurricular advances in technology. The World Wide Web and the Internet are really levelling the playing field for deaf people. Of course, I remind our students (and younger students when I travel) that in order to really take advantage of the emerging technologies, deaf people have to be highly literate. They must be able to read and write fluently! It is absolutely essential that students become highly skilled in reading and writing English. They have to. We talked about advances in computer technology, and how that makes for a level playing field for deaf people. So they have fantastic new opportunities. But that's only if they have highly skilled levels of English. So obviously literacy is a high priority, and it has to continue to be a high priority.

Q   Are college students in general—and Gallaudet students in particular—different today than they were in the past? And how must Gallaudet accommodate changes that are happening now and in the future?

A   Students are absolutely different today. They are empowered. They're activists. No more apathy or just allowing things to roll along. The students today know what they want and don't want to wait for it. Sometimes this is very challenging, but it sure beats the old stuff. We also have a different mix of students. We have many more non-traditional students. Many, for example, are students who had left Gallaudet before finishing years ago find are coming back now to complete their education. Others never attended college. They raised families and now that their children are grown and gone, they are coming back. Statistics of young deaf children in schools show many more are students of colour. Already, we have more students who are African American, Hispanic, and Asian American. Many of our students are from other countries. Gallaudet is still the only four-year university in the world for deaf people, so we could enrol many more international students. Congress currently limits us to ten percent of our enrolment, but I am working to remove that cap. More and more students are mainstreamed today, and more of them can benefit from a Gallaudet education. Many have never signed before they come to Gallaudet; some grow up oral, some grow up with Cued Speech, some with a sign system, some come from deaf families. Gallaudet has to be ready to provide for them a welcoming environment that supports their needs.

Already, we have done several things to address these changes. I created a position in my office for a special assistant for diversity. He is charged with creating an environment where we embrace diversity and value differences, where we learn from each other.

A few years ago, the University adopted language that recognizes we are a bilingual community where both English and American Sign Language are used. This statement on sign communication supports the idea of communication diversity and affirms our goal of meeting the visual communication needs of each individual. We have two centres on campus—one for American Sign Language literacy and one on English literacy. It is very important that everyone on campus can sign and understand sign. It is very important that everyone achieve high levels of fluency in English.

Q What are the most important challenges Gallaudet will face during the next decade? How do you envisage the University changing to meet those challenges?

A We must keep up with technology and be aware of how it will change the delivery of higher education. Distance education, for example, will be much more important.

Recently, a group of highly sophisticated technology people, representing all the different divisions at Gallaudet, developed a five-year information technology plan. The Board of Trustees endorsed it at their October meeting. The plan calls for an intense infusion of human and fiscal resources to support advances in technology. I put the word 'human' before the word 'fiscal' very intentionally. Faculty, staff, and administrators at Gallaudet are moving forward very fast with adopting new technology and adapting to technology. We will need to be sure that training keeps up with the acquisition of advanced equipment.

Gallaudet is all about visual learning. All of our students learn through their eyes. Many of the technology corporations are also all about visual information processing. We are working now to form partnerships with some of the major information technology corporations to advance knowledge about how all people learn best visually. By creating a sophisticated, interactive visual learning environment, we will not only enhance the way we teach our deaf students, but develop strategies that will help all people learn better visually. Being ready for the change in the pool of students, as I noted above, is essential. Funding will continue to be very important. Congressional support will continue to be our main source of support, but it is clear from the last ten years that we will not see big increases in that area. We will need to increase in other areas.

Q If you could say one thing to Gallaudet students and to future generations of deaf people, what would it be?

A It is a well worn expression now, but I have to say that it is important to keep preaching that deaf people have all the abilities and potential that others do and that if they work they can do anything they want. It is absolutely true that deaf people can do anything except hear.

Q One last question. A lot of options are available to deaf students today. They can go to many different colleges and universities. Why should they come to Gallaudet? What can Gallaudet offer them that they can't get at other institutions?

A If I had deaf children who were college age, I would ask that question myself. Why come here instead of going to a state university, for example? The short answer is that Gallaudet is the only university in the world where everything is accessible to deaf people. Here at Gallaudet you not only understand everything that is happening in class—you understand everything that is happening everywhere. You not only understand it, but you fully participate in it. There are probably a hundred different student organizations—fraternities, service clubs, student government associations, cultural organizations. Students have the opportunity to gain leadership experience. The editor-in-chief of the *Buff and Blue* student newspaper is a deaf person. So is the editor of the *Tower Clock* yearbook. The captain of the football team, the lead in the play are deaf. If they go to a state college, they're not going to be editor of the newspaper—they won't be anything other than a reporter.

Here, students can have a full range of experiences in an environment where they also have one-on-one communication and direct accessibility to all those programs. So they can put aside the struggle to understand and focus on learning. Then, when they've finished their four years here and go out and get a job or go on to graduate school, they have a really solid base of learning.

My Experience of Being Deaf

Gloria Pullen

The book entitled *Being Deaf: The Experience of Deafness* was published in 1991. My first impression of the book was surprise that so many people felt negative about their deafness and it made me realise that, for some deaf people, their ability to communicate with the hearing family in which they were raised is poor throughout their lives. Some Deaf people have terrible experiences because their parents are unable to accept their child being deaf and so the child is never given the opportunity to access the real world of the Deaf community.

The main problem for parents in terms of the best approach for their deaf child is the acceptance of the medical school of thought which is based on a belief that there is a cure for their child. Parents are looking for a cure, for the child to fit easily into their lives, to speak. I feel very sad for these parents but wish that there were some easy route for these parents to gain access to the Deaf community and thereby to an understanding of the positive lives of deaf people. It is only this understanding which will enable them to improve the situation in which they find themselves.

It is the medical school of thought which led to deaf children being sent to oral schools. These schools were devoted to the teaching of speech and lip-reading rather than having a full and proper educational curriculum.

This explains why deaf children did not develop the full understanding necessary for when they reach adult life, as an oral education not only does not provide a good education but also never meets the needs of a deaf child. The damage is done to the deaf child in three ways: as described above at school, and through the child's observation of their parents' struggle through the years. The third way in which damage is caused is through the isolation the child experiences growing up, watching the ease with which their parents are able to communicate with their brothers and sisters and the blame they impose on themselves for not making their parents' lives easy and pleasing them. The accounts in the book by Deaf people who have Deaf parents also described the horrible experiences they had of education and their accounts reinforced in my mind the two different ways of raising a deaf child.

I am profoundly deaf, culturally Deaf, my parents are Deaf, one brother is Deaf, the other is hearing. Both sets of grandparents were Deaf and I have Deaf uncles and cousins. I never had the horrible experiences that so many Deaf people describe of growing up deaf. I have never once felt regret at being deaf. I did have some bad experiences in education but the difference was that I had a great deal of support from my Deaf family because they understood the context of the oral education system, the struggles I would face and the oppression experienced by all deaf people. I did not go to a mainstream school but to an oral school for deaf children where, because of my status as a Deaf child from a Deaf family, I could teach the other children and influence them through signing.

Similarly, when I reached adulthood I did not feel regret about being deaf. When I started my first job I was the only Deaf employee there but each evening I was able to discuss with my family my difficulties at work and to receive a great deal of advice and support from my parents based on their experiences at work. Their willingness and ability to share their experiences with me to empowered me to develop into a confident adult.

I remember discussing these types of issues with a friend and she told me that she blamed her deafness for her lack of access to society. I remember how shocked I was and how I tried to disagree with her but I came to realise that it was too late for her to change her attitude because she was hurt so badly. The emotional damage she had sustained led her to block out from her memory all of the good things that had happened in her life and to focus only on the negative things and the experiences she might have had if her life had been different.

I left school at sixteen with no qualifications. I would have liked to be a secretary or a nurse but instead I worked for a number of years doing packing in a variety of factories. My first job was at the Wills' cigar factory. I was there for three years and I really enjoyed working there, but on my first day I felt that I'd been thrown in at the deep end in this enormous factory full of machinery. I was the only deaf person there and when I arrived they labelled me as 'deaf and dumb'. It was a month before anyone spoke to ask me my name and then they could not understand my reply.

So I wrote it down. Some of them could not read or write and they were amazed that I could write and that I'd been to school. It took a year to start to make friends. A woman called Dawn had noticed how I watched the others in conversation and she took it upon herself to write down what was being said. That broke the barrier. Then she invited me to play hockey with them. Well I knew how to play tennis, so I thought I could manage hockey and I'd give it a try. I had a wonderful time and by Monday everyone's attitude at work had changed as they realised that, not only did I know how to play, I wasn't afraid to join in and I was a good team player. People approached me who had only seen me as 'the deaf and dumb one', as disabled, and so I started to socialise with them, we'd all go out together. People started to learn how to sign. Dawn came with me to the Deaf club and started to see a different side of me: how I operated in my own environment where the language was my own, rather than spoken English. I spent most of the money I earned on clothes, mainly on miniskirts! I wanted to follow the fashions. In that I was different from my parents and it brought quite a bit of conflict. 'You're not twenty-one yet', my father would say.

It wasn't only our parents we were in conflict with: as Deaf young people we wanted the Deaf club to move with the times and to organise a monthly disco. The Deaf club committee wasn't buying it. We thought it was outrageous that they were so unresponsive to our needs in not providing us with what we wanted. We thought that they were dictatorial. In fact, they kicked us out, calling us cocky and arrogant. Well, there were other places we could go. There was a nightclub called The Glen. It was a rock and roll club. A group of us would go every Friday night. We loved rock and roll. It was the fashion at the time, of Teddy Girls and Teddy Boys. That's where I met my husband, Ian. He came up and asked me to dance. Although we became regular dance partners, there was so much noise he didn't realise I was deaf until the day we met in the street. The next Friday, after we had danced, we went to the cafe-bar and chatted by writing notes back and forward. When my father found out that I was dating a hearing boy, he wasn't very happy. In fact all my family were concerned about it, even the hearing relatives, until they realised that Ian was learning to sign. My heroes were in rock 'n' roll. I dreamed of marrying Tommy Steele and that's how my love of music was triggered. I have my own way of enjoying music—like a lot of Deaf people, I feel the beat. I go to the theatre and enjoy music there but a lot of Deaf people don't get access to music. I know that some Deaf people enjoy translating songs into sign from English words, my daughter's ex-partner, Colin, describes his interest in this in the book *Being Deaf*, but there's still no established way to encourage musical talent, no workshops or training in either 'sign-singing' or in the instrumental side of music in the years that have passed since he wrote that piece. I think sign-singing is a way to bring Deaf and hearing people together, to integrate and to influence hearing culture, but I would also really like to see the emergence of a Deaf music experience that is firmly rooted within the Deaf community and culture.

When my first child was born, I knew that she was deaf but I could not get the medical profession to believe me, although I should say that my family doctor had a very good attitude: the problem was not with him, he had to refer us to the Hearing and Speech Clinic. They tested Angelina, and because she was visually aware, she reacted to the bells and tests. It was a long time before I could convince them that she was, in fact, deaf. They thought I had an attitude problem, being from a Deaf family and that I was convincing myself that I had a Deaf child. On the other hand, when Kevin was born, they would not believe me that he was hearing and sent a peripatetic teacher to work with him from the age of nine months to two years old. They gave him hearing-aids and were just getting ready to admit him to the Deaf school when the teacher arrived one day and could hear him talking in the kitchen. Then they believed me. I had explained that Kevin just loves to sign and although he talks when he's alone with Ian, he always signs in my presence, it's so much a part of the culture of our household, and of course Ian was always at work when the teacher called. Well, after my experiences with Angelina and Kevin, there was no way that I would let them have any contact with Debs, my youngest. I just shut the door on them.

Ironically, Angelina had a similar experience with her first child, Ian, who was hearing but diagnosed as deaf. He was given hearing-aids, which damaged the hearing in one ear. Angelina attended the Deaf school but we weren't very satisfied with her education there. When she was seven, the concept of Partially Hearing Units was developing and the Head felt Angelina would be a good candidate. She visited the school and mixed well with the other children and so she started on a trial basis. After about six months, it was clear that she was struggling despite the support Ian was putting in but when he talked to the Deaf school, they refused to accept her back as the educational psychologist would not agree to her return. This was difficult for all of the family.

The Unit was vehemently anti-BSL and as all of my children attended the school, Debs and Kevin were also subjected to teasing. Debs reacted particularly badly when Angelina was bullied and became aggressive in her defence, upsetting the natural order of things that the older protects the younger child, rather than vice versa. Angelina was severely disadvantaged by her school experiences. When she left she had no qualifications, but working on a Deaf Information Project educating hearing young people in schools helped her to develop her confidence and skills.

Angelina's second child really was deaf, but again there was a struggle with the Education authorities. Ben attended a mainstream nursery in Nottingham and Angelina and her partner Colin had to fight to get a placement at the Derby Deaf school. Eventually they moved to Derby, hoping that would enable him to attend the School, but Derbyshire County Council also refused to support the placement, only conceding defeat when Ben's parents kept him home, and in the face of press publicity, backed down.

I feel that educational standards for Deaf children are not good enough yet. We need a Government minister to become really interested, and investigate the standards of Deaf education. That is the only way that action will be taken to bring the level of Deaf education to that experienced by hearing children. There are encouraging changes: more parents are signing when their children are very young. There are more Deaf classroom assistants, although I worry that many are not qualified. Many others are, of course, but usually it is the hearing staff who have the qualifications and therefore the power and influence in the schools and in the education system. My dream of Deaf people becoming teachers is coming to reality: there is a course at Leicester University and two Deaf people have qualified through the course.

I feel strongly that parents should accept their responsibility to learn

218 to sign. It is essential if the deaf child is to receive the encouragement of their family, access to the family's culture and life and to discipline, that the parents learn BSL to communicate with their child. Without sign, Deaf people grow up with the depressed and despairing attitudes of the friend I mentioned earlier. Many hearing parents feel that cochlear implants will solve the 'problem'. I fear that their children will grow up to be as damaged as my friend is. Parents must be helped to understand that it is essential for them to respect the natural language of their child, to respect BSL as an equivalent language to spoken English.

Deaf schools are not the natural choice of hearing parents for their deaf child. In some ways, I sympathise because I recognise that some Deaf schools have low expectations for their pupils. They need both to prepare children to expect a University-level of education and to develop their Deaf identities through the teaching of Deaf Studies courses. From a Deaf perspective, mainstream schools are not the natural choice for a Deaf child as they are places where the child's confidence and their Deaf identity is stripped from them. The opportunity for ease of access to language and Deaf culture is denied. All of this has severe implications for the child's right to equality of opportunities throughout their adult life. It also removes their access to inter-connecting networks within the Deaf community: we need to recognise and understand how important those Deaf networks are both for the Deaf individual and for the community and how they are based on the network of friends developed at school.

More young Deaf people are going to University. There are several reasons for this happening: some schools are using BSL and have Deaf assistants, there is more access to information, Deaf young people themselves have more confidence and are more determined to go to University. They can access University because there is an interpreting service. There have been so many Deaf people like Arthur Dimmock who have in the past been refused access to University. Arthur, and people like him, were thereby blocked from obtaining professional jobs in the Deaf community, but now that access is possible, we have a growing pool of Deaf professionals. While this is of course excellent for the Deaf community and especially for the development of services, I do have some concern about the development of elitism. In the past, people like Arthur Dimmock, excluded from professional work within

the Deaf community (I think he worked as a graphic artist in architec-
ture), brought their skills to the Deaf community as volunteers within
the Deaf clubs. Now there is a danger that Deaf professionals, who are
nearly all bilingual in BSL and English (and are not monolingual BSL
users) divorce themselves from Deaf community events and from Deaf
social clubs because these take place 'out of work hours' and they are
not strong members of the Deaf community. Where then does that
leave grassroots members of the Deaf community? Does that leave
them without access to professional employment serving the Deaf community? Is it possible that we might return to a two-tier situation, but
whereas in the past the Deaf clubs were served by hearing people, in the
future might sole-BSL users be served by bilingual Deaf people who do
not participate in the life of the Deaf community?

When I compare life nowadays to that several years ago, we do
have better access to the world because we have qualified interpreters
to support our communication needs. With interpreters I can see how
I can handle things myself, I am able to understand the choices being
presented to me and to make use of my options to improve my life.
In the past, social workers would make these choices for Deaf people,
recording the interviews and appointments in their case records so that
the information was available for future occasions. I still do not use
social workers because of this issue of confidentiality and the legacy of
disempowerment. Unfortunately many Deaf people's distrust of social
workers also affects their use of interpreters.

Lacking information about the training, qualifications and ethics of
interpreters, they avoid using their services because they fear the inva-
sion of their privacy. Of course I understand their feelings, but I am fully aware of the rules interpreters must keep and I know that interpreters
do not keep records of their assignments with deaf people.

I began to work for the University of Bristol on a voluntary basis
when the Centre for Deaf Studies was first set up in 1979 and then I was
employed by them in a series of research projects there concerning Deaf
people and communication and employment issues. I became interested in working in Africa after seeing pictures on television of Ethiopian
people during the famine—I noticed there were never any Deaf people
shown, though they must have been suffering too. I wondered if there
was discrimination against Deaf people there, and if Deaf people were

able to get employment.

I discussed the idea of going to Africa with Jim Kyle, Director of the Centre for Deaf Studies, and he suggested I get in touch with Action on Disability and Development (ADD), a charity supporting projects for disabled people in developing countries. Through ADD I was able to arrange a brief visit of two weeks to Uganda, accompanied by a hearing ex-ADD worker, Simon, and a sign language interpreter. We actually saw very few Deaf people during the two weeks, and met mainly ADD personnel. In the capital, Kampala, we went to the headquarters of the Ugandan Deaf Association, and did meet some very privileged Deaf people there—people whose parents could afford to give them a good education. Then we made a trip out to a rural area, to a town called Gulu where ADD had an office, and by chance met some Deaf people there in the street. Though poor, they were neatly dressed. We stopped to talk with them. They had a Deaf-blind woman with them; she had not been born blind but became so through river blindness. I wondered how a Deaf-blind person could possibly cope in Africa. Amongst the group they were communicating with her using hands-on signing—it was amazing. I was able to talk with her through her brother. But it seemed to me that some of the Ugandan ADD staff felt I should not have had anything to do with these Deaf people, because they were poor.

On returning to England I worked with Jim Kyle on raising the funds for a two-year project. Jim acted as my interpreter for meetings with the Overseas Development Agency (ODA) and other organisations. The ODA agreed to provide fifty per cent of the funding; the rest was obtained from Comic Relief and the Red Cross. It was clear from our meetings with these agencies that funding organisations knew nothing about the Deaf community, Deaf culture or sign language, or about the differences between Deaf cultures in different countries. They were not aware that sign language is not a universal language used by all Deaf people, but that each country or region has its own sign language. I had to explain to them that in Africa people cannot afford hearing-aids or batteries, and it is not useful to provide this kind of technology.

Once the funding had been organised I had to find a sign language interpreter to work with me for the duration of the project. I advertised and interviewed several people, and finally chose Mark Schofield, who worked with me for the first year. Chris Stone acted as interpreter for the second year of the project.

I went out to Uganda for two years, from 1996 to 1998. I went first as Mark was delayed for a couple of weeks. The Ugandan Deaf Association provided with me with their best interpreter, but he did not understand international signing and could not do voice-over. This made it very difficult to communicate with the local ADD staff who were meant to be facilitating my project. I had decided I wanted to be based in Gulu, as it was a rural area where Deaf people were poor and needed help and support. This was in a part of Uganda affected by the war, and the ADD staff did not want me to work there. They actually contacted the British Embassy in Kampala to arrange to send me home, without involving me in any of their discussions. When I asked what was going on, the interpreter told me the two ADD directors felt it was too difficult for me in Uganda, and that I should go home. It seemed to me they were discriminating against me because I was Deaf, and did not believe I had the intelligence and initiative to establish a project in Gulu. I protested strongly about the fact that these decisions were taken without telling me, and also told them they knew nothing about Deaf people. When Mark arrived I explained everything to him and there were further negotiations. So there was the problem of people's attitudes towards me, which were typical of hearing people's attitudes and behaviour towards Deaf people. There was further conflict about where I should be working.

ADD wanted me to work in Mbala, in the north-east of Uganda, so we arranged to have a look round. When we went there, it was a town: I said that was not what I was in Uganda for, and that I was going to Gulu. I was furious with them. I felt they did not realise I had the ability to undertake the programme I had planned. I chose the village where I wanted to work from the map: a place called Lira, near Gulu. When we visited it, we could see it was a typical rural area, with people living in huts. They had no water supply but had to carry water on their heads, no electricity, and they cooked on wood fires. This was exactly where I wanted to be. I wasn't interested in working with people who were well-off and had a lot of possessions. Because I had already been to Gulu and told Deaf people I would be working there, I knew they would be expecting me. The ADD staff told me they had cancelled the arrangement—but the Deaf people there would have had no way of knowing this. I suppose it is normal in Uganda, as in the UK, to ignore Deaf people in this way. I wanted to let them know what had happened, and felt I should go to Gulu to inform them and tell them what was going on, so I talked to ADD and persuaded them to let me do this.

ADD sent one of their staff to Lira to organise some accommodation for me there. But it took several months to get ready. In the end I went to Lira to take a look at the house and see what was going on. It was still far from ready, and needed a fence for security. I went to see the local government official, who was also an army commander with much power and influence in the area. He summoned the landlord of the house I was supposed to be staying in, and told him to get the necessary work done quickly. The man was shaking with fear. So my bungalow was ready soon after that. The government official decided that I should have my office next to his. Symbolically this was important, because it impressed local hearing people. He ordered his staff to allow Deaf people in to the compound. The soldiers came to learn sign language. I developed a good relationship with him; he would use signs to greet us whenever we met. He was a pleasant man but also very powerful—everyone was in awe of him. Wherever he went there were always four militiamen following him. He would have been a prize target for the rebels: if they had got him it would have been a severe blow to the government.

The war in Uganda has been going on for some time. The rebels kidnap children, brainwash them and train them to be soldiers. I never actually saw children being taken. But in the second year, when many soldiers and rebel forces poured into the Lira area, a man came to my house one day carrying his daughter on his bike. He wanted my help. His daughter had had her arms hacked at by the rebel soldiers, and he was trying to get her to hospital.

The child was wrapped up in clothes and I couldn't see her clearly, but she was soaked in blood, absolutely soaked. I had the use of a car for the project and asked my driver to take them to the hospital. The father came back to thank me later. His daughter had died anyway despite getting her to hospital. That's how I became aware of the rebels and what they were doing. The Deaf Development Project was my own conception and based on my conversations with Deaf people in Uganda, asking them about their situation, their chances of employment and so on. Developing communication was the first priority. Then education in basic skills such as handling money so they wouldn't be cheated when they went to the market. We organised women's groups, carried out counselling work and had discussions on healthcare. We worked with families with Deaf children. We tried to develop better behaviour towards Deaf people, and had the local police learning signs. We started a Deaf children's association, and a school for the children with Deaf people teaching them. The ADD staff did not approve of this, as they are an organisation supporting specifically adults who are disabled; but there were no schools in the area—how could you leave the children without any education?

During the two years we also trained two Deaf development workers, one male, one female, and a sign language interpreter. I met up to a hundred Deaf people every day, sometimes more, and visited outlying villages by car on specific days so they would know when I was coming and be there to meet me. They were enthusiastic about the project and eagerly anticipated our visits. They would walk long distances sometimes to come and see me. I remember one old woman walked seventy-five miles to my house; when she arrived it was pouring with rain and she was drenched. I wasn't at home that evening and a colleague asked her to come into the house and have something to drink, but she insisted on standing out in the rain until I returned.

When we first arrived we had to familiarise ourselves with Ugandan Sign Language and the local Deaf culture. Initially the Ugandan Deaf people were extremely respectful of me. They weren't sure they could trust me, and would watch what I did and follow me. Gradually they came closer. They would give me a hug or hold my hand. They might invite me to their home, show me the crops they were growing. Slowly they accepted me. At first they were proud to have a white person as a friend but later they stopped showing me off and treated me without fuss. By the end of the programme our relationship was such they felt they could argue with me—I felt this was good and just as it should be. They were shocked at the beginning because they didn't know that white people could be Deaf—they had no television and no access to the outside world. They only knew about what was happening in their own village.

I had a dog while I was in Lira, one of the native dogs, which I got as a puppy. In Uganda dogs aren't treated as they are in England or allowed inside the home. The Deaf people in Uganda were frightened of dogs—they thought it strange that I would feed a dog, stroke it, look after it and take it out on a lead. I told them about dogs in England—working dogs, dogs treated as pets and so on. The strange thing about my dog was it could identify whether a person was Deaf. During the day if a Deaf person approached, he would get very excited; if it was a hearing person, he would start snarling. I don't know how he knew—perhaps from the sound of a person's speech. One night he woke me up by jumping on to the bed—I got a torch, since we had no electricity, and followed him outside to see what was going on. When I flashed the torch around I could see someone waving their arm but had no idea who it was and felt a bit frightened. But I knew the dog would have attacked a stranger, and it seemed the dog knew the visitor was Deaf. It turned out he was a Deaf person I knew who needed help, so I woke up my interpreter and we took the car and went to the person's home to sort out the problem.

I had continuing problems with the ADD staff in Uganda because they didn't understand Deaf people or Deaf culture. To give an example of Ugandan Deaf culture: a Deaf colleague of mine from England came out to Uganda to visit me and as one of the visits planned, we drove to the nearest school for Deaf children, about thirty miles away from Lira. It wasn't a particularly good school, but it was better than nothing. It was a boarding school; the staff tried to inform parents and advise them to enrol their children in the school so they could get an education. That day we were taking with us a man from Lira, a Deaf man who was thinking of sending his daughter to the school but was worried about whether it would be all right for her: he went to see the school, met the Deaf people working there, and in fact got a job there later. Anyway, the children at the school knew I was coming because I'd written a letter saying I was coming that day. Some of the children knew me, some didn't. When we reached the school, the children crowded round the car.

We had to hold the hand of each child before they were satisfied—and my colleague said, 'This is how Deaf people are here'—this was part of their culture. The children felt it was very important to touch our hands, to make physical contact with another Deaf person. Now when the ADD official came to visit me and see my work, she drove into one of the villages and children came rushing up to the car. She was a well-

off Ugandan woman and had a hearing perspective: she wanted to shoo
the children away and called them beggars. I was very angry with her
and told her they weren't begging, that you should hold their hands as
this was their welcome. One old woman came up and hugged me. Then
the ADD person wanted to ask them questions about the project. But
the way she expressed herself was too difficult for the Deaf people to
understand, since they were uneducated.

I said to Mark, 'do we really have to ask these questions?' For example, she wanted to ask, 'Do you think the project will be successful?' But
they wouldn't have understood what she meant if she discussed it in
those terms.

So I tried to rephrase what she was saying, and the question became,
'When this car arrives, how do you feel?' They replied, 'We want you to
stay, before we didn't have signs, before we had people throwing stones
at us'. The ADD person didn't understand and I had to explain to her—
before these people were discriminated against. She said, 'But their level
of communication isn't very good'. I said, 'Whose fault is that? Where is
the school for them? Deaf people have no way of getting information.
This programme gives them the chance to access information, to learn
sign language, to make the community more tolerant so stones aren't
thrown at them and they can live in peace, to give Deaf people the
knowledge so they can buy food and seeds at the market, so they can
barter without being cheated by hearing people'.

The ADD staff expected Deaf people to be setting up their own businesses, since this is what they supported in their projects with disabled
people. But the Deaf people I was working with didn't understand
money, couldn't communicate and only knew a few signs. Their language was scarcely developed, so it would take at least two years to get
to the stage where you could start setting up businesses. It wasn't only a
question of language—some Deaf people had never seen money in their
lives; hearing people had managed everything for them, so it would
be a long process to acquire basic skills. It was a completely different
situation for Deaf people than it was for disabled people. I found it very
stressful trying to get this point across to the ADD personnel.

I worked in different villages on different days of the week. People
knew that sun or rain I would be coming. Sometimes the rebels would
be close and the government official would tell me that I should stay in

226   Lira that day because I was an easy target in the car. But if I failed to arrive in the village as planned they would send two or three Deaf people all the way through the bush to find out where I was and ask me why I hadn't come.

That's how important it was to them. During the second year of the project the rebels came to Lira. Chris, my interpreter, was very ill and I had taken him to the doctor who said he had to be taken to hospital in Kampala. I carried on working the next few days with the Ugandan interpreter Chris had trained, getting about using a vehicle I had borrowed from a Dutch aid worker. People had expected me to accompany Chris to Kampala because the rebels were in the area, but I said, 'I've got my work, I'll stay here'. I felt responsible for the Deaf people. Later I wondered if I was safe, but by then I had made my decision. I talked to the house girl, who was Deaf. Neither of us knew what was happening. None of the other Deaf people knew what was going on. It was very risky—the huts offered no protection. It would be easy for the rebels to creep up on the Deaf people as they wouldn't hear the twigs snapping in the bush and their response would be far too late. I felt very anxious. I now knew what the situation was like for them. I asked them what they wanted me to do. They seemed apathetic. So I decided that all the Deaf people should gather in my house for protection. I felt responsible for them: I forgot that my Ugandan interpreter felt responsible for my welfare, and there would have been implications for him if I had come to any harm.

We went out in the car; outside there were crowds of people packing up their goods to leave Lira. Deaf people saw me and greeted me. When I told them the rebels were coming, they panicked. I told them to bring their family and bring some food and get in the vehicle. They were worried about their farming tools—we had to wait while they buried them. Other Deaf people greeted me—they did not know the rebels were coming even though all round them hearing people were packing up their goods and possessions. The hearing people had neglected to tell the Deaf people the news. They were sitting targets. We drove home with them. Then I realised there was one group of Deaf people who would be at real risk, so even though I didn't know whether I would be able to reach them, I set out. We got to their village, and when we saw them we saw they were not at all worried. I signed that the rebels were coming, and asked them, 'Where's your family?' All the huts had their doors bolted, all the people had gone, leaving the Deaf people behind. I told them to get their things and get into the vehicle. On the way we saw a line of men who turned out to be the soldiers from Lira. I saw the Lira government official in a rough army uniform—I hadn't recognised him at first. He told me I was mad to go out to the village, that that was exactly where the rebels were. But I told him I had to look after the Deaf people, and reassured him I was going back to the house and would stay there.

Back at the house we all had something to eat. We had to make sure there were no lights on and everybody was quiet, so they had to try and stop any of the children crying. We agreed who would sleep where—one room for the men and one for the women. We tried to sign in the gloom, to reassure each other. I told them that if the rebels came, I would go out the front door and they were to get out the back, go over the fence and run as fast as they could. I felt angry at the stupid hearing people who hadn't bothered to warn them and tell them what was going on.

The interpreter was looking out and heard shooting outside. I told him to keep calm so the Deaf people wouldn't panic. I made sure all the lights were out so we wouldn't attract the attention of the rebels. The dog was rushing backwards and forwards. We didn't know what to do. We just waited and waited. The next day, at sunrise, I was up to get a drink of water. The dog was pricking up its ears.

The interpreter told me a vehicle was coming. The dog's hair was standing on end so I knew a hearing person was approaching. It was a soldier sent by the local army commander to stand at my gate. Later the commander himself arrived and told us we were very lucky—he had seen hundreds of people dead in the bush. The same thing would have happened to the Deaf people if they had stayed in their homes. He told people which areas were safe and which were still dangerous, so some people went back home. They were worried about their families—even though these were the very people who had never told them the rebels were coming.

Chris recovered from his illness—he had had a bad bout of malaria—and returned to Lira, although the British Embassy warned him not to go back there. He ignored them and took the ordinary bus back to Lira. The situation went back to normal, although the threat from the rebels flared up from time to time. The ADD staff never understood the danger Deaf people were in, that they couldn't see the rebels coming because their

228 huts were surrounded by trees and they couldn't see the roads. Unlike hearing people, who could pick up the latest news by word of mouth, Deaf people had no access to spoken or written information, so they never knew what was going on.

During the two years of the programme the Deaf people proved they could achieve a great deal. They became much more confident and assertive, so that by the second year they would tell me sometimes for example that there were matters that I as a white Deaf person did not understand about their experience as black Deaf people. The basis of the programme was the community work, trying to improve quality of life, and developing language for communication. We did video a lot of the sign language in Lira so the material could be analysed later as part of research into Ugandan Sign Language, but this was secondary to the other activities of the programme.

I think the biggest single achievement of the programme was the video we made in sign language about HIV/AIDS. The actors in the video were Deaf people involved in the programme. The beginnings of this project were discussions we had with groups of Deaf people about sexually transmitted diseases (STDs). They had to talk about this in their terms—Deaf women would talk about people who had lost weight as a sign of STD. Although the Deaf women discussed these issues among themselves, unlike hearing women in Uganda they wouldn't discuss them with their men folk, this being almost socially taboo for them. So Chris and I started the discussion off with a role-play between us, so I was the woman asking Chris whether he had any sexually transmitted disease, and he was the man discussing his side of it, and so on. This broke the ice and got the discussion going. We then worked hard with the group on a story line that would inform people about the dangers of catching HIV/AIDS, and warning them of the kind of situations in which this could happen. Basically a husband goes out on the town and goes into a bar where he meets up with a prostitute. He spends the night with her, and after this incident falls ill. His wife doesn't know what's going on but calls in a doctor to see her husband. Fortunately he turns out not to have HIV but another sexually transmitted disease which the doctor discusses and the relevant treatment is also described in detail. The scenes were rehearsed over and over, and we also did the necessary background research to get the prostitute's outfit and the doctor's clothes and equipment right.

The final video was made without any retakes or editing and was absolutely excellent. It was very important that Deaf people showed they could do this themselves. The video was shown to the Ugandan health authority, who thought it was very good, and felt it could be used to inform all the tribal groups in Uganda about HIV whatever their spoken language because the message was expressed so clearly. The local Member of Parliament who saw it was also very impressed.

I feel the Deaf Development Programme achieved an enormous amount, despite the obstacles and frustrations we encountered. Many of the Deaf people we worked with would have been in a position to move on and do something like start a business or find a way to earn their living. For example, one of the initiatives we undertook was to encourage Deaf people to produce pictures and carvings which were then sold, the money being ploughed back into supporting their work. At the end of the programme, Deaf people told me that they were no longer being shot at by the army or being stoned as they went about their daily business.

However, I feel it would be very useful for the agency that facilitated the Programme in Uganda, ADD, to employ a Deaf person full time in their UK office so that any projects undertaken with Deaf people can be properly assessed. Programmes for Deaf people are going to be completely different from projects for disabled people. And it was the case that the ADD personnel in Uganda, accustomed to assessing projects for disabled people, seemed to look down on Deaf people and their language. They need to be educated in Deaf awareness so that they can support and enable Deaf people rather than trying to control and direct them.

I feel that comparisons between countries are useful. In some of the Scandinavian countries, particularly Norway, Sweden and Denmark, it doesn't matter if you are deaf or hearing because what is considered important is communication. If BSL was really recognised in Britain, Deaf people would have the chance of an equal life. If we look back in history to how English governments have abused Welsh and Scottish people, denial of their languages was fundamental to their disempowerment. Now that their languages have been recognised and valued, their sense of national identity and equality can come to fruition. I feel that

230   my children and my grandchildren have an equality of attitude with re-
       gard to Deaf and to hearing people; this sense of equality has developed
       because of the status BSL has in our family culture.

Being Deaf and Twenty-five

Asif Iqbal

There are six children in my family. After the first three children were born hearing, my mother was suddenly confronted with my profound deafness. She was very shocked and expresses the disappointment she felt at the time, but later my younger sister, Shazia, was born profoundly deaf as well. The final member of the family was born with Down's syndrome.

My father approached our doctor for advice on how to manage a deaf child and was told they could operate on the inner ear to improve my hearing. However, my parents were made aware of the risks of the operation and so decided against it. They resolved to treat me as a normal deaf child, although my mother continued to pray to Allah that I would miraculously become hearing. Really this was a natural parental response. They hadn't met any Deaf adults who could act as role models for me and there was no information in any of the Asian languages that might explain and help them to understand the issues and needs of deaf children. My parents' first language is Urdu and English is their second language.

Luckily, my oldest sister, Perveen, had a friend who lives in St. Albans and knew about Heathlands, the deaf school there. She went along to the school and got information from them to pass on to my parents, recommending to them that Heathlands would be suitable for me. My parents accepted her advice and I entered Heathlands as a weekly boarder when I was just two years old.

Heathlands uses the method known as Total Communication, a combination of sign language, speech and listening. The contact with other deaf children increased my own confidence as understanding each other through sign language was easy, and by participating in the educational and social life of the school I began to build my own cultural identity as a Deaf child. I remember when I was seven years old my class went to the church in St Albans as the Queen was visiting. I had to

232   present a flower and bow to the Queen. Afterwards I was so excited to receive a letter of from Buckingham Palace and I am sure my fascination with the Royal Family was inspired on that day.

I had to stay at the residential school from Mondays to Fridays. This was very difficult for my mother who, despite reassurance from the deputy head that I would be fine, missed me terribly and worried about me. In part I am sure my mother was influenced by the Asian community's viewpoint that deaf children are disabled and that disabled children are in need of protection, that the best way to treat disabled children is to keep them safely at home at all times.

Every Friday during the school term, the taxi would pick me up at the school to take me home. While I was at home, my family would speak Urdu and imperfect English. I have always felt that clear communication within our family is important so, in addition to English, my parents had to learn a third language, British Sign Language. My two oldest sisters can use basic sign language to communicate with me and of course I always use sign language to communicate with Shazia. I remember I had a problem with my older brother as he usually spoke to me with very little lip pattern and of course I found it very difficult to understand what he was saying. I had to tell him to please speak up and open his mouth more clearly. He has some use of sign. I am very lucky with all my sisters because they can all sign. Shazia is special because we find it easier communicating with each other. We have a very strong relationship and over the years we have worked together to develop and boost each other's confidence. We can catch up with the news together, share information, support each other on deaf issues within the family and develop our family's knowledge and understanding of deafness. For example, when my parents speak to each other in Punjabi, Shazia and I don't understand what they are saying. Sometimes that might be deliberate if they want to have a private conversation, but obviously we find it very frustrating when we can't understand what they are talking about. When I use sign language to talk to Shazia then my parents do not understand what we are talking about and my parents experience the very frustration that Shazia and I feel.

My father taught me some Urdu. Unfortunately, he started before I was ready, since I was too young even to learn English at the Deaf school. He gave me a book of the Koran in which there was a translation from Arabic into Urdu side by side. I would copy out an Urdu sentence in writing but as I didn't understand the meaning, it was impossible for me to read and speak it as my father hoped. It was confusing for me too.

My father regularly took me to the mosque at weekends where we wore Pakistani clothes to demonstrate respect. All the other boys there of all ages were hearing and I felt lost and self conscious as I was the only deaf person in the mosque and felt that everyone was looking at me. The leader of the mosque was an Urdu speaker. It's a bit of an old fashioned system, but the Asian community prefers to elect a mosque leader from Pakistan. He could not speak or write in English. I was expected to read the Koran in Urdu by lipreading the leader as his finger followed the words in the book and copying what he said. I had no idea of what the book said and the mosque leader had no conception that Urdu was not my first language. I was under a lot of pressure and in fear because the mosque leader used a wooden stick to hit pupils he thought were not reading well enough. I feel that it was awful that I should have been punished like that.

Of course, now as an adult I realise I need to use an interpreter in the mosque so that I can have easy access to religious teaching. However, I need to be sensitive to the rules of the mosque: obviously a white interpreter or an Asian woman would not be acceptable to the mosque leaders. On the other hand, the religious community needs to face the reality of deaf children's religious and other needs and to accept some deaf awareness training in order to allow equal access by providing communication support in the mosque. Although there is one mosque leader from Birmingham who is an English speaker and has an understanding of British culture, generally the system of importing a mosque leader from Pakistan concerns me greatly because of the lack of information, education or knowledge about deaf people. The persistent belief that deaf children are a punishment and need to be cured of their deafness denies the human rights of Deaf children. Lack of changing attitudes within the Asian community is compounded because they haven't yet seen any successful Deaf people with high status occupations. Until the Asian community have experience of Deaf politicians, teachers, business leaders and other professionals, they will not accept a Deaf person to be an equal part of the Asian community and the traditional belief that all hearing people are better than Deaf people will continue.

234   On the Asian calendar, the month of Ramadan is followed by the festival of *Eid Al Fitr*. During Ramadan we follow the timetable given by the mosque waking early in the morning to eat breakfast before sunrise and then fasting until sunset. Although we can eat anytime during the hours of darkness, I find that I get a bit hungry in the middle of the day when most British people have lunch. Each morning we must have a bath to ensure that our bodies are very clean and then at *Eid* we put on the shalwar clothes and hat. I accompany all my male relatives to the mosque where the leader urges us to donate money to the impoverished third world. When it comes to the prayers, I simply follow the other men. Although I don't have any real access to the mosque as they don't consider a deaf person's needs, I do not refuse to attend as I respect the values of my family and the Asian community.

At the close of prayers, we call to Allah and hug each other, shaking hands to say 'Eid Mubarak', ('Blessed *Eid*' or 'Happy *Eid*') before we go home where all the women are waiting in their finest Kameeza and Dupatta and wearing their jewellery. Traditionally the men give money to their sisters, mother and wife and gifts to the children. We then share a big family meal. The afternoon is usually spent at a special event or on some kind of trip like bowling or to the funfair and the evening is spent eating dinner with friends. The traditional *Eid* meal is colourful rice with lamb curry, chicken curry, tandoori chicken, samosas, yogurt, mint, salad, kebab, with rice pudding and halva to follow. Often families have a secret recipe to provide something that is different.

My nine nephews and five nieces are learning BSL to enable them to communicate with their Deaf aunt and uncle. I am very lucky have a wonderful family with an interest in deafness who are emotionally close enough to each other to be able and willing to communicate with each other.

When I was ten years old my parents decided to transfer me to Burwood Park School in Surrey. The school has closed down now, but it was a school that used the oral method of teaching and you had to pass an exam to be accepted. The school was very good academically and encouraged both study skills and sports. I had a good group of friends there.

The Duke of Edinburgh Award scheme is a great way to meet people from different walks of life, to do and see new and exciting things and to gain valuable experience for later life. I took up the scheme as a pupil at Burwood Park School and completed the bronze and silver awards there, completing the gold award later at college. The bronze award is divided into four sections: service, physical recreation, expedition and skill. For the service section, I worked as an audiology assistant, supporting deaf children with headphones and testing hearing-aids. For physical recreation I took up weight training with a hearing group and for the expedition three of us who were deaf went camping with a hearing group in Dorking, Surrey. To pass the skill section, I learnt about gardening including garden design, planting, tending and arranging flowers and vegetables. Our class went to the Painshill Park in Esher where we helped with planting. The Duchess of York came to open the waterwheels there. She met our group and following that, we corresponded with her. When it came to the silver award, I also learned to cook in the school kitchens and provide a dinner for school pupils and I took up table tennis, now my favourite sport.

In 1992, I got involved with Friends for the Young Deaf's Sport Festival at Crystal Palace where I played badminton and football. I was surprised to see how many deaf children attended sport activities. FYD is an organisation which encourages deaf and hearing children to integrate, to work together and to learn skills from each other. I maintained some involvement with the FYD and helped to raise funds through a sponsored walk. I became the assistant leader for the Sport Festival held at Crystal Palace in 1993.

One of my friends at Burwood Park had a Deaf family. It was a real experience for me to see a family who used sign language to communicate with each other and I envied him his Deaf family, particularly having Deaf parents to look up to. Deaf parents understand so much better how to bring up a deaf child and to be supportive in the deaf child's attempts to develop his education and independence. The Woolfe family was so flexible compared to mine, and I realised that this was partly due to the restrictiveness of Asian culture which insisted that I must stay at home and did not allow me to go out by myself. The time came when I had to make my first step away from the family and the Asian tradition. Tyron suggested that we meet up at Euston station on a particular Saturday. I told him, 'Yeah, why not? I will ask my father if I am allowed to meet you'. My father was very concerned at the idea because I am deaf but my mother rejected it completely as she felt I would get lost in London and that travel was impossible without hearing.

Tyron phoned my father to ask him for permission for us to meet up. My father agreed to take me to Euston. I was so excited at the prospect of the whole experience and of catching the train. My father left me with Tyron and other friends and I promised that I would be at home by 3pm. When I arrived home safely, my mother jumped for joy in her relief. For myself, I was aware that I was starting to overcome the problems which I faced in respect of the Asian community's attitudes to me as a Deaf person. I had taken the first step towards breaking down the barriers the family had established around me and replacing them with trust.

I began to get very actively involved in many deaf organisations and in public service. I found that this provided me with a sense of challenge and some real life experience. As well as learning a great deal from the organisations in which I was involved, the contacts gave me confidence and took me out of my own home.

I was keenly involved for five years with the National Deaf Children's Society (NDCS) Youth committee. Their aim was to consult the youth voice, to find out what deaf young people wanted from NDCS so that they improved their youth services. I also got involved with the Deaf Broadcasting Council and the British Deaf Association and later with the BBC's Children in Need appeal and Comic Relief. I also had an opportunity to visit the Great Ormond Street Hospital and I was delighted to be able to help sick children. I was introduced to an organisation in Preston called CAST which provides a 24-hour helpline and aims to provide people with Aids or HIV with total care in the home if possible. I learned lot from this organisation; the opportunity to meet a diverse range of communities and people with different interests raised my awareness and understanding of the range and connections between issues of difference, whether they are religious, or to do with ethnicity, disability, deafness, gender and so on. This realisation has profoundly influenced my life and the direction in which I have moved.

In 1993, Deaf Accord organised a visit for deaf and hard of hearing people to the Houses of Parliament. There was a reception hosted by the Liberal Democrat MP Malcolm Bruce where the Minister for disabled people, the Hon Nicolas Scott, made a short speech and answered questions. In all, nearly 30 members of parliament attended, including many of the young deaf people's constituency members of Parliament. I can date my interest in politics from there. I got involved at my local MP's office and in his office at the House of Commons. My job was to sort out the leaflets, type letters and so forth. I learned a lot from him, including details of Tory politics.

At about this time Channel 4 screened a programme about Gallaudet University, a Deaf University in Washington DC where the American President, Bill Clinton, was attending their graduation ceremony. I was struck by two things: Bill Clinton used American Sign Language and the President of the University, Dr Irving King Jordan was a deaf person. I was staggered that the President of the USA could sign. Can you imagine a British Prime Minister signing? I decided I wanted to go to Gallaudet University for the ten weeks between finishing school and starting at college. When I arrived at Gallaudet, I was met at the door of the college by a Deaf security guard; that was incredible! The students there are truly international and there are deaf people at every level on the teaching staff. I met Dr King Jordan, the first Deaf President of Gallaudet, and asked him how he felt when he was selected. He said he had been truly amazed and couldn't believe it. Then he said: 'Deaf people can do anything except hear'.

Gallaudet is a complete Deaf world. With Deaf people there from many different countries, it feels like a Deaf United Nations. Deaf people work there in every role imaginable: teachers, researchers, caterers, sports coaches, secretaries. The point I would make about Deaf role models is that not only are they necessary for deaf people, they are important for hearing people too, to help them to realise that deaf people are capable of equal levels of achievement.

On my return, I started at Derby College for Deaf People (DCDP) where I initially studied for the BTEC 1st Diploma Business and Finance. At that time I thought I would follow in my brother's footsteps and he was setting up his own business. Later I decided to change course because I realised that business and finance were not the best career direction for

238 me and so, with the support of my parents, I took an access to higher education course to enable me to develop the study skills necessary for university entrance. The College for Deaf People is based on the campus of the Royal School for the Deaf and it provides the communication support needed by the deaf students—in my case a sign language interpreter. The teaching takes place in a mainstream college and DCDP provides tutorials to back up the mainstream teaching. I was residential in the student house along with thirteen others. They suggested I become the house representative. I hadn't a clue what being a house representative involved so I thought I'd take the opportunity to find out! Actually it involved being the advocate for the group, getting a consensus on the resources needed by the students in the student house, for example a closed caption video and kitchen equipment, and then developing ideas for fund raising to obtain them.

In my second year at DCDP, I was appointed a Vice Chair of the student committee and the following year I became the Chair. The students at DCDP were fortunate in being provided with a full and varied programme of activities by our student committee; these included the Duke of Edinburgh Award Scheme, Raleigh International, British Deaf Sport Council, outdoor pursuits weekends and student reunions. I feel student reunions are important. They encourage former students to come back to Derby to keep in contact with old friends. Current students benefit from the experiences of those who have left, and they learn the ways in which people change, grow, get married or go to university. I feel that the rest of the activity programme is equally important as it provides young people with information, encourages them and provides them with strategies to maximise their potential.

As I was still in contact with the Duchess of York, I decided to invite her to the celebration of the centenary of the Royal School for the Deaf in Derby, and as I doubted that she would come, the principal, Tim Silvester, was totally unaware of the correspondence. When she replied and I informed him that she had accepted the invitation, he was gob-smacked! The secret was shared across the school and everyone was really excited especially as she arrived by helicopter. She met the interpreter, Ben Steiner, and the governors followed by the staff and was given a tour of the school to meet the children and then the students. I gave a speech to thank her for coming and the primary children put on a signed singing performance. The Duchess thrilled them by using some signs to communicate with them, she seemed very relaxed, warm, friendly and confident when communicating with us and thanked us for inviting her. The Duchess asked us to join her in wishing Ben a happy birthday since it was his birthday too. One of the outcomes of the visit was an arrangement by the Duchess of a work placement for one of the students, Cheryl Matthews, at Nicky Clarke's, a famous hairdresser.

I also became involved in promotion activities within Derbyshire, with a focus on the Derby media, encouraging them to include positive stories which demonstrate the abilities of deaf people and raising the level of Deaf awareness. For example, on one occasion Dean Jones, Captain of Derby cricket club invited me to meet the players and in particular to meet Asif Iqbal, who was a star for Kent and Pakistan in the 1970s and whose name I share. It made my day to meet them and I especially enjoyed meeting Devon Malcolm because I think he is the best cricketer in the world. Four of us were lined up for the local paper so that Devon Malcolm was photographed using the sign 'Derby', I signed 'Cricket', Phillip De Freitas signed 'Club' and Dean Jones appeared on the end signing 'Fantastic'. The association between the local paper and the College continued after I left and that gives me great satisfaction.

I continued with the Duke of Edinburgh's Gold Award by working as a community care assistant in the Royal School for the Deaf Derby, completing a residential project with Friends for the Young Deaf which involved Initiative Training and Leadership courses and by organising with others an expedition to Sweden and Finland. Pouring rain, midge bites and an uphill haul couldn't dampen the spirits of twenty-five determined youngsters who tramped 160km across Finland and Sweden. High spots on the trip included reindeer spotting, a visit to Santa's grotto on the Arctic, teaching sign language and finger spelling to hearing students, and a tour of the Royal Palace Stockholm. But the highlight of the fourteen days camping trip was completing the hike. We arrived in Abisko finally, at the end of the four-day, 80 kilometre trek from Nikkalvoka. I was so tired and so happy successfully to complete my expedition. Isn't it strange that people often think that deaf people can't do these things?

I went to St James Palace in London with 350 other people to receive the award. I was one of the few who were introduced to Prince Phillip.

240 He asked about the expedition and was amazed that I was the only deaf member of my group; he asked how I was able to communicate with the others. I met Major General Hobbs, the director of the Duke of the Edinburgh Award scheme and we discussed how we could adapt the Award scheme to make it more accessible to the Deaf community as it has potential for opening up doors for deaf people if the communication barriers are addressed.

I wanted to continue my political and social activities while I was studying for my BA Hons. Deaf and Education Studies at the University of Central Lancashire in Preston, and I was horrified to discover that the Student Union would not provide an interpreter so that I could attend meetings and activities. I had to arrange for a policy to be agreed at their Annual General Meeting. It was agreed unanimously and I later became the disabled students officer. My work influenced the university to improve accessibility for deaf, hard of hearing and disabled students, particularly by increasing the text phone network on the university campus; but I think my greatest achievements were in increasing Deaf and disability awareness within the Student Union itself by providing training for staff and members. We also produced a video called *What is the Student Union?* The video is also accessible to deaf students who use BSL. I wrote deaf awareness guidelines on how to communicate with deaf students for the Student Handbook. Over ten thousand copies were published.

I used my experience in Derby to involve the Lancashire media in promotion work to encourage greater awareness of Deaf people. Preston North End's players were treated to a lesson in British Sign Language. Kurt Nogan, Colin Murdoch and Dominic Ludden all tried their hand at signing the name of the football club before I was shown around the ground and met the manager David Moyes. It made my day to meet Mike Atherton, the Lancashire Cricket club captain Wasim Akram and the other players. I especially enjoyed meeting Mike as I think he is the best English cricket captain ever. Really, he is my hero. I taught him how to spell 'Lancashire' in sign language. He is a fantastic player and good at sign language as well.

The Mayor of Preston, Councillor Rose Kinsella and Mayoress Elaine Lloyd also learned to communicate in sign language as part of a promotion campaign to urge town hall staff to use BSL.

The *Deaf Nation* Symposium was a major international conference held at the University of Central Lancashire during my time there. It was organised by the Deaf Studies team from the Department of Education Studies and I was a voluntary conference helper.

Shazia attended the West Herts. College and her student days were very different to mine. She enjoyed the GNVQ Advance Art and Design course she took but she was not happy with the communication support the college provided as she was missing a lot of information. She asked me to come to an urgent meeting with the Head of the Fashion course, her tutor, my mother and my hearing sister, Perveen. The college considered that the communicator was qualified as she was able to use sign language but she had no qualifications in communication support work and had passed the CACDP Stage I qualification ten years earlier! In the meeting it was evident that because the communicator was very slow and could not give all the information, Perveen and the college staff were making the decisions on behalf of Shazia. I had to intervene to stop the meeting and to ask Perveen to facilitate the rest of the meeting in the absence of a qualified interpreter.

The solution the Head of Fashion course came up with was to suggest that Shazia attend a lip-reading class. Apart from this being an unhelpful response, she made it without even consulting her so I asked Shazia if she preferred to attend lip-reading classes or to have a properly qualified communication support worker. I am sure that you can guess her response! Finally, the college agreed to advertise for a proper communication support worker with the result that Shazia successfully passed the course, so my family were over the moon with delight. I am so proud of her.

Later Shazia made the decision to apply to university. I had something of an argument with my parents over this as their preference was for a local university. I had to explain to them the importance of finding the most suitable university in terms not only of the provision of communication support, but also the right course for Shazia's academic needs and her future career. It accords with Asian tradition to encourage women to remain in their home area but my modernist theory is to encourage British Asian women to experience the challenge of university life in the diverse nature of the wider community and to live independently. She found the right fashion course and communication

242 support at the University of Northampton. She passed the course and the whole family went to her graduation day. I was so emotional when I saw my deaf sister collect her Diploma.

I feel that I belong to three cultures and these are each equally important parts of my life. The Asian culture I acquired through my family background includes food, clothes and a sense of community life in which the languages of Arabia, Urdu, Punjabi are shared by my relatives. I love to watch the Asian films produced in Bollywood, India and to see Asian people dance, sing and act in roles such as a fighter, but unfortunately as few of the films are subtitled, I don't have full access to the storylines. So while I am attracted by the strong visual element, I also feel excluded.

I am part of the British culture because I have had access to it through the education system, through work and my social life, my interests in the Royal Family and British politics. I have a one hundred percent British identity because I was born in England and I am certainly a fan of the England football team. I feel offended when people assume that I come from another country on the basis of the colour of my skin. This is a very sensitive situation but I feel it is important that when people need to establish my family background, they bear in mind that I may have been born in England.

I realise that some people find it impossible to imagine living without sound but Deaf people find that life is perfectly fine without it and adapt equally well to a life where getting someone's attention is done through tapping on the shoulder, switching the light, stomping on the floor or the wave of a hand. We can meet as a Deaf community through travelling to conferences, Deaf clubs, social events and through deaf organisations. I am so proud of what the Deaf community has achieved, for example in the development of Deaf arts and I support their aims for the improvement of education and employment and for the recognition of BSL. The Federation of Deaf People organised the BSL march on 7th July 2000 in which 9,000 people took part, which boosted our confidence and encouraging further regional actions.

Although the three cultures are equally important to me, in terms of identity I am first of all a Deaf person. My second identity is that of being

British because I was born in England and my third identity is of being Asian given that I was brought up within the Asian community. I realise that society runs on identifying people in terms of visible images and stereotypes and, as people cannot so easily identify me as Deaf or British because these factors are invisible, they first of all identify me as Asian.

The traditional Asian believes that, as an arranged marriage worked best for previous generations, the tradition should be valued and continued. Many arranged marriages are, of course, very successful despite the failure of others. It is important to remember and consider the choice of individual parents rather than stereotyping all Asian parents as operating the same practices, for example some parents seek spouses for their children in the country where they themselves were born, whether this be Pakistan, India or Saudi Arabia. Some parents will decide to choose the person they feel is suitable for their daughter or son to marry without giving the young person a right to express their view or to meet the potential partner. Some young people respect their parents' judgement in these matters, but others fear to refuse their parents' decisions. I support the principle of choice based on full information and clear direct communication.

At the *Ethnic Minorities Open Day* held by National Deaf Children's Society in 1996, Sabina Chowdry, Deaf Adviser at Newham Social Services, and I led a presentation and discussion group of deaf young Asians about their experiences of growing up and why they feel good about themselves and their identity. Examining aspects of their own personal development, they explored concepts such as Deaf culture and Deaf identity as well as ethnicity and culture.

I have given presentations to parents at the East Lancashire Deaf Society and at Thorn Park School for deaf children in Bradford which has a significant number of Asian children. My presentation discussed education, communication methods, my family's experience, the issues confronting Asian teenagers in respect of Deaf and Asian culture, arranged marriage, careers and work. The parents were very receptive, they seemed more comfortable in being able to discuss these matters directly with a deaf Asian presenter and benefited from the opportunity to meet a successful Deaf professional.

I received an invitation to an event at Buckingham Palace being held to recognise the efforts and achievements of young people in all fields,

244 including voluntary, academic and sporting success services to the community or in overcoming adverse personal circumstances. The Queen seemed so pleased and interested to hear about my work with the Deaf community. I also received a commendation for my achievements from the Duchess of Kent. She pointed out the wider social importance of having excellent Deaf role models. I agree with her as without the evidence provided by role models within the Deaf community, the low self-esteem and low expectations amongst deaf youngsters will continue. I also believe that the diversity of deaf people needs to be made more visible and that all types of deaf people need to be more fairly represented in high profile jobs such as politicians and teachers.

I would like to offer up two parallel lines of advance: one by society generally and one by deaf people themselves. Often the hearing community seems to encourage deaf people, while ignoring or even discouraging deaf people from expressing themselves in their own ways. One of the ways that Deaf people are ignored and discouraged is by labelling them as disabled. Society should recognise the Deaf community in a tangible way in order to encourage Deaf participation and to remove the barriers which we have faced for so long. We need to change this system urgently.

Hearing people need to be encouraged in their positive attitudes, to improve Deaf awareness. The Deaf community has, of course a very important role to play in changing society and in raising Deaf awareness amongst hearing people so that the level of employment of deaf people is raised. This would be to everyone's benefit, but in order for it to happen, Deaf people need to consider their communication skills and social involvement and not just sit passively waiting for things to happen. We need to raise our own awareness and be pro-active! We also need to be critical of ourselves as a community. The tendency we have to make deafness our main focus of identification can ignore and deny diversity, individual differences, problems and the spectrum of discrimination. I believe in a partnership with the hearing community which combats the ignorance and prejudiced attitudes in the Deaf community and challenges instances of negative Deaf behaviour whenever they occur.

An Independent Life

José Antonio Libros Solaz, with Antonio M. Ferrer Manchón

I was born in 1969, in a very small town about eighty kilometres from Valencia, Spain. The town had about a hundred inhabitants (a maximum of 300 in summer), most of whom were elderly and worked in agriculture. My parents tell me that when I was a six-week-old baby I was taken to a doctor in Valencia, the capital of the province, due to a severe head-cold. They detected serious heart problems that required a three-month course of injections. My parents prayed with all their strength that the injections would make me better, but they had no idea that those injections were the start of my deafness. A couple of years passed and they began to worry that I was two and didn't talk. Some people commented to my parents that I couldn't hear. My mother didn't think I could be deaf because I would turn around at loud noises: a glass smashing, bangs...

I went to the local school but didn't understand anything. I was the only deaf child in the school and, in addition, the only deaf person in the town. Faced with this situation the priest, a very influential figure in small towns, told my parents that he'd heard of a special school for deaf children in Valencia where I would get along a lot better. When I was six I started going to the special school. It was run mostly by nuns and I went there on a boarding basis: I ate, studied, and slept in the school. I only went back to my home town during holidays. I cried inconsolably every time my parents left me to return home, I didn't want them to abandon me. This is how it was for two years. My father was always worried about what would become of me, especially once they were no longer alive. It was uncertain as to whether after finishing school I could find work in my hometown where most jobs were related to farming. These worries, together with the fact that the new school suited my needs better in the eyes of my parents, culminated in their decision to follow the example of many of my classmates' parents and move to Valencia.

So, at eight years old I returned to live with my parents in a flat near

246 the school. I still attended the school but no longer as a boarder. This situation brightened my outlook somewhat as I was no longer subject to the strict rules of boarding and went back to having some privacy; I wasn't in a big room with lots of beds and other children, I had a bedroom to myself. The move to Valencia also brought about my first experience with audiometric tests and using hearing-aids. When I was about six or seven they placed an instrument in my ear, which would now seem very antiquated. I couldn't hear anything in my right ear, although the doctor insisted I could, whereas I did hear certain things in my left: I perceived differences in the intensity with which people spoke or shouted at me and I believe I could distinguish some sounds.

We were with the nuns for the first few years of special school. I remember that they showed us pictures and then wrote words and sentences related to the pictures on the blackboard. Then they asked us to orally repeat what was written down. We really had to try to repeat the words properly. I remember, with disgust, that when I made a mistake they would hit me. They would grab and pull my hair, hit my head against the mirror that they placed in front of me to repeat the sounds and they would smack my fingertips with a ruler...

We couldn't use sign language in the lower school. We were obliged to use oral language and to write, even though the nuns would use sign language at times and they let us use it to ask for basic things: going to the toilet, asking for water. We signed in secret when their backs were turned and they couldn't see us. We also used sign language at break time to communicate amongst ourselves. That's where I first learned to use sign language. I began to understand, thanks to my classmates, that one sign meant 'Dad', another 'Mum' and so on. I couldn't communicate with hearing people and felt marginalized, but when I found other deaf people I began to feel comfortable in that I could finally communicate.

At nine-and-a-half I began my primary studies, three years later than hearing people, and by eighteen I had finished, four years later than hearing people. Things were better in the primary studies classes. We no longer had nuns but had teachers who would always sign when they were talking. Also, instead of being at desks, one behind another, we sat in a u-shape giving more importance to visual communication. We had

five deaf teachers who gave classes in manual crafts: carpentry, needle-
work, shoemaking, pottery and drawing. The Deaf teachers preferred to use sign language, but I remember that the headmaster didn't like it and he would make them use bimodal communication. Sometimes, when we were happily working in the classroom whilst the teachers were using sign language, we noticed a sudden switch to bimodal communication, which to begin with, we couldn't understand. We later understood: the headmaster was nearby.

The hearing maths, language, natural and social science teachers gave priority to oral language in their lessons although they managed to use bimodal language. They didn't use sign language strictly; just a few signs while they were talking that at least helped us understand a bit more. Nevertheless, sometimes I couldn't stop writing down things the teacher put on the blackboard, although I didn't understand what they meant. Someone who did always make continuous use of sign language was the priest who taught us religion in class, as well as when preaching and taking confession. The religious nature of the school had a big impact on our schooling. We always had to go to Mass on Sunday. It was curious the way in which Mass changed: when it was time to bless the body and blood of Christ, the priest, unlike hearing priests, had to leave the communion cup and wafers on the altar instead of raising them in the air, in order to express himself with his hands. In December we always did a play with a theme related to Christmas and used sign language.

It was when I was eight or nine years old, when I stopped boarding and moved back home with my parents that I began to communicate better with them. It's surprising that having lived the first six years of my life with my parents, I was able to communicate earlier with the nuns than with them. At times my mother still turns her head away when she's talking or speaks very quickly whereas my father tries to speak more slowly and pronounces things better. Of all my family I communicate best with my only brother, who is five years older than me. He has always taken care to look at me directly, speak slowly and pronounce clearly. I do feel that I understand almost everything we talk about. However, no one in my family uses sign language, communication in the family has always been based on my lip-reading, as they never learnt to sign. We still have family gatherings where I don't know what's being said. My brother always explains to me what's hap-

248 pening and helps me with television programmes. My mother gets annoyed when she sees me communicating in sign language to my deaf friends because she doesn't understand what we're saying, but I always reply that I don't understand her either when she speaks. On that point, although it's my brother who has helped me most with communicating, insisting on teaching me the proper structure of oral language, he's never got involved in learning sign language to communicate with me and he doesn't like me using it either. I have offered to teach him some sign language in exchange for all of the time he dedicates to me with oral language, but he's never agreed to it. We argue about it sometimes; he doesn't consider it to be a language, he sees it as mime.

My entrance into the workplace was slightly unusual. I began to work after finishing my schooling in August 1987. My brother was working as a postman and combined this with his studies. He didn't get enough time for his studies so he suggested that I replace him in his job. When he suggested it I thought it would be impossible. I couldn't do that job: there were too many names to read on the letters, on doorbells, I would have to talk to the doormen of buildings. It would be too much. My brother convinced me in principle that I too could do the job and he even became my trainer. I went with him on his rounds for a few days and he explained how I had to do it: he showed me the streets that were part of his assigned route and he introduced me to some of the doormen of the buildings that he delivered to...

The problems started when he left me alone. The first few days were very discouraging. When I rang the doorbell and called out 'It's the postman!' my voice gave me away. Many people were suspicious and wouldn't open the door. I returned with lots of letters. I thought I just wasn't cut out for it, that it was too difficult. However, my brother didn't let me give up and insisted I could do the job. After a while people began to find out who the 'strange' new person was that delivered their letters, and when they heard me coming they would say, 'Ah, it's the deaf postman!' and would let me into the house. Later my brother got a job at another firm, but tried to convince his boss at the postal depot that I could easily take over his work. To begin with he was sceptical and asked how a deaf person could work as a postman. What he didn't realise was that I'd been doing the job for a while already, because my brother had to study and so had left me in charge. He finally agreed to give me a trial period and I worked there informally for a time. In 1989 they formally contracted my services and I joined the social security scheme. I've stayed with the same firm since then. I'm the only deaf person in a depot of about eighty to ninety people but the job doesn't require a lot of interaction with colleagues as I work independently. I communicate well with around five colleagues by lip-reading and also with one of the managers that I talk to now and again.

I don't wear my hearing-aid very much outside of work but I always wear it at work, although it doesn't really help me to understand spoken language. I feel nervous if I'm not wearing it because it helps me to distinguish sounds, to be aware if someone replies through a door intercom. My tendency not to use the hearing-aid stems from my first meetings with the Deaf Persons' Association of Valencia; older people would ask me, 'Why are you wearing a hearing-aid? We all communicate with sign language here'. It's a situation that is changing amongst younger deaf people who have a more open perspective and don't see anything wrong with hearing-aids.

I was nineteen when I first came across the Association. I generally went on Fridays and some Sundays. At first it was as much about playing different sports, going on trips and excursions, as gaining access to information. From Monday to Friday I received no news. At work everybody went about his or her business and there was no real communication. But at weekends the Association represented a forum to receive information about what had happened during the week and gave us a chance to talk it about amongst ourselves. It was our primary source of information, together with seminars that were organised now and again on history, cultural topics, and social issues: drug taking, refusal to do military service and more currently, the change of currency and the use of the Euro. It also allows me to keep abreast of new technologies, such as the text mobile phone, etc.

In terms of my social life, I'm most comfortable at the Association because I feel I can communicate totally; it's where I have one hundred percent understanding of what's going on. Its role has changed though, as new developments in communication have given me other ways of accessing information. Apart from the newspaper that I read every day, I mostly use teletext to keep me up to date. This medium, together with subtitling, which although still insufficient has increased a lot in the last few years, helps me to stay informed with what's happening in society. In this way, I've come to depend less on the Association and now I only go there for leisure activities: excursions, sports practice...

Another key aspect of having a feeling of independence has been the decision that I took two years ago to leave my parents' house and live on my own. My deafness has never made me fear living on my own without the company of hearing people. I rely upon environmental aids and therefore have many in my house. I have an illuminated doorbell and an illuminated alarm clock; I've just installed a DTS (Telephone Device for the Deaf) that I'm about to try out and I'd like to incorporate more, like for example an illuminated alarm device that responds to crying, in case I have children in the future. Thanks to these devices, the only changes in my life are the same as for anyone else: getting used to shopping, cooking, cleaning and taking full responsibility for my living costs.

Something that I would mention about my independent life is my participation as President of the residents' committee of my building. Annually and rotationally each neighbour has to take on the administrative tasks related to the building and the responsibility to keep the residents informed about any incident or repair affecting it. Last year was my turn. It is common for many deaf people living alone not to assume these functions and the neighbours all promptly 'understand and forgive'. I didn't want to escape that responsibility and accepted the role on the condition that I would have the help of a neighbour in the event of having to make an emergency phone call for lift or lighting repairs. For my neighbours this has meant learning a lot about deaf people. Some of them didn't seem to think I could do the job and were surprised that I didn't live with hearing people. I had to explain the modifications I have in order to satisfy their curiosity about how I know there's someone at the door, how I wake up, etc. Through the residents' meetings they also came to know about the interpreter and they learned how to interact with me in their presence. I took my dad along to the first meeting and as usual, I only got his 'summary' at the end. I requested an interpreter for the second meeting and it took some convincing for the interpreting service to provide me with support.

Interpreters are usually requested for things like appointments with doctors or lawyers, but until that point no one had requested one for this purpose. I finally managed it and at the residents' meeting I had to explain who the person was and what they were doing. It's hard for me to explain to others the usefulness of an interpreter, to make them see the importance for me to receive all the information at the same time as everyone else. My neighbours quickly got used to seeing me with the interpreter. At the start, my family didn't understand why I requested an interpreter to go to the doctor. There are some things that I reserve the right to find out alone, information I want to receive without the presence of my parents or any other family member and using an interpreter to receive information or express myself doesn't take away my privacy.

Another factor that has transformed my present life is my relationship with my partner. She is also a profoundly deaf person but was born hearing. I communicate in sign language with her although her most usual form of communication is oral language and all of her family, like mine, are hearing. This has changed a lot of things in terms of my relationship with oral language. Sometimes when I was small, just playing about, I used to say, ' I wish I could speak like a hearing person!' It's something that I consciously think about today, that I'd like to be able to communicate well using oral language. It's also something that I've shared with other deaf friends. They respect my opinion but don't feel the same way.

My interest to become more familiar with oral language has increased a lot. I've made the decision to review the only hearing-aid I use because I've had it for seventeen years and never changed it. Eight years ago another deaf person with some hearing told me they tried to listen to the radio everyday to practice and understand more. I'd also like to try it. In addition, ten years ago I got some headphones for the television and I noted some progress. I came to understand adverts because they were more visual but not, for example, the news. They broke after a while and I stopped using them. Now I have a new set and I use them everyday. I want to make a bit more of an effort to practice understanding oral language. Without doubt, my partner has influenced me decisively to be much more aware of the need to be bilingual.

Taking Pride in Who I Am

Andrew Charles with Rachel Coombs

When I was seven years old I was sent to a Catholic boarding school for deaf children. I had spent my earlier years living in a children's home after my mother left me there and had also spent some time living in a foster home so I was used to adjusting to new situations. However I was totally unprepared for the experience of being a boarder at this school.

Although I had not been able to understand a lot of what was being said in the children's home I had experienced kindness from the nuns and from the other people that worked there. At this boarding school the teachers were strict but usually fair. However, some of the people who looked after us when we were not in lessons were very different. One woman, in particular, was very cruel to the young boys and seemed to enjoy humiliating us. These incidents happened on a daily basis so that they became part of our normal everyday life. For example, every morning we were woken up and had our beds and pyjamas inspected to see who had wet their bed during the night. If you were found to have wet pyjamas or sheets, the housemistress would take you to the bathroom where all the other boys would be lined up to look whilst she wiped the wet pyjamas over you and wrung the urine out in your face and mouth. If you struggled she would hit you hard round the face and the head. I think that perhaps this was supposed to teach us a lesson and stop us from wetting the beds in future. But it certainly didn't work for me as I found it very difficult to wake and go to the toilet in the night, and as I became more nervous about the punishment and the ridicule the more I seemed to wet the bed.

I also needed to go to the toilet quite often during the day and when I asked permission to go was often told that I couldn't, and I would end up wetting myself and suffering the same punishment as I endured most mornings. Very often the housemistress would hit me very hard and would encourage the boys to laugh at me.

At school the staff members were very keen on the boys being clean and put a great deal of effort into this. There were no mirrors so we had to rely on the staff to tell us if our faces were clean enough. If I didn't wash my face thoroughly enough for the housemistress she would scrub at it herself and hit me hard with the back of the brush on the back of my hands or arms or my legs. Some of the white boys used to say that we black boys could get away with being dirty better than they did because the staff couldn't tell whether or not we were dirty. Certainly it was true that when they inspected our bottoms to see if we had wiped ourselves thoroughly after going to the toilet the housemistress would make remarks about not being able to tell if I was clean or not. They seemed obsessed with this bottom inspection and would usually do this in front of the other boys. There was no sense of privacy or respect at all.

I never told anybody about the cruelty I experienced at school and nor, as far as I knew, did the other boys. We did not think that those at home would believe us and we were frightened of the school and thought that we would be punished for lying.

My life at school improved when this house-mistress left some years later. Although there was still a lot of physical punishment it was not as persistent or as violent as it had been before. Years later I discovered that she had had to leave following a police enquiry. At the time I knew that a boy at the school had run away and that not long afterwards this house-mistress had left but I never knew these two incidents were connected.

Years later I discovered that this boy had run away because he could no longer bear the brutality. When he did not return to school the police were contacted. Eventually the police found the boy and interviewed him to find out why he had run away. The boy had quite good speech so they could understand what he said and they believed what he told them about the cruelty he had suffered. They also saw the extensive scarring criss-crossing the boy's back that had been caused by being whipped by the housemistress. The police then contacted the school and saw the headmaster. I think that the governors then told the house-mistress she had to leave. I don't know if the police took the matter further. The boy never returned to the school.

I only found out why the house-mistress had left when I was much older. At the time I had no idea that anything could be done about the cruelty and that anyone outside would believe us or take us seriously. In

254 fact I became used to it and took it for granted. I used to cry a lot when I was younger but I stopped myself from crying when I was twelve because it only seemed to make matters worse and I got bullied more, and instead I learned how to fight and take care of myself.

There were good times at school, especially as I got older. I made some strong friendships with other deaf pupils who have continued to be important to me after I left school. Although the school was an oral school and I could lip-read reasonably well, I learned British Sign Language there and learned a lot about Deaf culture and what deaf people could achieve and this has proved to be really important and positive in my life. I received a good academic education and training for employment as a joiner.

When I got older we were allowed to mix more with the girls which I enjoyed very much. I fell in love with one of the girls in the school and she became my first girlfriend. We used to arrange to meet and go on long walks in the grounds of the school. I thought our relationship would continue for a long time and my girlfriend wrote and told her mother about us. When the school had an Open Day in the summer, my girlfriend pointed me out to her mother. It was then that her mother realised that I was black and she told my girlfriend that she would have to break off her relationship with me because she didn't want her daughter to go out with a black man. When my girlfriend protested about this her mother told her that she had a simple choice—she could either choose her or me but if she chose me her mother would never speak to her again. One of my friends tried to help and told her to ignore her mother and tell her that I was a decent person and that my (foster) parents were white, but my girlfriend's mother was determined and my girlfriend wrote me a letter saying that she would have to finish with me because she loved her mother and couldn't go against her.

When I think about my schooldays I feel sad and angry about the cruelty, but I feel pleased that I had a good education and learned a lot academically. The weekends were the worst times and sometimes I felt that I would have would have preferred to go to the school during the week and to have gone home and been in a 'proper' family for the rest of the time. I was worried about leaving school because I was upset about saying goodbye to my friends and thought that I might never see them again. I had been at the school for many years and it was difficult to imagine my life without it.

For the first few years of my life I had been brought up by nuns in a children's home. I was then fostered by a family and spent the remaining years of my childhood living for some of the time in the children's home, some time with my foster family and the rest of the time at my boarding school. My birth mother had stopped visiting me at the children's home when I was very, very young and I had had no contact with any other member of my birth family. Although I was close to my foster parents and tried to take their advice to forget about my birth mother, I could not do this and I always wondered about her, what she was doing and why she never came back to see me during all those years. I will never forget how scared, upset, frightened and lonely I was when she left me and I felt that there was nobody to comfort me.

I made several attempts to find my mother over a number of years when I became an adult. I couldn't find out any information about what had happened to her and I didn't know if she was still living in this country or if she was dead. In the end it was a chance meeting that led me to find her. A couple of years ago my wife went for a dental appointment and when she was there she noticed that the surname of the dental nurse was the same as her's so she remarked upon it and asked about her family explaining that her husband had lost touch with his family of the same name. The nurse explained that she was married into the family and that she would ask her husband to meet with me if my wife would let her have my address. It turned out that her husband was my cousin. He came to visit me at my flat and it felt strange meeting with a blood relative after so many years. He told me that he would bring my mother to see me the following week and I asked an interpreter who I had known well for many years if he could interpret for me at this important meeting.

The following week my cousin called with my mother, and his mother, as he had promised. I felt very emotional seeing my mother again. I had so many questions to ask—why had I been left at the children's home? Why had my mother not come back for me? Did my mother know that I was deaf? Where was the rest of the family?

I learned that my mother and her boyfriend were always fighting and there was a lot of violence. She left him and was on her own, young, isolated and frightened with no money and didn't know what to do with me. The only thing she felt she could do was to leave me at the children's home where she knew I would be looked after. I learned that a year or two after this she met the man who was to become her husband. He was a very strict person and she felt she couldn't tell him about me. She started a new life with him and stopped coming to see me at the children's home. She and her husband went on to have a family of their own but she never told any of them about me. My aunt knew about me but my mother had sworn her to secrecy and she felt unable to do anything as her husband didn't know about me. My mother said that she hadn't known I was deaf when she left me at the children's home.

Even though I hadn't known what to expect and I had learned a lot of new information, I felt close to my mother and wanted our contact to continue. My mother wanted this too although she said that we would have to meet in secret because she did not want her husband to find out. Over the following year we met often, sometimes weekly, sometimes fortnightly and I enjoyed spending time with her. One day I met her by chance in a shopping centre and I embraced her in my usual way. She, however, was very different with me. She pulled away and was very formal with me, acting as if she didn't know me very well. I then noticed that she was with a man who asked who I was and I think she told him I was a friend and they walked away. I don't know if the man was her husband—I can only assume it was. I waited for my mother to make contact again to arrange for us to meet again but weeks passed and she did not make contact. I contacted my cousin and asked him to find out what was going on. He said he would find out and when he got back to me he told me that he had some bad news for me. He told me that my mother had decided that she wouldn't see me any more, that it was too risky. He went on to say that she had decided to move from this country and to live permanently in Trinidad.

I believe it was wrong for my mother not to tell her husband and family about my existence when I was little and to leave me on my own with no contact. Perhaps if she had told him about me he would have come to accept me and I could have been part of their family. I feel very confused and angry that she has left me again without any way of contacting her again and without giving me any warning. Even though I'm an adult now she has left me in the same way that she did before and I now have even more questions to ask about her.

I sometimes reflect on the things that have happened in my life and think why did all this happen to me? In some ways I feel as if I have been tested by the experiences that I have had, and I think they have made me a strong person who works hard and has made a contribution to the Deaf community and to the hearing community, both through being a good citizen and through my particular achievements. I have been very lucky in that I have travelled all over the world taking part in sporting events and on visits to Deaf communities in faraway places. I also enjoy my job and my hearing colleagues treat me with respect.

Although my birth family has not stood by me I do have had the experience of another family, my foster family, taking me on and supporting me. I continue to have a loving relationship with my foster parents and foster brothers and sisters.

The Awakening

Amparo Minguet Soto

Imagine what it means for a six year-old girl to wake up after a severe headache and think that due to her being in a hospital her mother's talking so quietly she can't hear her. The step from the hearing to the deaf world is difficult. You begin to have previously unknown feelings: a loss of balance, using your eyes to understand the world around you, thinking you can hear your mother's voice sometimes but it's just your auditory memory confusing you, thinking that maybe one day you'll be completely cured of your 'illness' and regain your hearing because hearing loss is a disease that has to be overcome, and generally feeling lost in a world that you once knew but that has now escaped your grasp.

There was a before and after for me. The natural way that close friends spoke to me turned into falseness—they didn't know how to approach me—I felt lost. It's difficult to remember if that period of my life was very traumatic because many years have passed, but I imagine that I shed many tears and never knew how to distinguish between someone looking at me through pity or because they were interested in me as a playmate or a person. I learnt how to repress a lot of feelings, which I knew broke my family's heart, and most of all I disguised my deafness and what it meant to me.

These first feelings tend to die down when you finally find your place in another world, also close but very unknown: the world of Deaf people. Nevertheless, I still hadn't discovered this new world and felt alone, like I was the only deaf person. I asked myself if anyone else lived like me or if I was unique in not hearing well, because I didn't say I was deaf then—it was a taboo word. I simply couldn't hear like everyone else—it was my problem.

For a child like myself that had already acquired oral language, it was difficult to come into contact with other Deaf people that I was yearning to meet. The special education school didn't allow me to attend on the basis that I spoke too well to go there and at that time integrated schools didn't exist, so a relentless search begun for a primary school for me to go to. In the end I went to a school where all of my classmates were hearing.

Now I reflect on the importance of those years, from zero to six. I had a linguistic foundation and although I still had a lot of concepts to learn, I was able to begin school with sufficient knowledge to progress in my education.

I sometimes ask myself if schooling was complicated for me and the truth is that weighing up my memories, the positive experiences far outweigh the negative, but it is also the case that memory is our ally and it often erases painful experiences. I know that I received a lot of support from one of my teachers who had confidence in my capabilities as a person. Despite educational integration not being regulated and not having resources or support from the management, she, from the position of a teacher, tried to rescue me and made me realise that although I would find many, many people who didn't believe in me there would always be some that would help me see the positive side of things.

She dedicated her attention to making sure I could follow the classes free of problems but in all honesty the exclusivity of being the only deaf student gave me excessive limelight and that hindered my going unnoticed by the other children. I enjoyed benefits—I was in a glass case that made certain privileges available to me of which some children were envious. However, in the long run, it was at the cost of my independence. It was hard for me to face the outside world and overcome the adversities that one faces throughout life. It was difficult to spread my wings but I managed it nonetheless. This feeling accompanied me throughout my education. I think that like any other deaf child I suffered the taunts of some of my classmates, but the biggest problem was not having other people like myself, feeling different and not being able to understand a lot of things. I was constantly around hearing children, I played with them, communicated with them more or less, but something was missing from inside of me.

I spent many hours reading, going to the doctor and to the speech therapist. Even today I'm still scared of white coats—they frighten me. I needed to grow as any other child. I wanted to play, have fun, and have

260   spare time. A period of isolation began. I rode my bike, took my dog for walks and I went out with my childhood friends although I didn't understand a lot of what was said. My most intense feelings came through books, where we're all subject to the same conditions, and they were also the main way for me to receive information. At that time films weren't subtitled and I felt stupid if I paid for something that I didn't understand, and the television bored me although my family explained some of the goings-on but in a summarised fashion. Therefore my motivation for reading was very strong and I searched for other ways to increase my knowledge. This interest allowed me to teach myself a lot of subjects.

Nevertheless, my need to meet other Deaf people, to find a place in this world where I would feel secure and be amongst equals, remained inside of me. To begin with I didn't know how to read my feelings— something was missing and I didn't quite know what it was. My mother made it possible for me to get in contact with other Deaf people by enrolling on a sign language course run by the Deaf Persons Federation, taking me with her so that I would get to know other people like me. That's where my journey towards the discovery of my own identity began. I started to use the 'prohibited' word, 'Deaf'. I got rid of the medical hope that, until then, had revolved in my head that one day I would recover my hearing, and I finally stopped laughing at those jokes I didn't understand but pretended to enjoy like the rest of my group of friends. Through the theatre and the friendships I made at the federation I began to acquire sign language skills. Sign language gave a richness in my life that was missing, a visual language that enabled me to understand and express ideas, feelings, and concepts that to me were subdued in oral language. Finally I didn't have to look for adequate words to transpose ideas, communication began to flow effortlessly, and I could interrupt conversations with my hands and understand the interruptions of others in the group.

Sign language brought me light, and therefore the worth that Deaf people feel, for it is indescribable to everyone else. Lack of communication, communication in pieces, constant communicative errors wear away at you inside and that's why it's a big personal step when your insecurity turns into communicative assurance and you never forget or stop being grateful to the thing that made it possible: sign language.

As I began meeting Deaf people, I realised that situations I endured before in the hearing world didn't happen with them and so I became a nonconformist. Contradictory feelings emerged inside me and I could no longer stand to not follow a conversation or not laugh when others laughed. I still had, and still have, hearing friends but it was utopian to be able to share everything with them—I needed Deaf people. These needs that exploded inside of me provoked a thirst for knowledge, to make up for lost time. I worked with the young people at the Federation, I became a member of the Association at sixteen, which was the allowable age then, and from that day I felt that I was full member of the community. To learn, discover and communicate were my priorities during that time. I wanted to spend as much time as possible with Deaf people, but I had to study as well. It was difficult because I hated to spend so many hours of my life in class not understanding what the teacher was saying and I missed Deaf people, I longed for the weekend to arrive, to finish school in the afternoon in order to return to the Federation or to the Association and to share.

My yearning for knowledge made me get in contact with other young Deaf people in Europe. An exchange in Ireland allowed me to discover the conditions in other European countries where education for the deaf had already changed, sign language was used as a linking language and bilingualism, something I hadn't given attention to before, was well established. There were studies on sign language. It had the same status as oral languages, and in some countries it was valued as a real language of the same standing as other languages. I got to know sign language interpreters, hearing people that didn't just do you a favour by going to the doctor with you but that worked at it professionally. It was inevitable to make comparisons and I asked myself why the same thing wasn't happening in my country?

Therefore, I suppose irremediably, for any young Spanish person travelling to Europe, the discovery of certain attitudes, advances or services that didn't exist in Spain was a revelation that made you reflect on lots of things. Also if we're talking about an unknown group, as was the Deaf community, and we bear in mind that there was no social policy or specific legal framework in Spain like the ones that exist today to address diversity, but rather policies of charity, the surprise and anguish you feel by not having the same opportunities explodes inside you in such a way that you make a firm commitment as a Deaf person and as a member of a group that had to be resurrected one way or another. This commitment firmly unified me to the protest movement of the Deaf community.

Within the Deaf community that I had previously known, most people didn't know how to read and write properly. They asked me to write for them and saw themselves as slow and incapable of becoming skilled in the Castilian language. They labelled me as 'brainy' merely because I studied and knew how to read, a fact that, compared with the social majority, had no significance. I didn't understand why this happened and why Deaf people assumed this situation was something inevitable that formed part of their persona. These young Europeans, teachers, psychologists, linguists, made me see that the illiteracy I'd observed in my country didn't belong to Deaf people but rather the educational opportunities offered to them. To always be faced with the same choice, of being incapable, of having limitations, the negativity of being deaf, makes you accept that it's unavoidable to not be able to reach objectives that other people, with other conditions, can. The vast difference that existed between Spain and the rest of Europe made living in this situation more intense. The comparison between the Deaf community in Europe and in Spain was a difference of light years. We weren't a Deaf community, we were united, we fought, we signed all day, we criticised the education we received, the same blood ran through our veins, we did the same as our European brothers and sisters but in a more intense way with our hearts, without professional arguments or scientific nomenclatures. In essence, the seed that was planted in childhood that made us believe we had limitations, that we weren't capable of having a place in society, remained. Only when we cut the seed down at the root did we discover how far the true abilities extended to and how their growth had been prevented.

Deaf leaders gave names to my feelings: Deaf community, culture, identity, sign language, sign language interpreters: that was when I wholly understood the conflicts that flowed through me when I began to have contact with Deaf people. The Deaf awakening is common in many people like me. You live knowing that something isn't as it should be, that we're protesting about something without a name. When you semantically classify these feelings everything takes on its own light and, as always, when you come out of the dark the first reaction is to either protect yourself against the fear that clarity brings you, or face the pain and the anguish of having been blind for so many years. I awoke and from a period of ignorance I came to radicalise my ideas—I crashed against the society I lived in: why hadn't society understood my needs? Why did it hinder deaf people, some of my friends, from being fulfilled? Why had it prevented them from reading and writing properly? Why weren't there any deaf psychologists or teachers here? Like a small child I was at a stage of asking, 'Why?'

The difference is that nobody answered my questions—deaf people went unnoticed in society. We were the great unknown and there were no answers, so I attempted to make our voice reach even the smallest nook, for our pain to be 'heard', our reproaches. Enough of settling for what we had been given; Deaf people can succeed and it was hearing society that had prevented our access.

I was convinced that society was to blame for everything, I had given meaning to my life, I could have discovered it a lot earlier but it had been forbidden. There are numerous deaf people that have experienced these feelings: Deaf Power, radicalise our protests. It's like an inventory of claims that's impossible to keep within and you have to expel it. I suppose the majority of young people go through this feeling of going against the grain, of rebelling against established power and if they've also seen their rights diminished and carry around that repressed pain, in the end it filters through the pores of their skin. It's a necessary transition, it's part of life, of maturity, of an emotional stability that every human being needs to fulfil themselves: it's essential to clean away all of the hatred and resentment in order to work for and achieve harmony. I guess that now it seems a bit exaggerated, even extremist: was society that bad? At that time I thought so and I think it's appropriate to radicalise feelings at a determined moment, as any protest movement has to go through a an extremist stage that strengthens the foundations for future battles.

That was one of the most intense and difficult periods, society didn't understand what we were saying, it wasn't right for us to feel united, to feel like brothers and sisters, to reject anything that disguised our iden-

264   tity. It was important to be Deaf, it was our essence, if it were taken away from us we would turn into a cheap perfume that no one would want to buy. The theatre was one of our weapons to fight against everything. We prepared plays that took our feelings to the extreme, we transformed the hearing world into a Deaf one in which the hearing suffered repression when they wanted to express themselves in their natural language, oral language, they created associations to struggle against the Deaf world that disabled them. Our intention was to get them to empathise with our feelings; of course at that time we didn't understand that we provoked the opposite effect. They categorised us as having a ghetto mentality, a closed community, not integrated due to our own social rejection and this stigma still pursues us today. How can you not understand that the majority of Deaf people don't have sufficient tools to argue their positions, they feel things they don't know how to classify?

When a Deaf person expresses their feelings about oral language it's interpreted as a rejection of oral language, but it is what they themselves have become that is rejected: living through the continuous disguise of their deafness in order to be the same as the majority, those efforts invested solely in speaking well, prioritising their oral rehabilitation against their development as an individual, their integrity. That is what is rejected, not the learning of another language, oral language, that they understand needs to be known in order to live in this world, a language that provides them with an indescribable wealth. But of course we didn't know this, we weren't speech therapists or psychologists, we were simply young people that could only play with our feelings and the contradictions that invaded us.

Possibly for deaf people, that awakening is inescapable and essential. Not everyone arrives and it's always accompanied by a sense of uneasiness that they don't know how to describe, that they can't put a name to as I could: to go from unconscious to conscious conflict and to do it with pain, but afterwards with understanding.

This period pervaded with radicalism is the least understood by society but one of the most important in order to achieve well-being as a deaf person, to reach a place in the world, to find yourself as an individual and clarify who you are and what you want to do in life. It helps you to understand your limitations and accept them in such a way that they no longer cause you pain because to be deaf is not shameful, your role models are no longer hearing people, you don't feel as if you should be something impossible for you: to hear. You go from the homogenisation of society to understanding diversity, the richness of being different to the rest, and valuing everything you can give and others can give to you.

Little by little your anxieties are liberated and you begin to understand that society has to be transformed via other more rational positions. Youthful intensity gives way to the calmness of reason, continual work and the constant fight by guile, by gaining the empathy of hearing society. But there is something that never abandons you and that is commitment, the responsibility that as Deaf people we have to change the world, to achieve tolerance and respect for our differences. Through the Federation of Deaf People I arrived at the conclusion that the associative movement can change circumstances that it didn't share. I began to work in posts of responsibility at a political level, learning from other Deaf people that showed me what leading this movement means. I understood that the world I once heard and then saw remained the world in which I had to live and therefore accept. I lived in a majority where there were some social rules that I had to follow, and political work was a weapon that I should learn to use. I learnt to unravel myself in society as part of it, without forgetting my concerns, the concerns of my community, without losing the direction of the objectives that we had to achieve but looking for appropriate strategies to achieve them.

I learnt about the huge misunderstanding of society towards Deaf people and this made me remove the guilt from the people that formed it. I knew that this pacification was the start of something, it was going to be the seedling of future fruits that maybe I wouldn't enjoy, but that other children like me would reap. Inevitably, this commitment to social change was linked to my profession. I studied teaching because I understood that education is essential for my growth as a person. It was important to show other young deaf people that we can achieve more so they are able to develop a spirit of transcendence, of professional fulfilment. You have to overcome the barriers you face in education with a tremendous effort, an effort that many allow abandon them, and that is why I wanted to show and prove to myself that I was capable of achieving it, that the stigma of having limitations was something fabricated that wasn't adjusted to the reality of deaf people.

It's true that the benefit of having a good level of reading and writing has helped me in achieving this goal, but above all, it was the fact of having discovered myself as a Deaf person, the fact of being able to tell my colleagues to repeat something because I didn't understand it, the fact of speaking to the teaching staff and negotiating my needs as a deaf student. Some responded adequately, others ignored my requests, but in general it was positive. It's been like this for many other deaf people that haven't been able to or allowed to discover their vocation and their abilities.

Of course my training doesn't end here, it never ends. I keep on learning, taking courses, reading, and I'm positive that having knowledge opens a lot of doors. Even today, I know that the biggest problem for Deaf people lies in their education and that's why I get angry when certain reactions of adult Deaf people who haven't had any educational opportunities aren't understood, because at times I have been on the side of misinformation, on the side of impossibility to argue what's wrong with you, what you feel and it's a dark side that no one sees or wants to see, but that expresses many feelings for which no one wants to be responsible.

My professional work has always been linked to the Deaf community and this is why I don't know what it's like to experience the daily the barriers at work that other Deaf people have told me about. I find it hard to understand what a lack of professional fulfilment is like, or working to survive no matter where, things that don't enter into my realm and I think that a majority of Deaf people haven't had any other way out.

The fortunate thing is to be surrounded by deaf and hearing people in my work that share the same objectives of our community. They have made me believe in integration, in the possibility of treating each other as equals, which is what I'm pursuing. I am an ambitious person and this ambition has shown that we can excel ourselves. Currently, in general I'm aware of the changes I have gone through as a person and those that the community has been through. We have many achievements: studies on sign language, sign language interpreters, some initial bilingual experiences, our social presence. The goal I set years ago, that 'our voice will be heard in society' has been achieved, although I suppose that I've had to pay a price. The price of being accused of being a rebel even though today I've chosen the path of negotiation, of conscience-raising, of education.

I still think that Deaf people aren't seen as professionals, but rather an uncompromising group that defends its ideas from the radicalism of its feelings. Previously I had commented that you have to go through and overcome the extreme period, but society is not capable of forgetting. I've reflected on the difficulty of arriving at a total understanding of these feelings that are so intense if you don't live them through your own eyes, but I think that if I have been able to understand, to forget and to dismiss reproach then so can others. It's easy for some social bodies to hold onto the excuse of the radicalism of the Deaf community in order to ignore its demands. To recognise this mistake is not easy but it's the foundation on which to build.

If we continue finding ourselves with those mental barriers that prevent us from examining in greater depth the inside of every person that forms part of our society, we will never arrive at our destination, at equality and respect for our differences. Fortunately today, just as my teacher told me, I still find myself with people who are worthwhile and who are worth continuing the fight for.

To a Deaf Child

by Dorothy Miles

You hold the word in your hand;
and though your voice may speak, never
(though you might tutor it forever)
can it achieve the hand-wrought eloquence
of this sign. Who in the word alone can say
that day is sunlight, night is dark!
       Oh, remark
the signs for living, for being
inspired, excited—how similar they.

Your lightest word in hand
lifts like a butterfly, or folds
in liquid motion: each gesture holds
echoes of action or shape or reasoning.
Within your hands perhaps you form a clear
new vision—Man's design for living;
       so giving
sign-ificance to Babel's tongues
that henceforth he who sees aright may hear.

You hold the word in hand
and offer the palm of friendship
at frontiers where men of speech lend lip-
service to brotherhood, you pass, unhampered
by sounds that drown the meaning, or by fear
of the foreign-word-locked fetter;
       oh better,
the word in hand than a thousand
spilled from the mouth upon the hearless ear.

Index